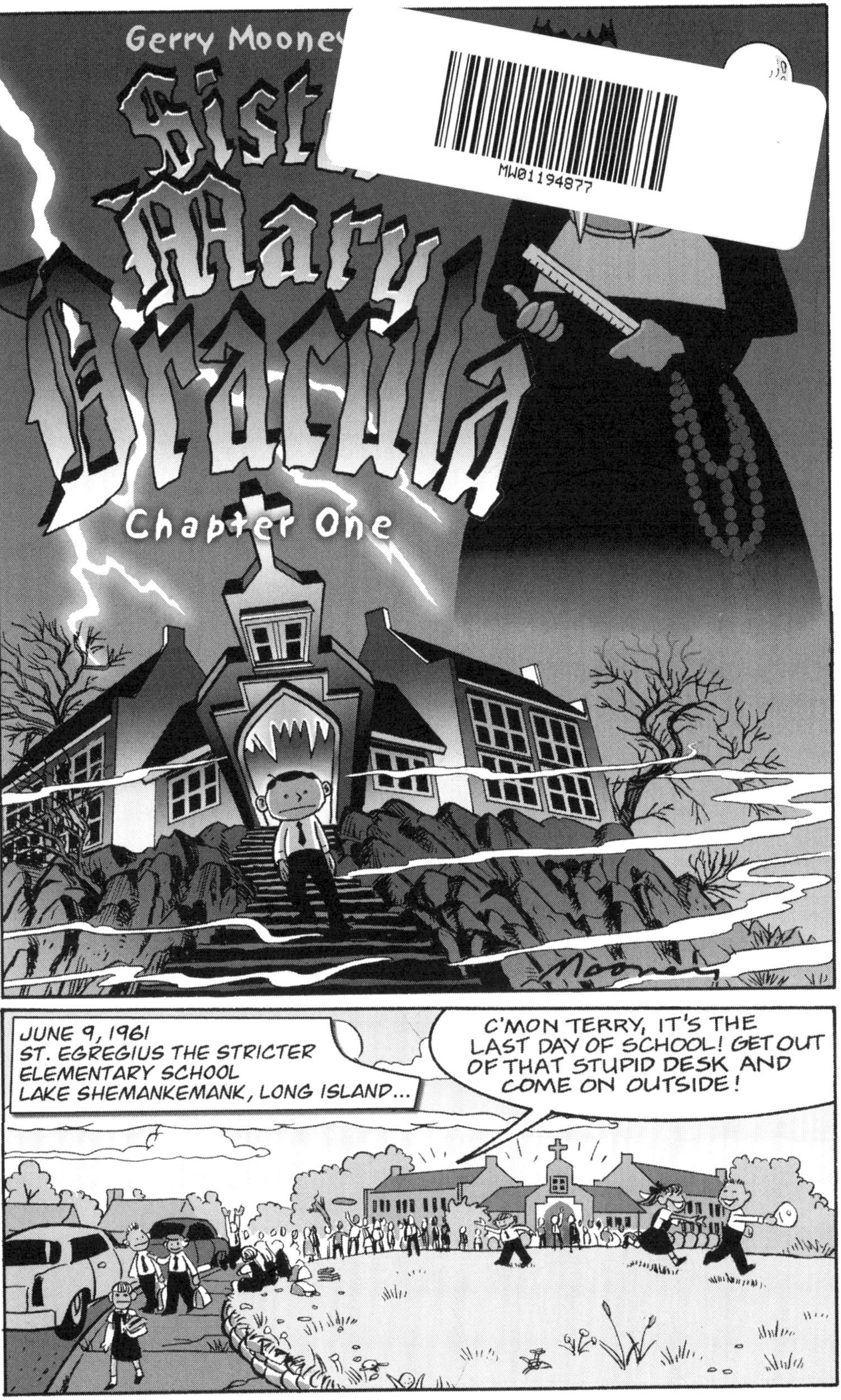
Gerry Mooney
Mary
Dracula
Chapter One
Mooney
JUNE 9, 1961
ST. EGREGIUS THE STRICTER
ELEMENTARY SCHOOL
LAKE SHEMANKEMANK, LONG ISLAND...
C'MON TERRY, IT'S THE LAST DAY OF SCHOOL! GET OUT OF THAT STUPID DESK AND COME ON OUTSIDE!

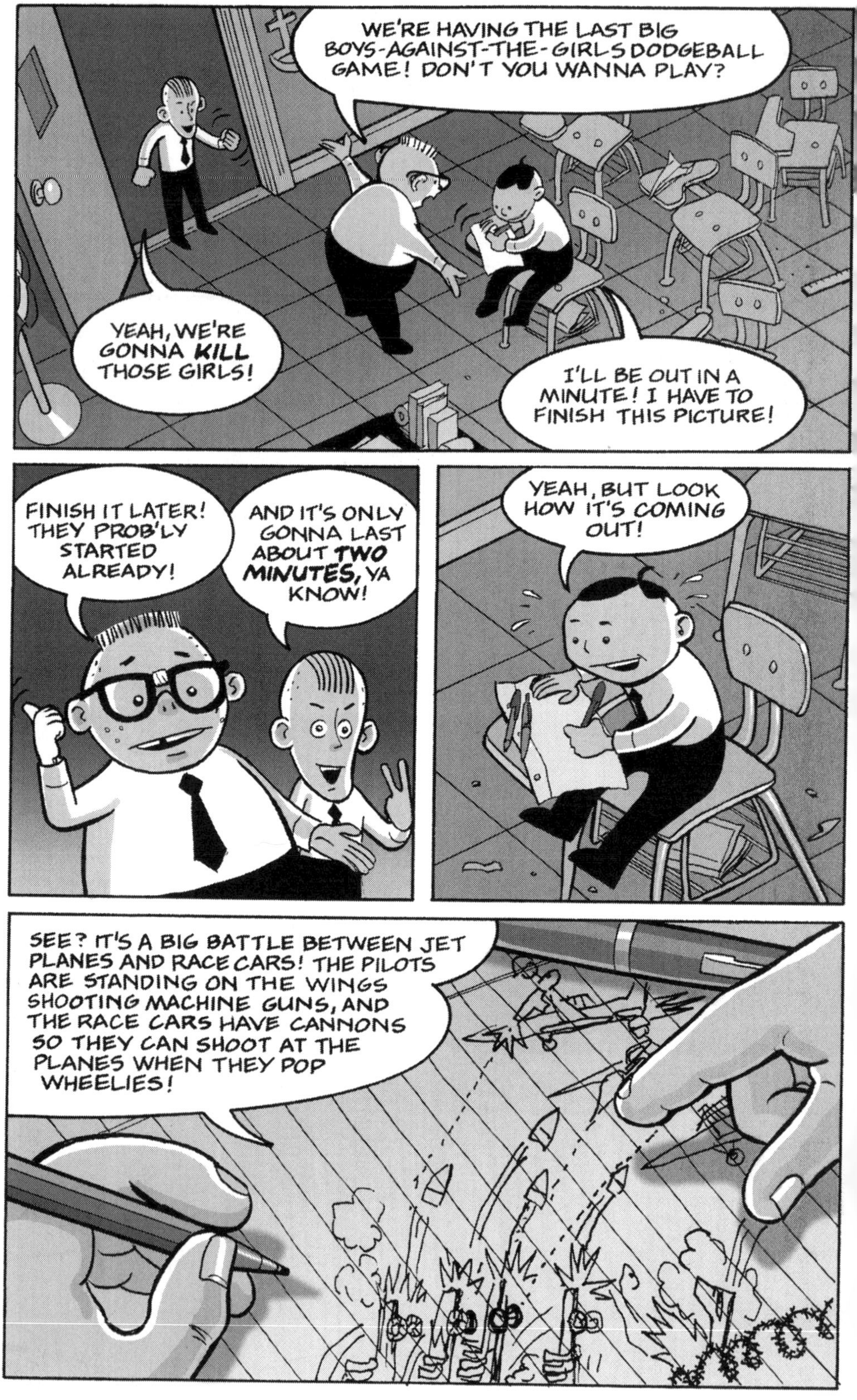
WE'RE HAVING THE LAST BIG BOYS-AGAINST-THE-GIRLS DODGEBALL GAME! DON'T YOU WANNA PLAY?
YEAH, WE'RE GONNA KILL THOSE GIRLS!
I'LL BE OUT IN A MINUTE! I HAVE TO FINISH THIS PICTURE!
FINISH IT LATER! THEY PROB'LY STARTED ALREADY!
AND IT'S ONLY GONNA LAST ABOUT TWO MINUTES, YA KNOW!
YEAH, BUT LOOK HOW IT'S COMING OUT!
SEE? IT'S A BIG BATTLE BETWEEN JET PLANES AND RACE CARS! THE PILOTS ARE STANDING ON THE WINGS SHOOTING MACHINE GUNS, AND THE RACE CARS HAVE CANNONS SO THEY CAN SHOOT AT THE PLANES WHEN THEY POP WHEELIES!

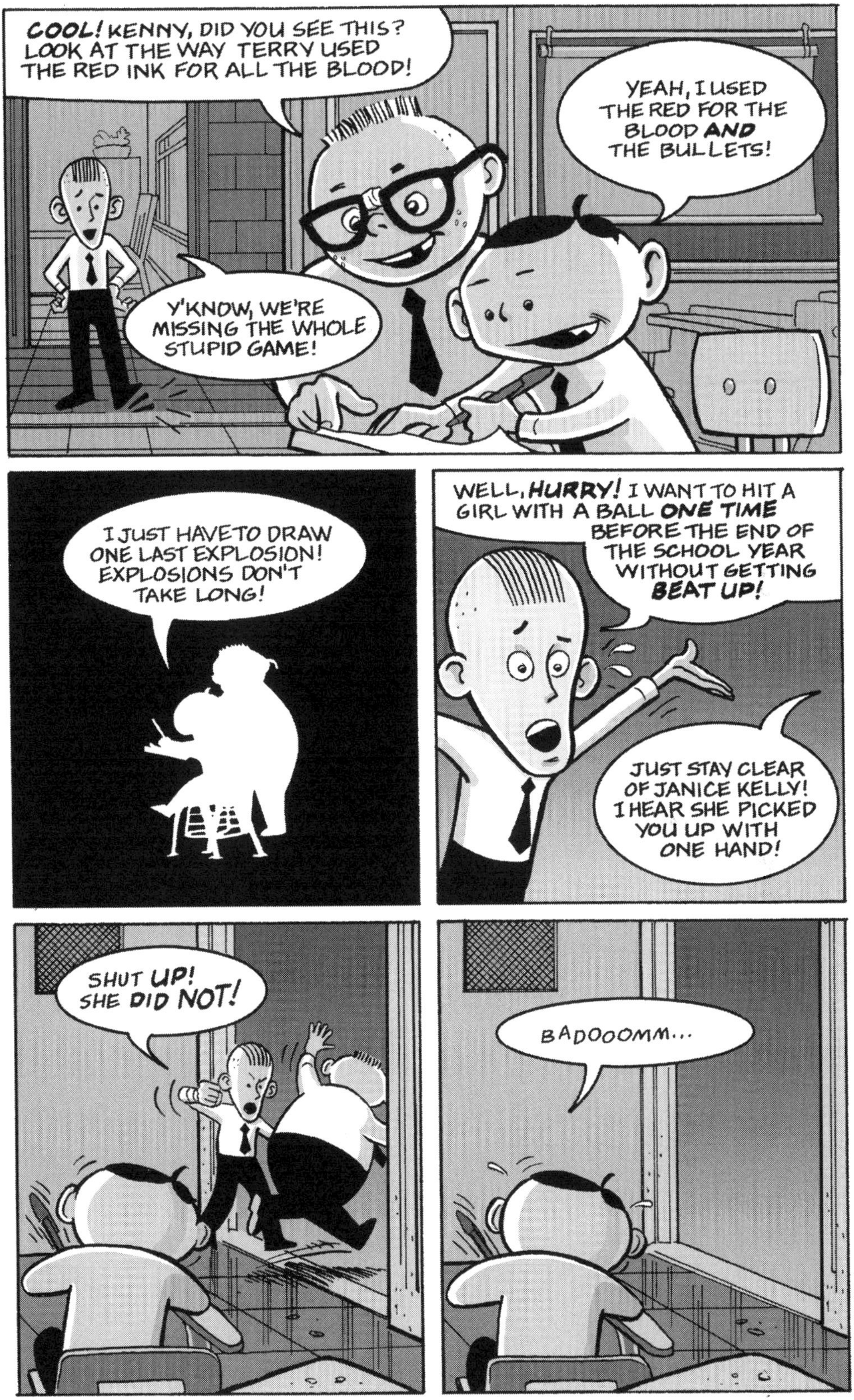
COOL! KENNY, DID YOU SEE THIS? LOOK AT THE WAY TERRY USED THE RED INK FOR ALL THE BLOOD!
YEAH, I USED THE RED FOR THE BLOOD AND THE BULLETS!
Y'KNOW, WE'RE MISSING THE WHOLE STUPID GAME!
I JUST HAVE TO DRAW ONE LAST EXPLOSION! EXPLOSIONS DON'T TAKE LONG!
WELL, HURRY! I WANT TO HIT A GIRL WITH A BALL ONE TIME BEFORE THE END OF THE SCHOOL YEAR WITHOUT GETTING BEAT UP!
JUST STAY CLEAR OF JANICE KELLY! I HEAR SHE PICKED YOU UP WITH ONE HAND!
SHUT UP! SHE DID NOT!
BADOOOMM...

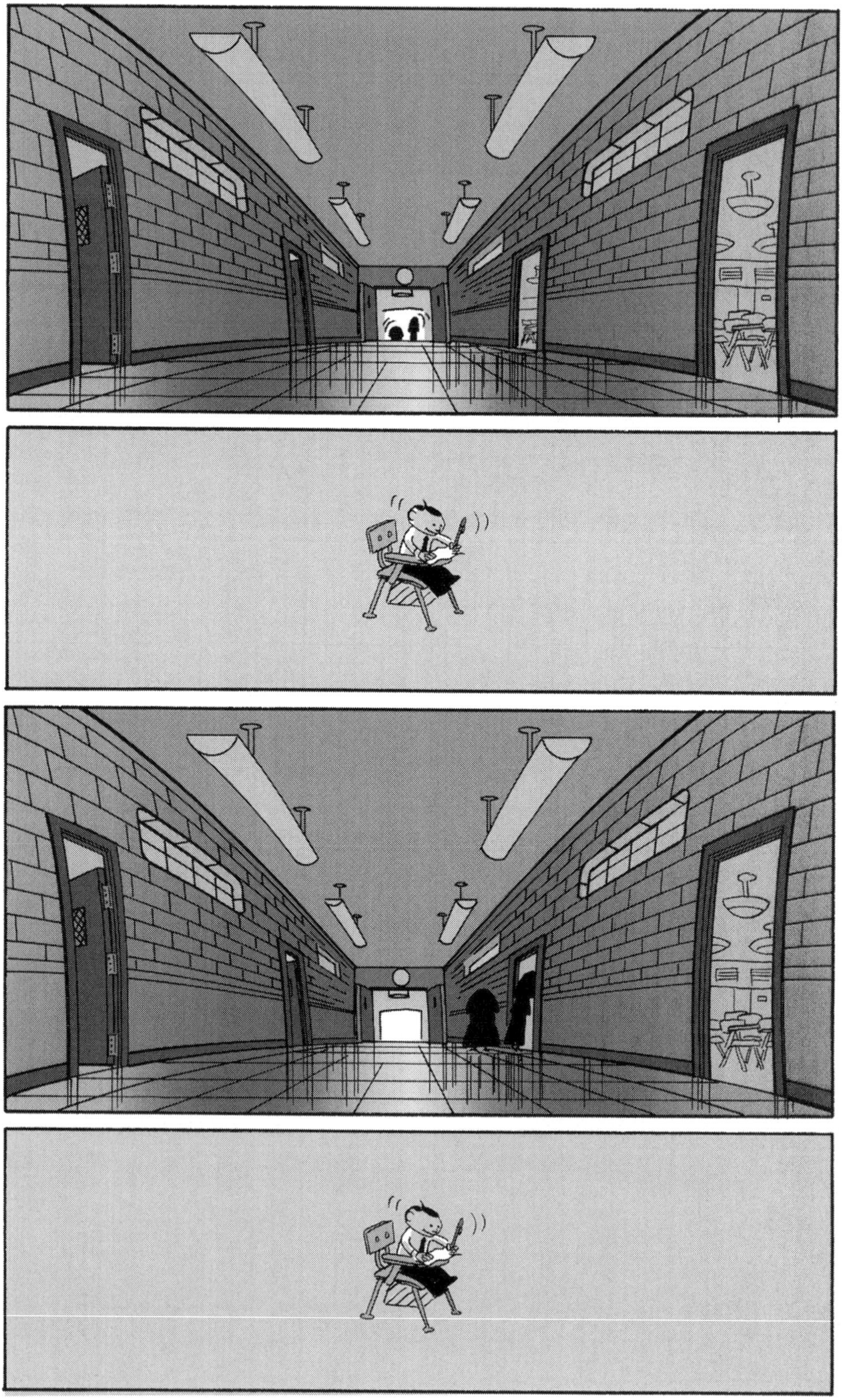

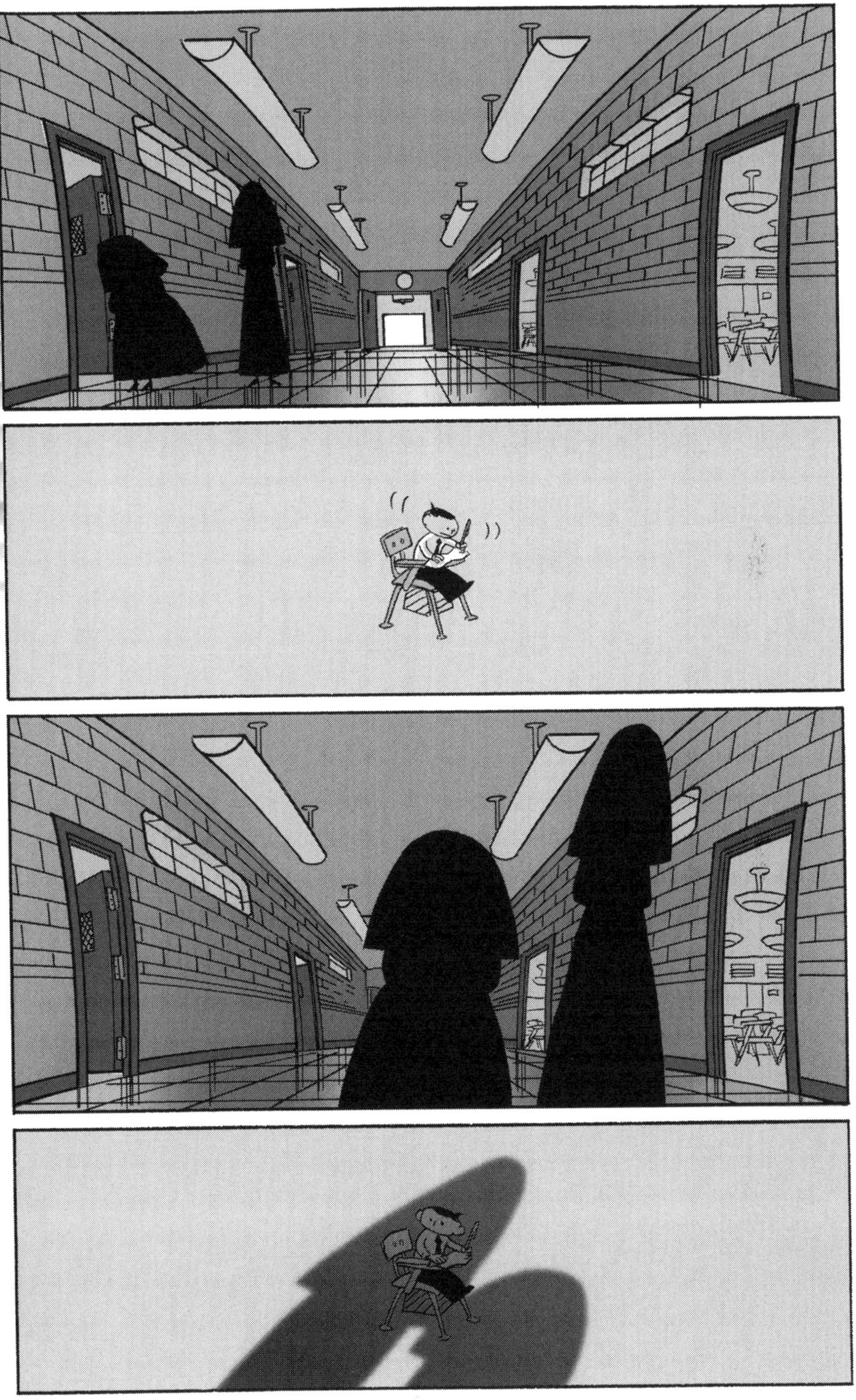

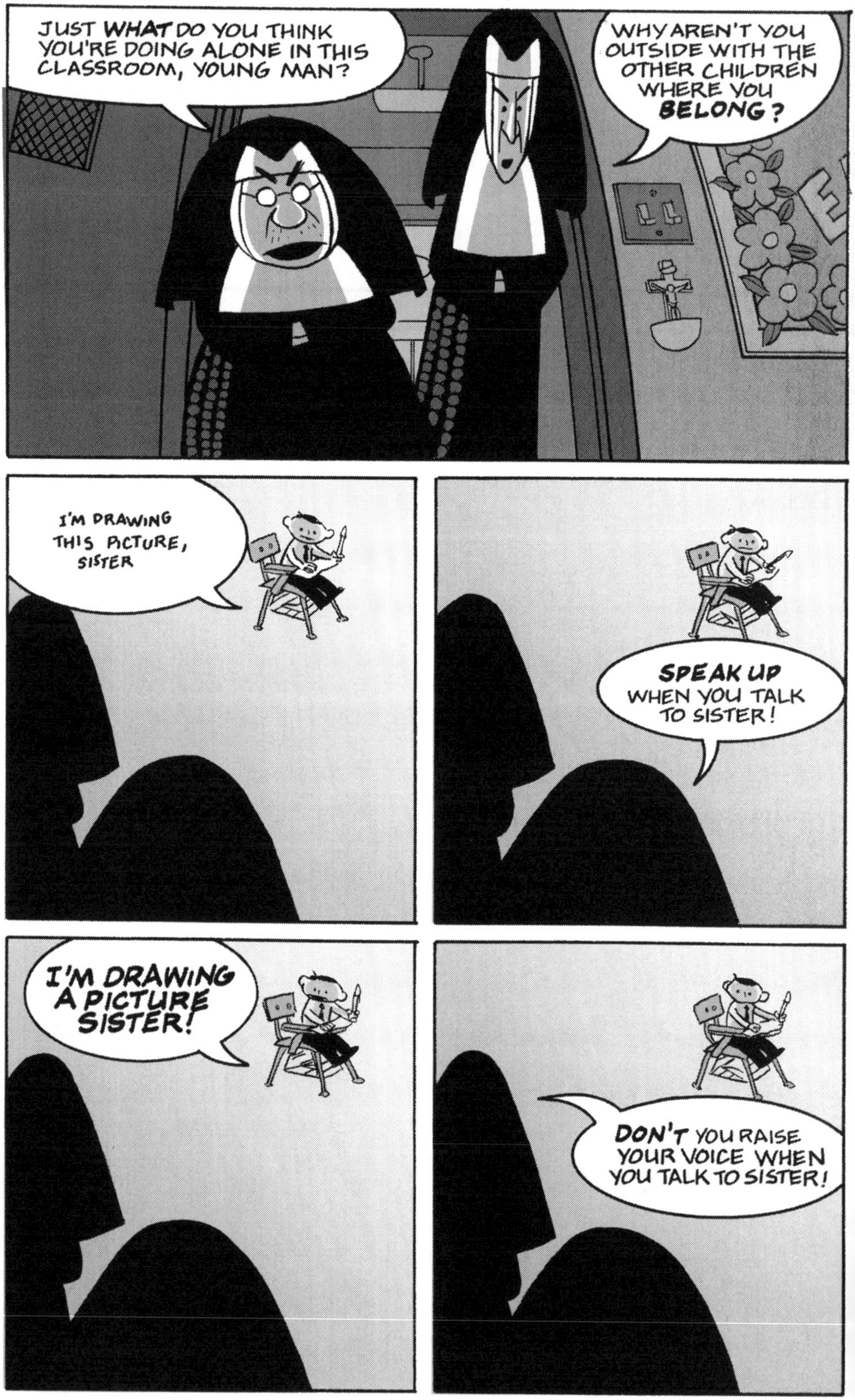
JUST WHAT DO YOU THINK YOU'RE DOING ALONE IN THIS CLASSROOM, YOUNG MAN?
WHY AREN'T YOU OUTSIDE WITH THE OTHER CHILDREN WHERE YOU BELONG?
I'M DRAWING THIS PICTURE, SISTER
SPEAK UP WHEN YOU TALK TO SISTER!
I'M DRAWING A PICTURE SISTER!
DON'T YOU RAISE YOUR VOICE WHEN YOU TALK TO SISTER!

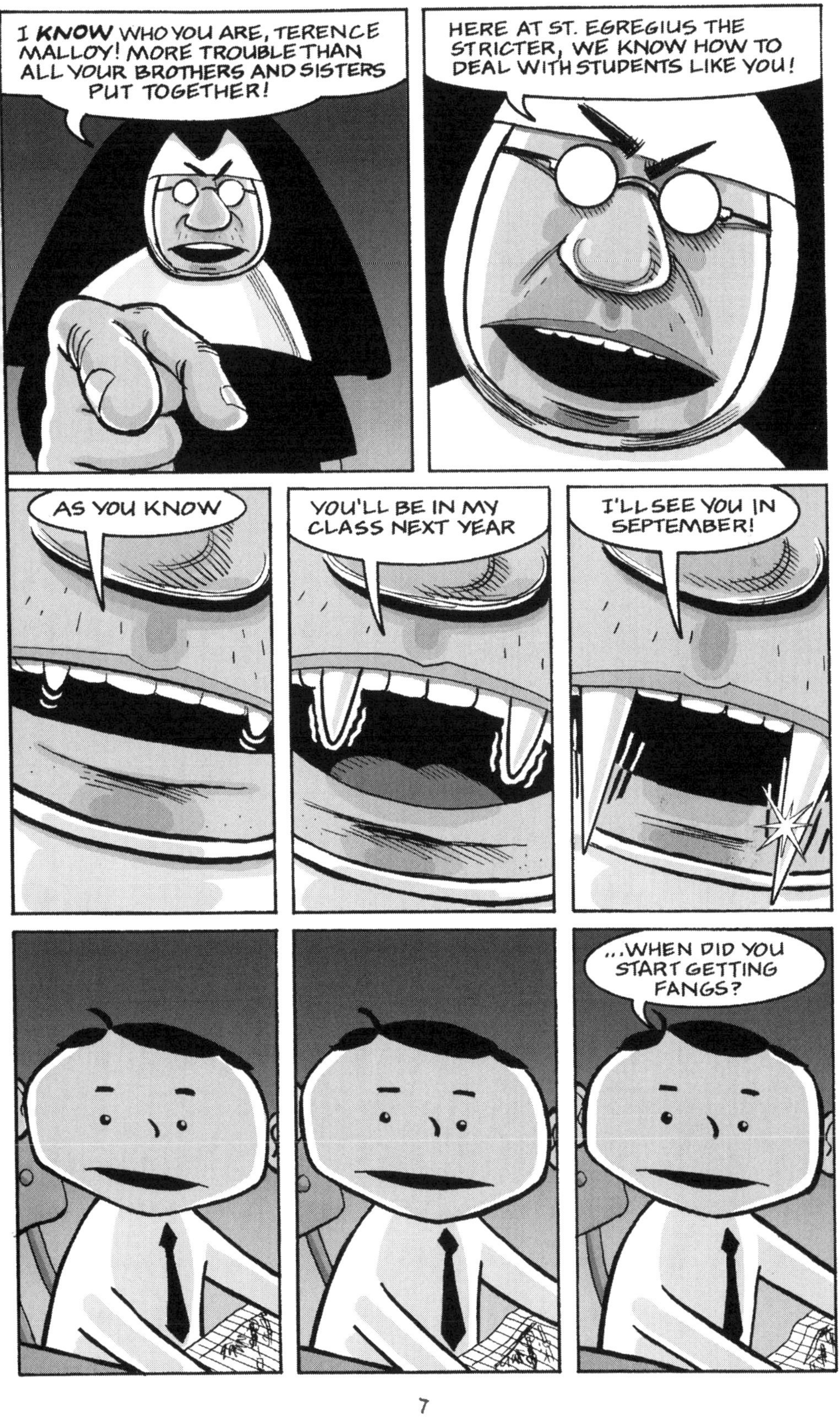
I KNOW WHO YOU ARE, TERENCE MALLOY! MORE TROUBLE THAN ALL YOUR BROTHERS AND SISTERS PUT TOGETHER!
HERE AT ST. EGREGIUS THE STRICTER, WE KNOW HOW TO DEAL WITH STUDENTS LIKE YOU!
AS YOU KNOW
YOU'LL BE IN MY CLASS NEXT YEAR
I'LL SEE YOU IN SEPTEMBER!
...WHEN DID YOU START GETTING FANGS?

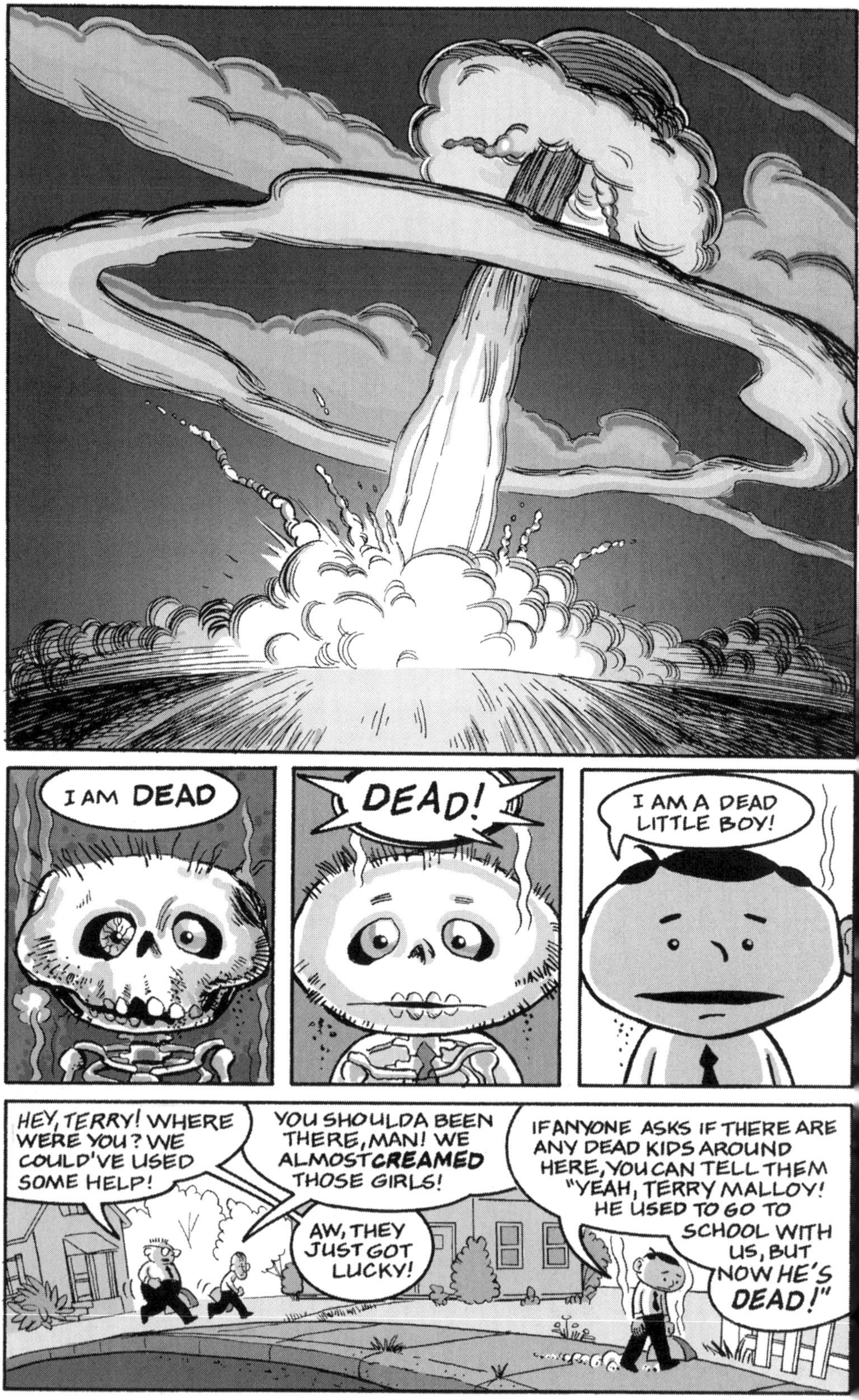
I AM DEAD
DEAD!
I AM A DEAD LITTLE BOY!
HEY, TERRY! WHERE WERE YOU? WE COULD'VE USED SOME HELP!
YOU SHOULDA BEEN THERE, MAN! WE ALMOST CREAMED THOSE GIRLS!
AW, THEY JUST GOT LUCKY!
IF ANYONE ASKS IF THERE ARE ANY DEAD KIDS AROUND HERE, YOU CAN TELL THEM "YEAH, TERRY MALLOY! HE USED TO GO TO SCHOOL WITH US, BUT NOW HE'S DEAD!"

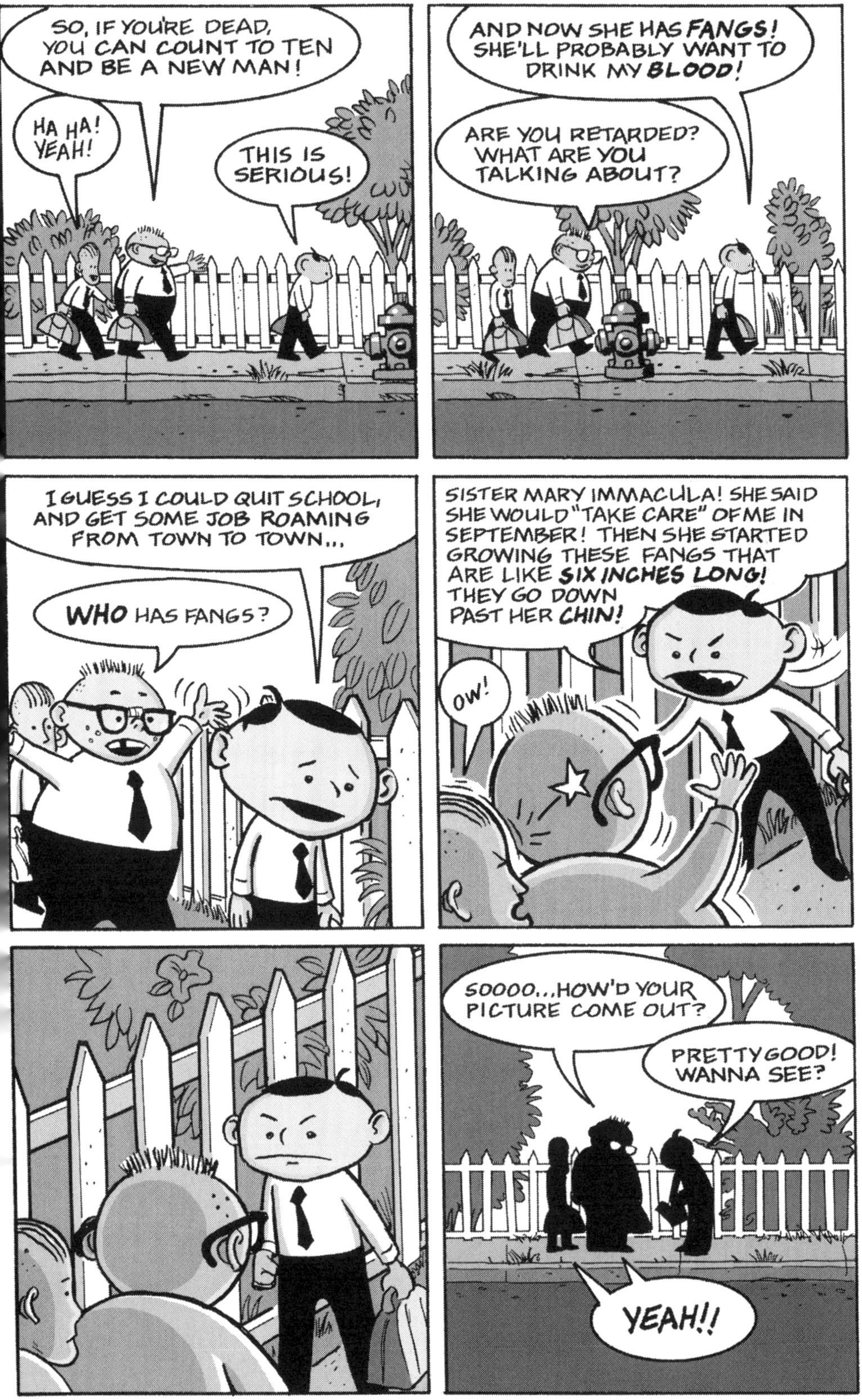
SO, IF YOU'RE DEAD, YOU CAN COUNT TO TEN AND BE A NEW MAN!
HA HA! YEAH!
THIS IS SERIOUS!
AND NOW SHE HAS FANGS! SHE'LL PROBABLY WANT TO DRINK MY BLOOD!
ARE YOU RETARDED? WHAT ARE YOU TALKING ABOUT?
I GUESS I COULD QUIT SCHOOL, AND GET SOME JOB ROAMING FROM TOWN TO TOWN...
WHO HAS FANGS?
SISTER MARY IMMACULA! SHE SAID SHE WOULD "TAKE CARE" OF ME IN SEPTEMBER! THEN SHE STARTED GROWING THESE FANGS THAT ARE LIKE SIX INCHES LONG! THEY GO DOWN PAST HER CHIN!
OW!
SOOOO... HOW'D YOUR PICTURE COME OUT?
PRETTY GOOD! WANNA SEE?
YEAH!!

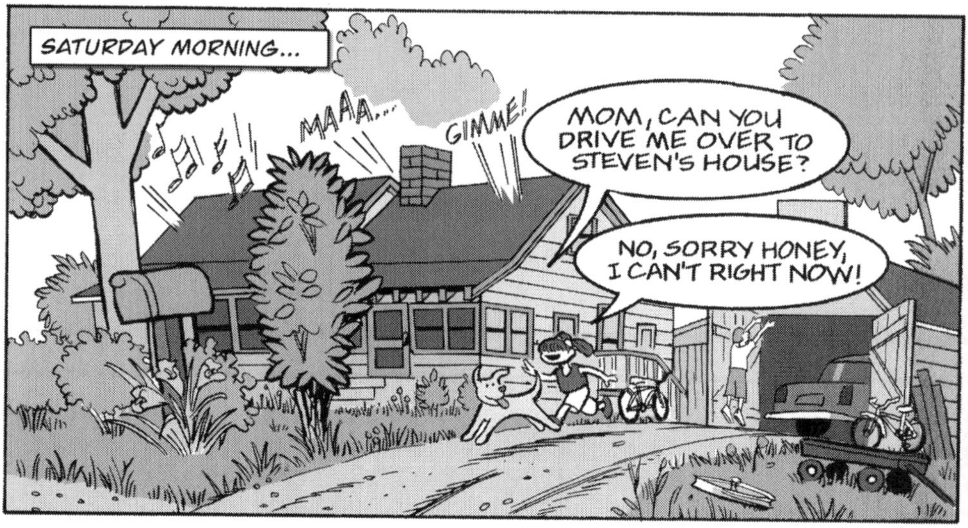
SATURDAY MORNING...
MAAA...
GIMME!
MOM, CAN YOU DRIVE ME OVER TO STEVEN'S HOUSE?
NO, SORRY HONEY, I CAN'T RIGHT NOW!

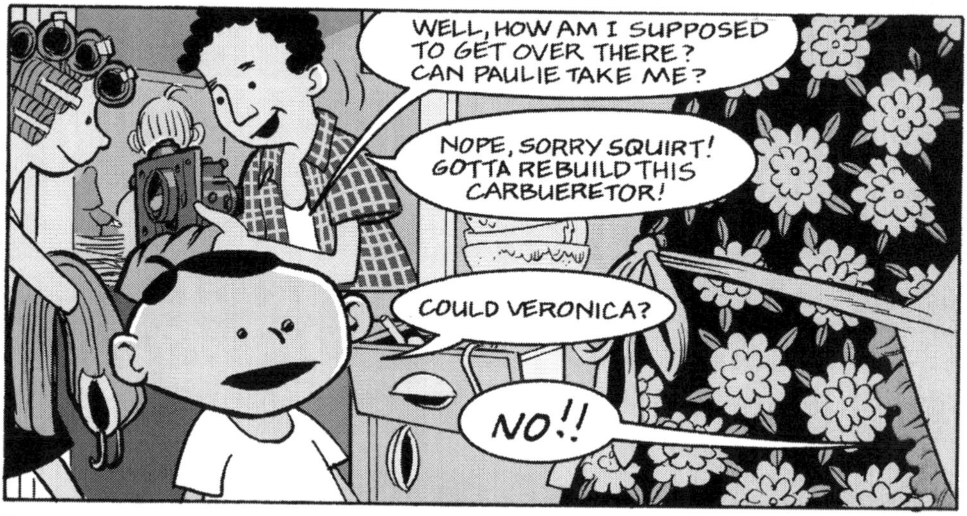
WELL, HOW AM I SUPPOSED TO GET OVER THERE? CAN PAULIE TAKE ME?
NOPE, SORRY SQUIRT! GOTTA REBUILD THIS CARBUERETOR!
COULD VERONICA?
NO!!

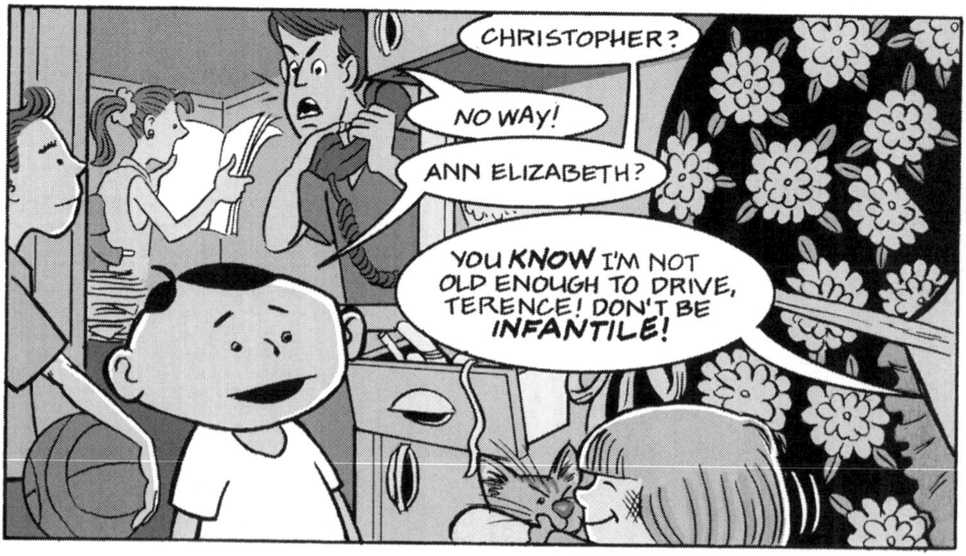
CHRISTOPHER?
NO WAY!
ANN ELIZABETH?
YOU KNOW I'M NOT OLD ENOUGH TO DRIVE, TERENCE! DON'T BE INFANTILE!

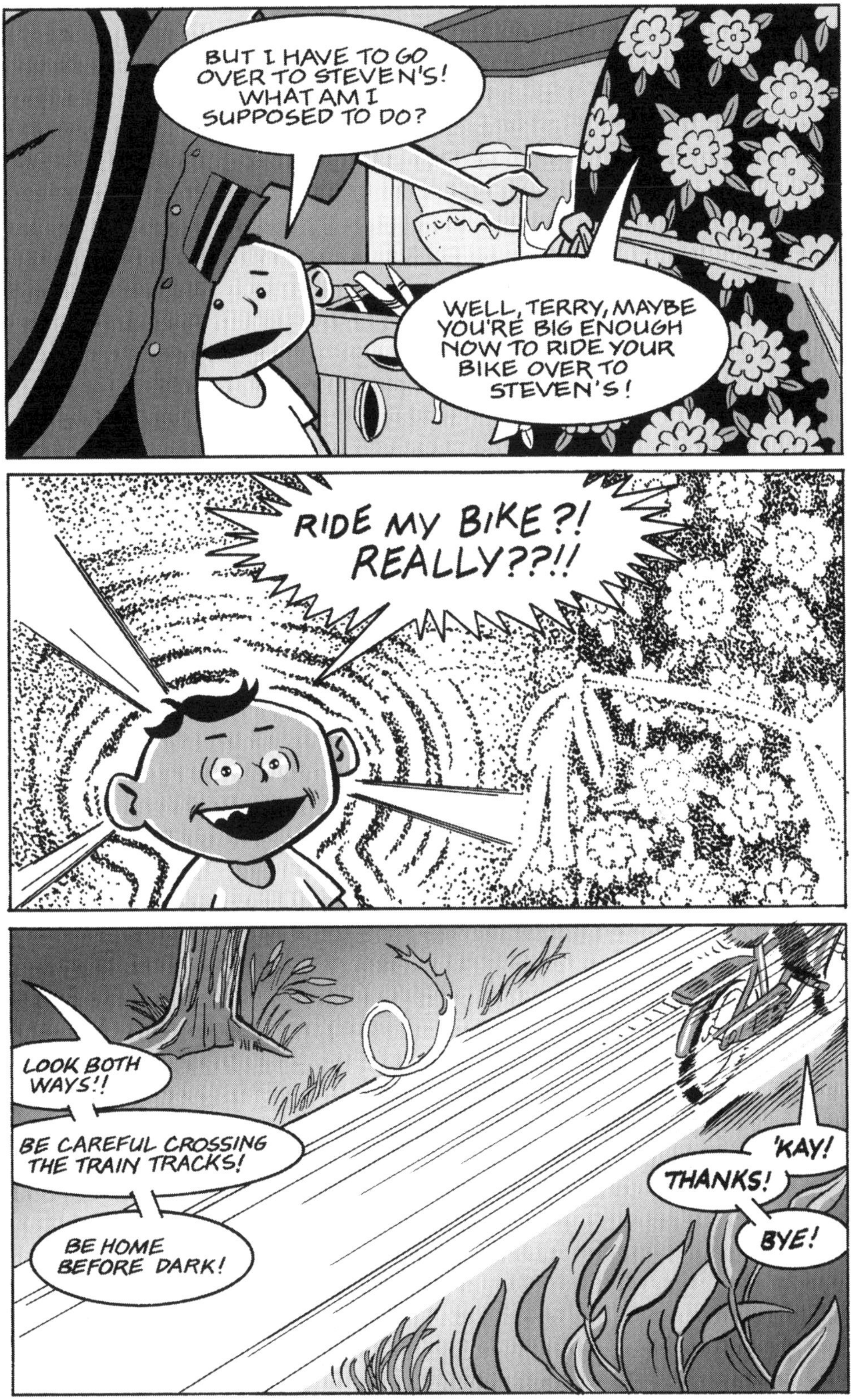
BUT I HAVE TO GO OVER TO STEVEN'S! WHAT AM I SUPPOSED TO DO?
WELL, TERRY, MAYBE YOU'RE BIG ENOUGH NOW TO RIDE YOUR BIKE OVER TO STEVEN'S!
RIDE MY BIKE?! REALLY??!!
LOOK BOTH WAYS!!
BE CAREFUL CROSSING THE TRAIN TRACKS!
BE HOME BEFORE DARK!
'KAY!
THANKS!
BYE!

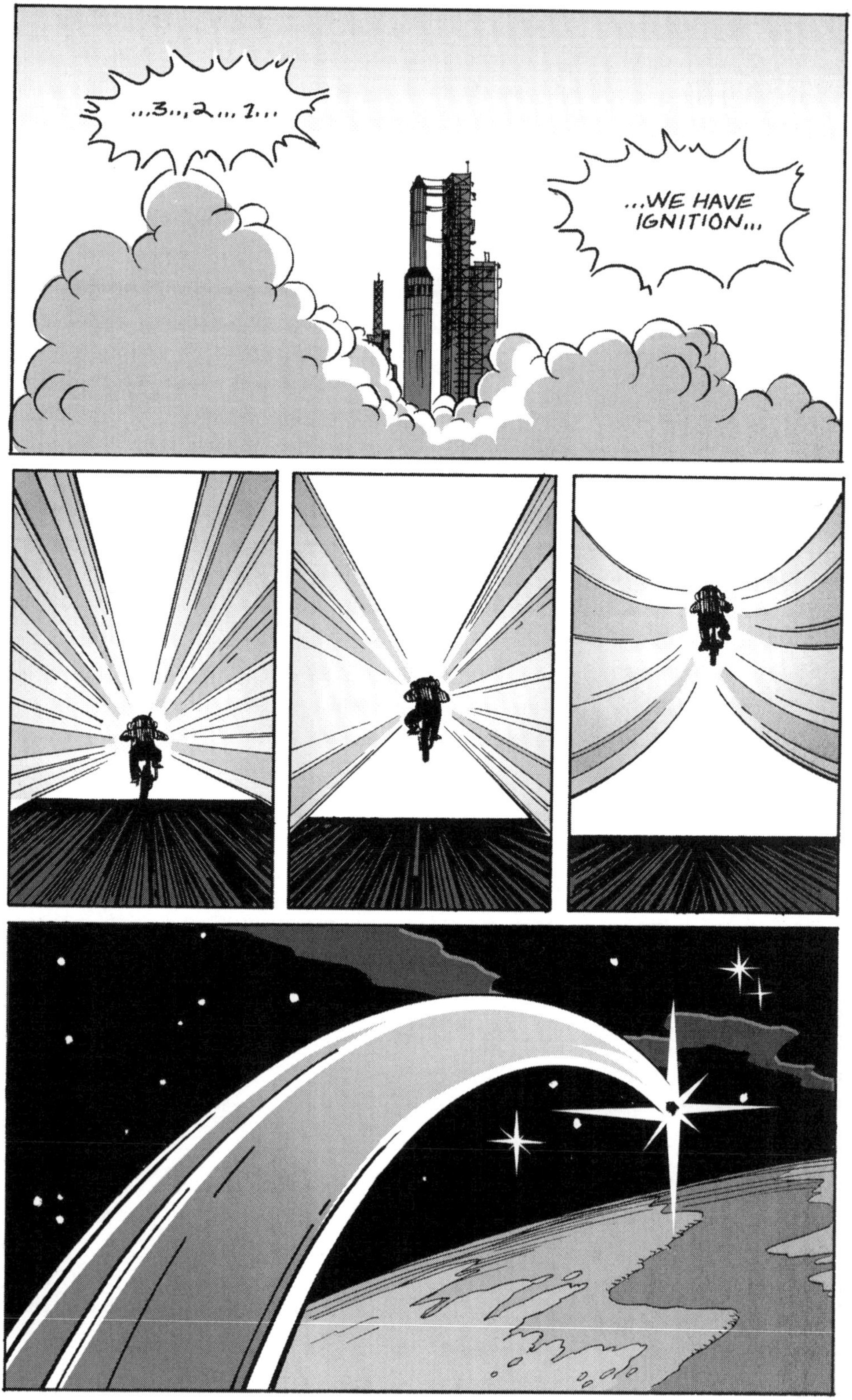
...3...2...1...
...WE HAVE IGNITION...

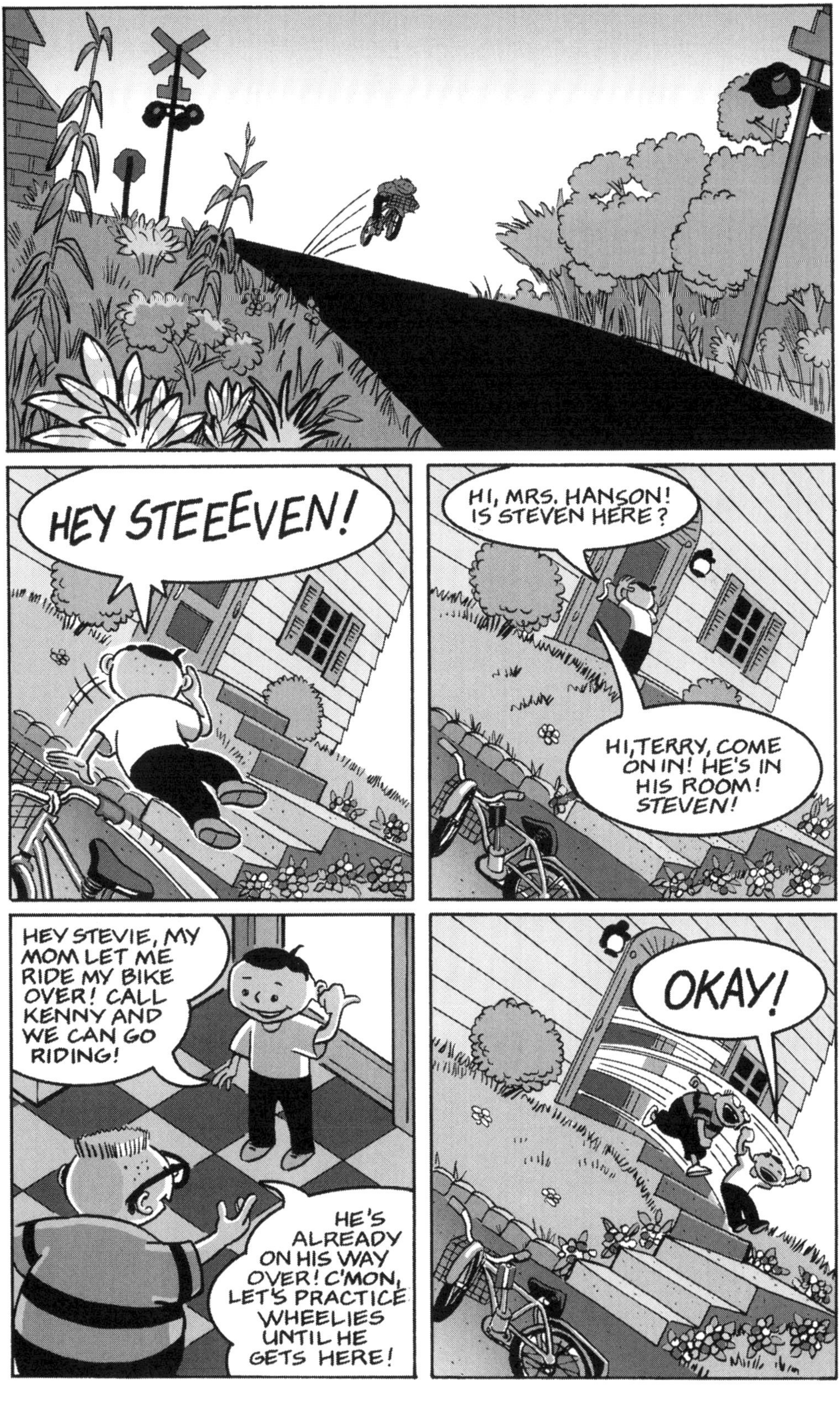
HEY STEEEVEN!
HI, MRS. HANSON! IS STEVEN HERE?
HI, TERRY, COME ON IN! HE'S IN HIS ROOM! STEVEN!
HEY STEVIE, MY MOM LET ME RIDE MY BIKE OVER! CALL KENNY AND WE CAN GO RIDING!
HE'S ALREADY ON HIS WAY OVER! C'MON, LET'S PRACTICE WHEELIES UNTIL HE GETS HERE!
OKAY!

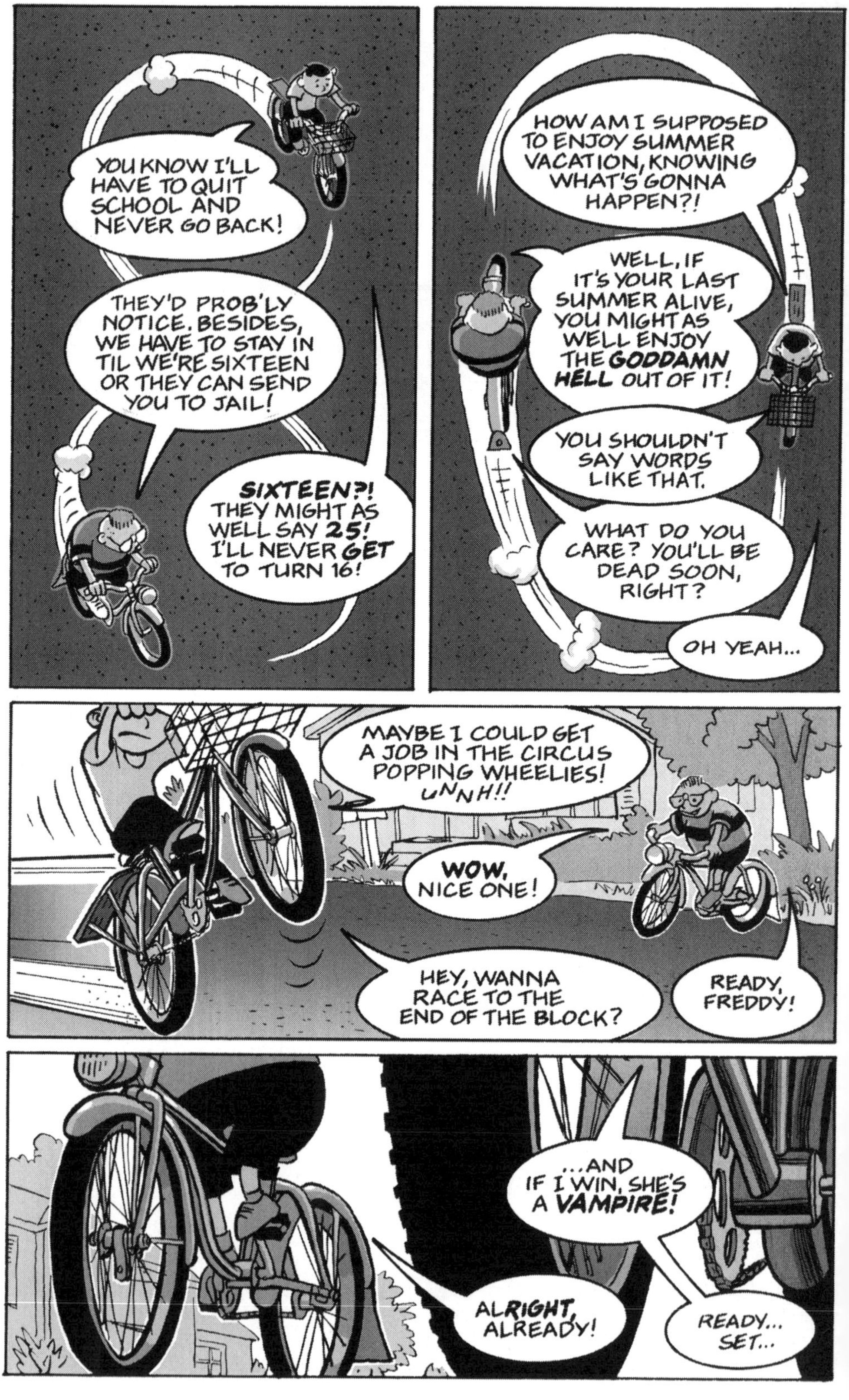
YOU KNOW I'LL HAVE TO QUIT SCHOOL AND NEVER GO BACK!
THEY'D PROB'LY NOTICE. BESIDES, WE HAVE TO STAY IN TIL WE'RE SIXTEEN OR THEY CAN SEND YOU TO JAIL!
SIXTEEN?! THEY MIGHT AS WELL SAY **25!** I'LL NEVER **GET** TO TURN 16!
HOW AM I SUPPOSED TO ENJOY SUMMER VACATION, KNOWING WHAT'S GONNA HAPPEN?!
WELL, IF IT'S YOUR LAST SUMMER ALIVE, YOU MIGHT AS WELL ENJOY THE **GODDAMN HELL** OUT OF IT!
YOU SHOULDN'T SAY WORDS LIKE THAT.
WHAT DO YOU CARE? YOU'LL BE DEAD SOON, RIGHT?
OH YEAH...
MAYBE I COULD GET A JOB IN THE CIRCUS POPPING WHEELIES! uNNH!!
WOW, NICE ONE!
HEY, WANNA RACE TO THE END OF THE BLOCK?
READY, FREDDY!
...AND IF I WIN, SHE'S A **VAMPIRE!**
AL**RIGHT,** ALREADY!
READY... SET...

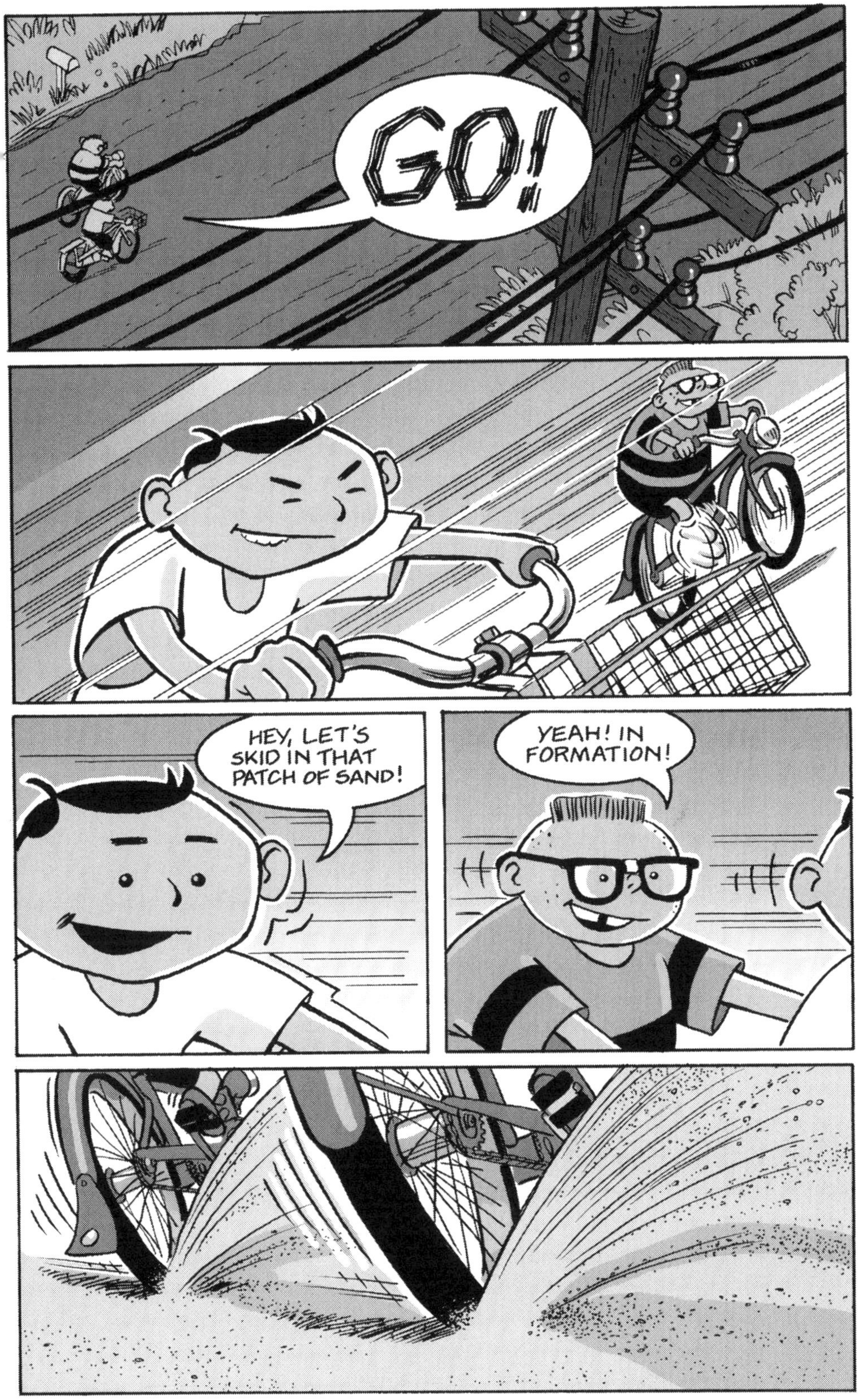
GO!
HEY, LET'S SKID IN THAT PATCH OF SAND!
YEAH! IN FORMATION!

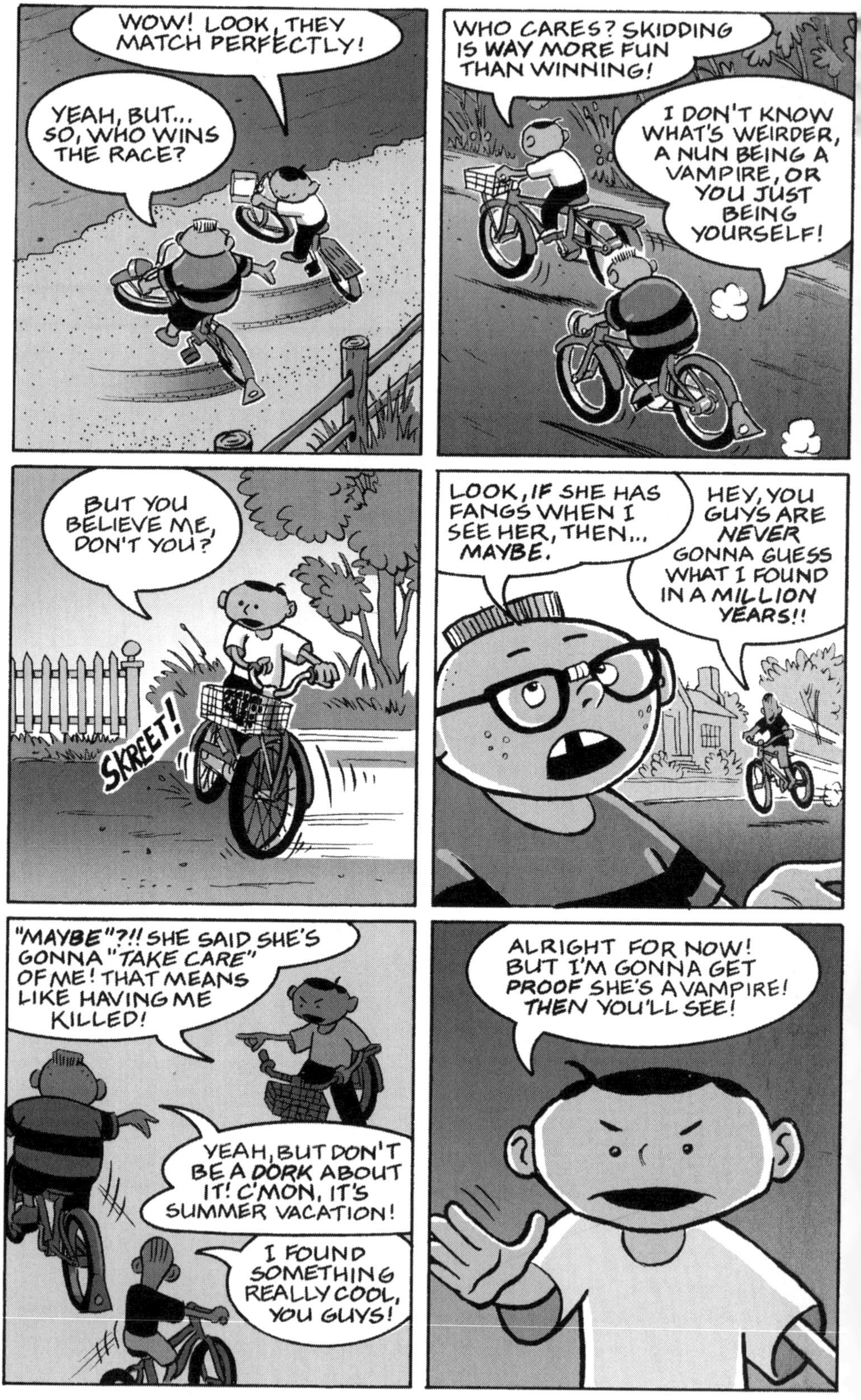
WOW! LOOK, THEY MATCH PERFECTLY!
YEAH, BUT... SO, WHO WINS THE RACE?
WHO CARES? SKIDDING IS WAY MORE FUN THAN WINNING!
I DON'T KNOW WHAT'S WEIRDER, A NUN BEING A VAMPIRE, OR YOU JUST BEING YOURSELF!
BUT YOU BELIEVE ME, DON'T YOU?
SKREET!
LOOK, IF SHE HAS FANGS WHEN I SEE HER, THEN... MAYBE.
HEY, YOU GUYS ARE NEVER GONNA GUESS WHAT I FOUND IN A MILLION YEARS!!
"MAYBE"?!! SHE SAID SHE'S GONNA "TAKE CARE" OF ME! THAT MEANS LIKE HAVING ME KILLED!
YEAH, BUT DON'T BE A DORK ABOUT IT! C'MON, IT'S SUMMER VACATION!
I FOUND SOMETHING REALLY COOL, YOU GUYS!
ALRIGHT FOR NOW! BUT I'M GONNA GET PROOF SHE'S A VAMPIRE! THEN YOU'LL SEE!

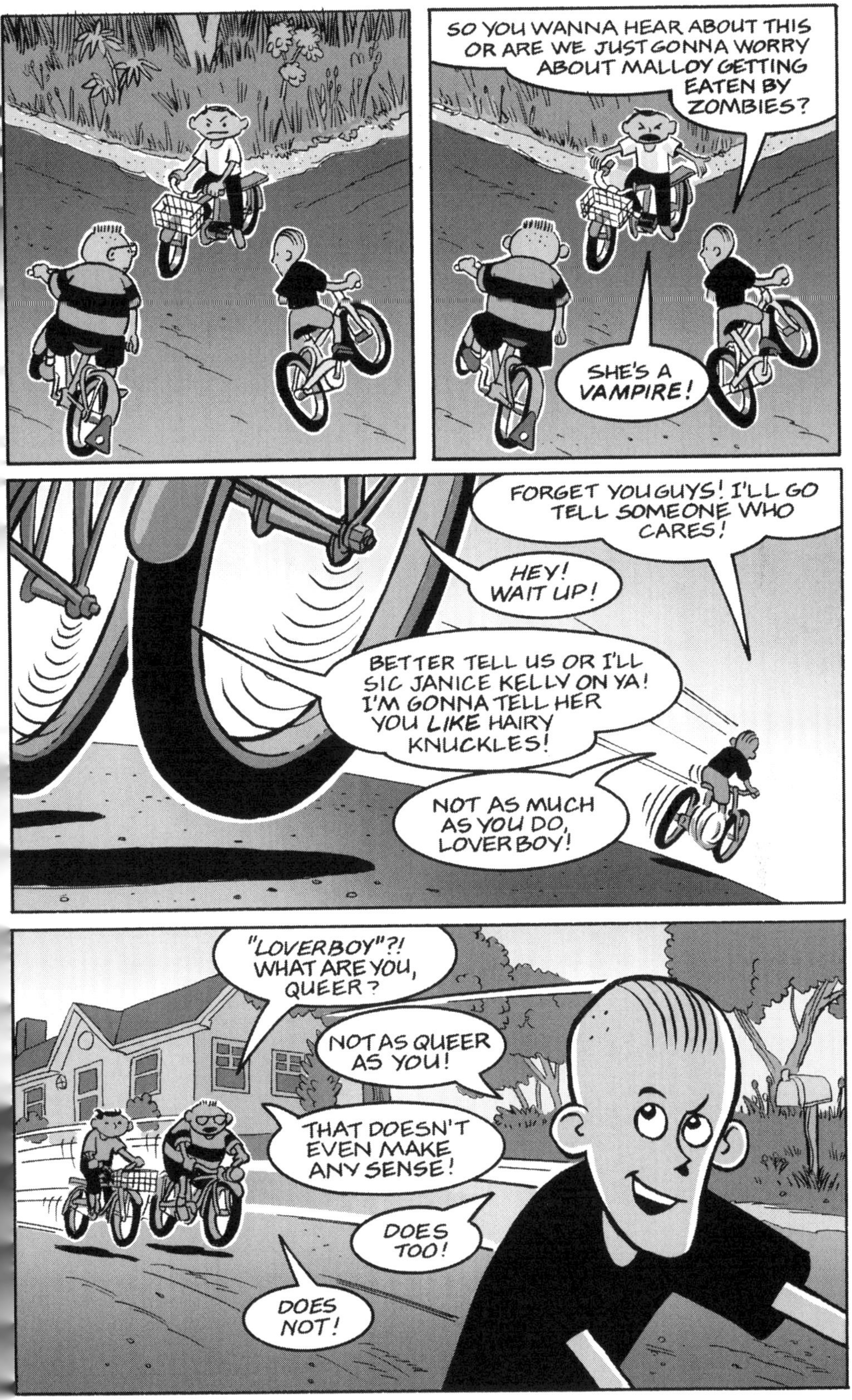
SO YOU WANNA HEAR ABOUT THIS OR ARE WE JUST GONNA WORRY ABOUT MALLOY GETTING EATEN BY ZOMBIES?
SHE'S A *VAMPIRE!*
FORGET YOU GUYS! I'LL GO TELL SOMEONE WHO CARES!
HEY! WAIT UP!
BETTER TELL US OR I'LL SIC JANICE KELLY ON YA! I'M GONNA TELL HER YOU *LIKE* HAIRY KNUCKLES!
NOT AS MUCH AS YOU DO, LOVERBOY!
"LOVERBOY"?! WHAT ARE YOU, QUEER?
NOT AS QUEER AS YOU!
THAT DOESN'T EVEN MAKE ANY SENSE!
DOES TOO!
DOES NOT!

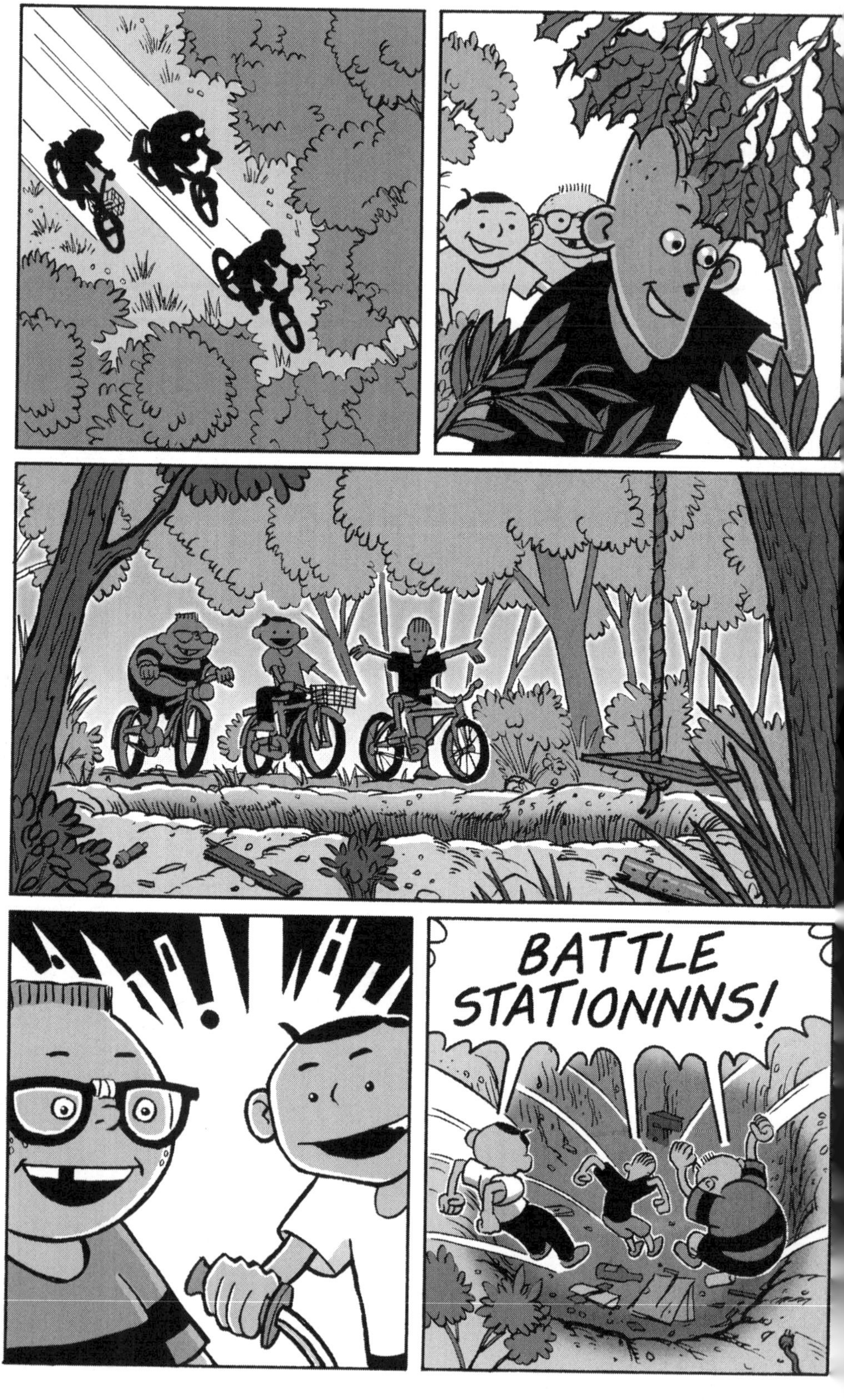
BATTLE STATIONNNS!

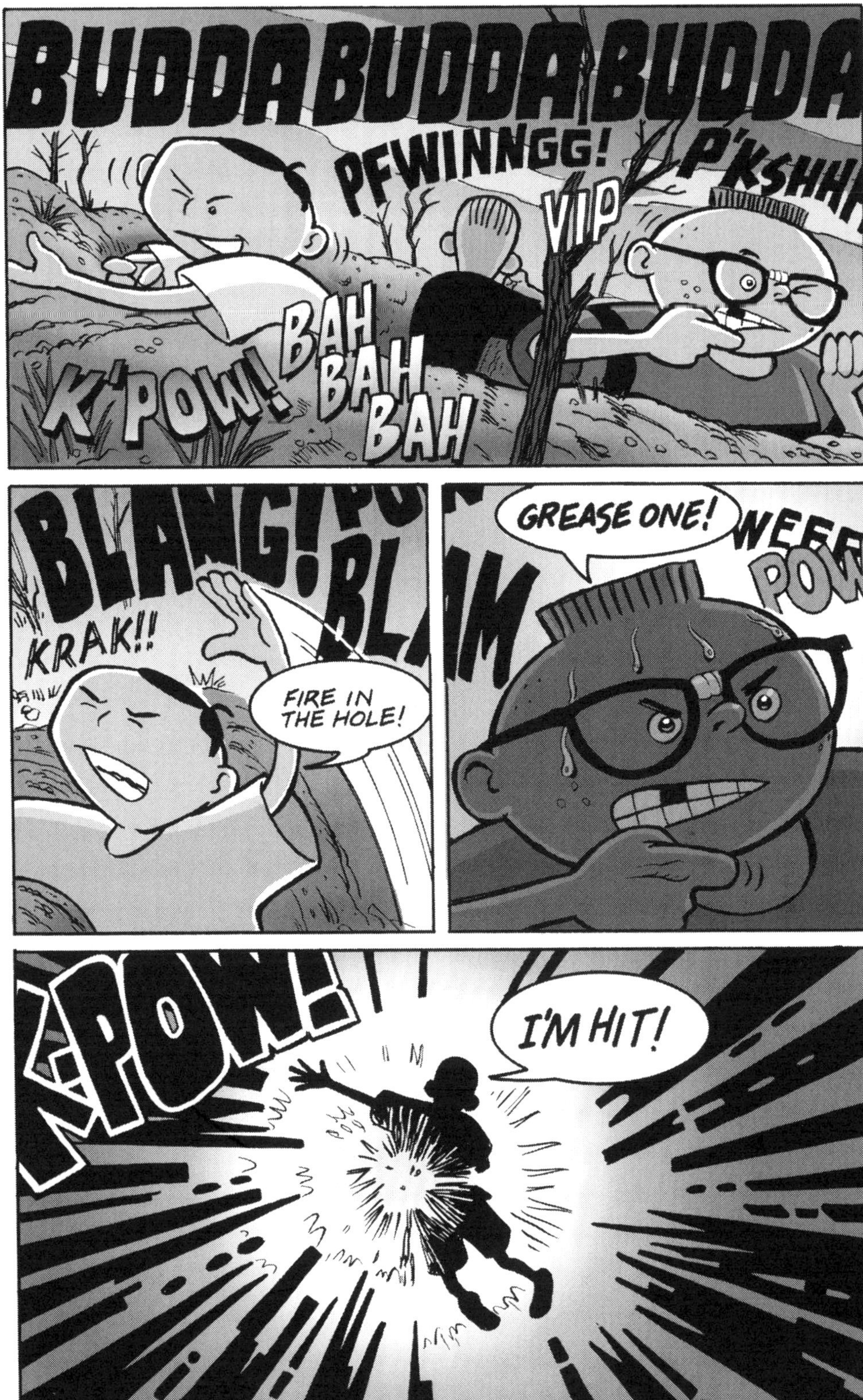
BUDDA BUDDA BUDDA
PFWINNGG!
P'KSHH
VIP
K'POW!
BAH BAH BAH
BLANG!
BLAM
KRAK!!
FIRE IN THE HOLE!
GREASE ONE!
POW
K-POW!
I'M HIT!

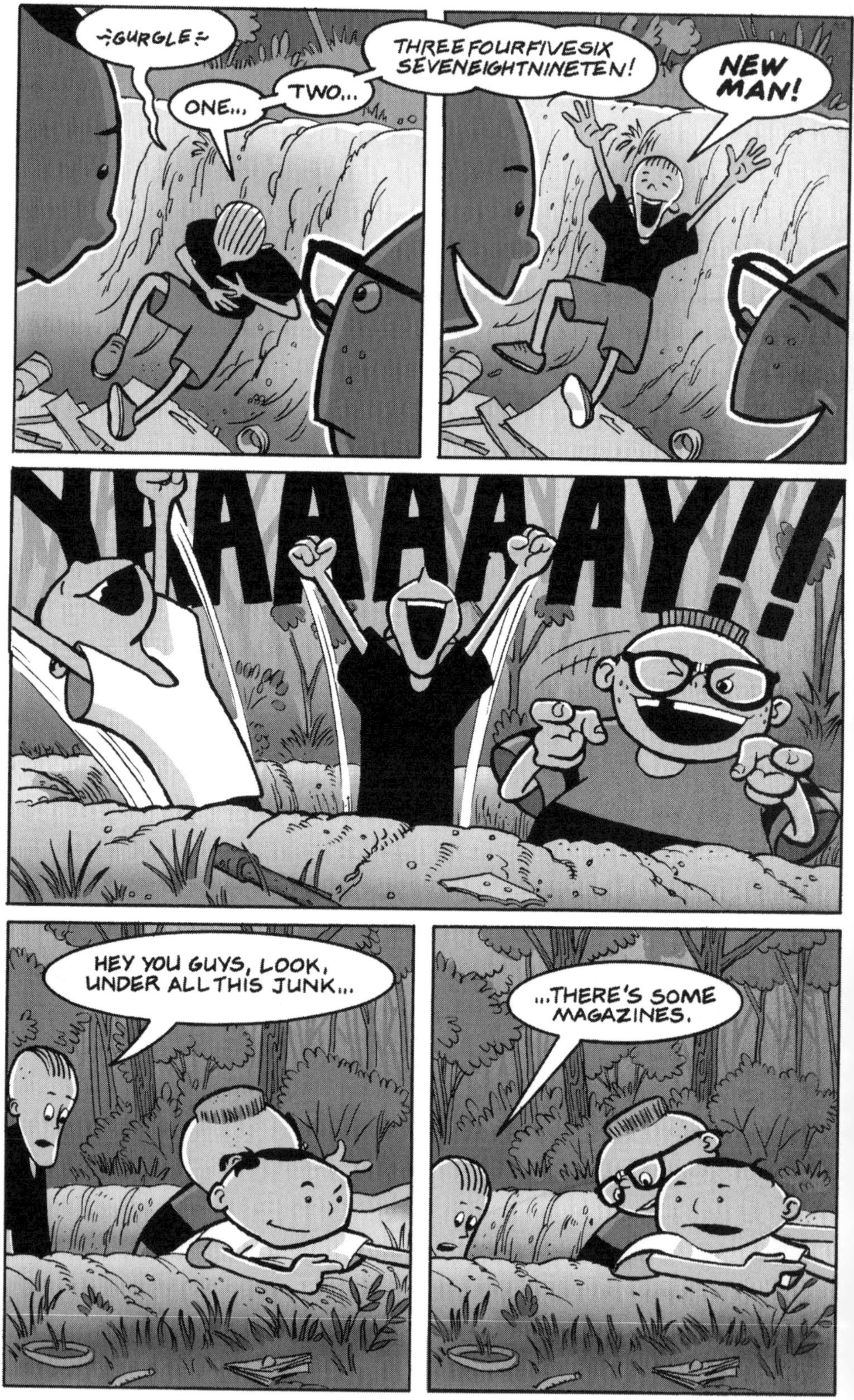

GURGLE
ONE...
TWO...
THREEFOURFIVESIX SEVENEIGHTNINETEN!
NEW MAN!
YAAAAAAY!!!
HEY YOU GUYS, LOOK, UNDER ALL THIS JUNK...
...THERE'S SOME MAGAZINES.

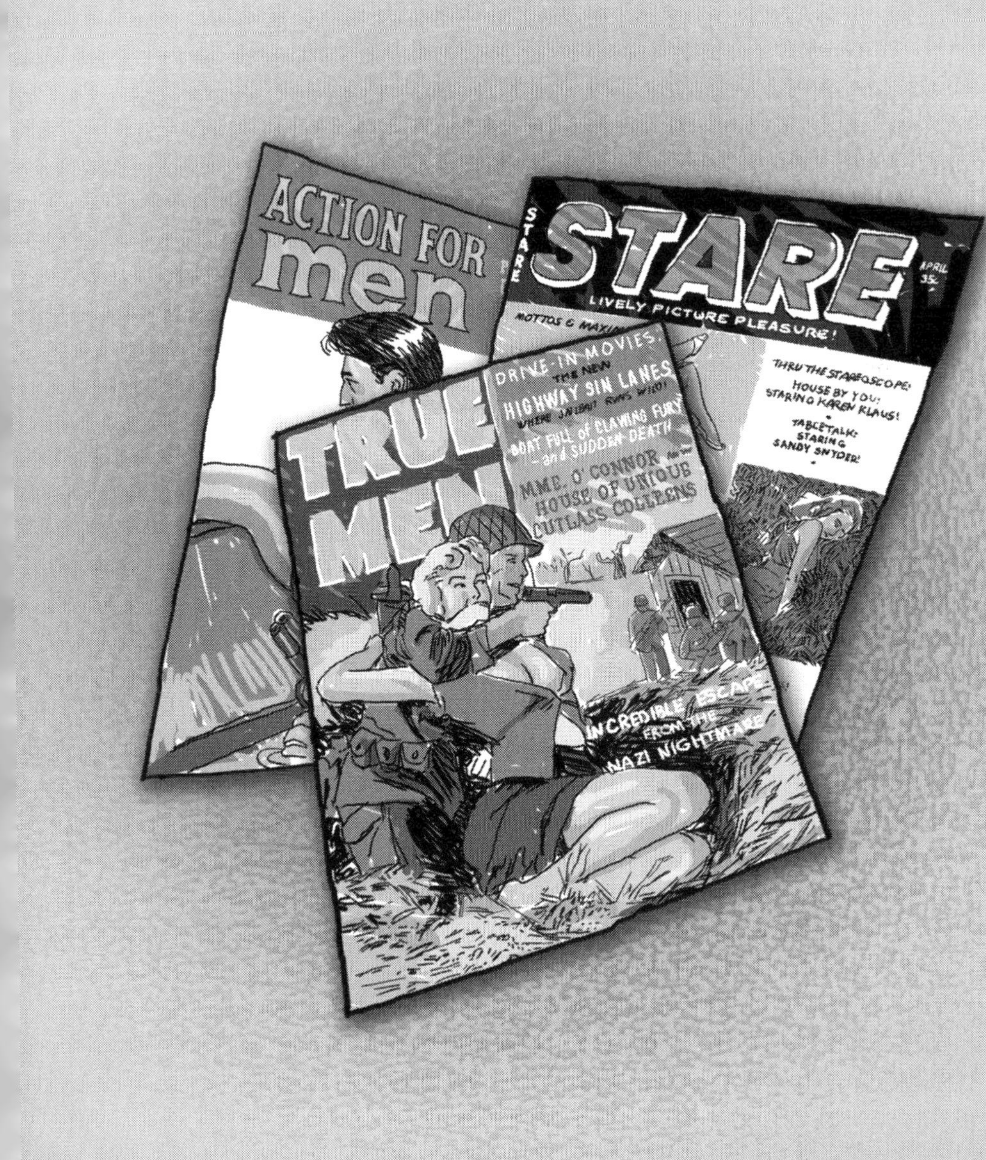
ACTION FOR
men
STARE
APRIL
35¢
LIVELY PICTURE PLEASURE!
THRU THE STAREOSCOPE:
HOUSE BY YOU:
STARING KAREN KLAUS!
TABLETALK:
STARING
SANDY SNYDER!
TRUE
MEN
DRIVE-IN MOVIES:
THE NEW
HIGHWAY SIN LANES
BOAT FULL of CLAWING FURY
- and SUDDEN DEATH
MME. O'CONNOR
HOUSE OF UNIQUE
CUTLASS COLLEENS
INCREDIBLE ESCAPE
FROM THE
NAZI NIGHTMARE

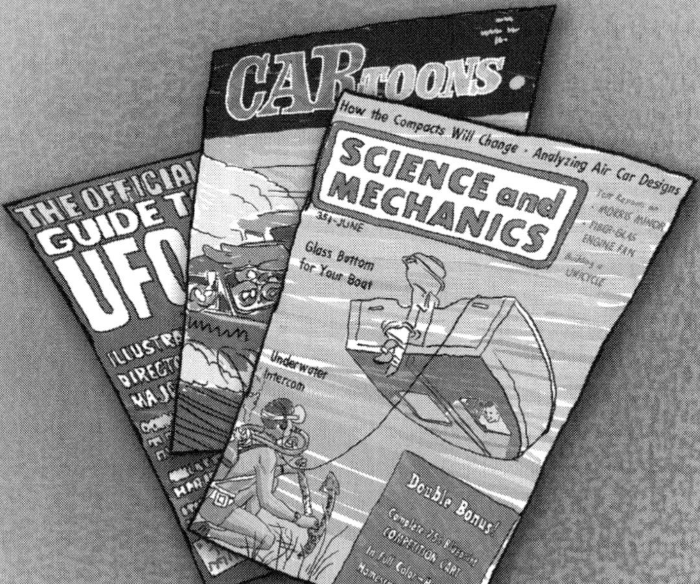

CARTOONS
How the Compacts Will Change · Analyzing Air Car Designs
SCIENCE and MECHANICS
35¢-JUNE
Glass Bottom for Your Boat
Underwater Intercom
Double Bonus!

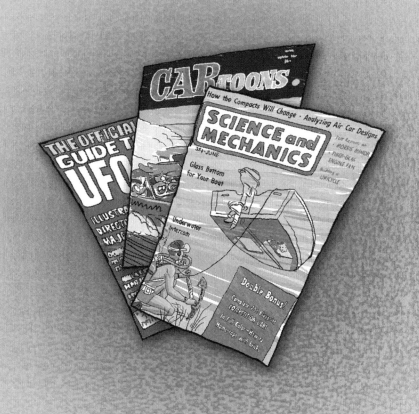

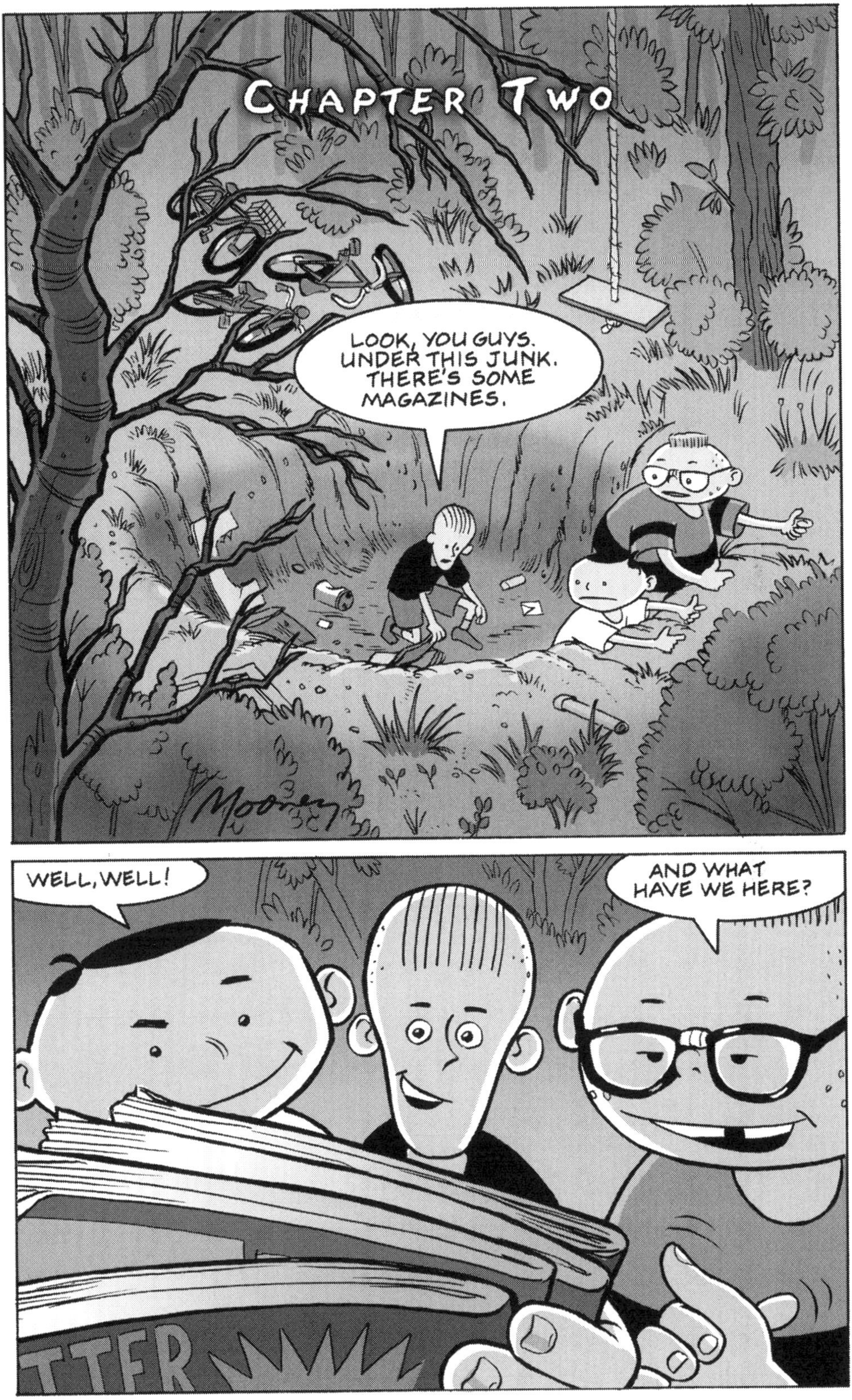
CHAPTER TWO
LOOK, YOU GUYS. UNDER THIS JUNK. THERE'S SOME MAGAZINES.
WELL, WELL!
AND WHAT HAVE WE HERE?

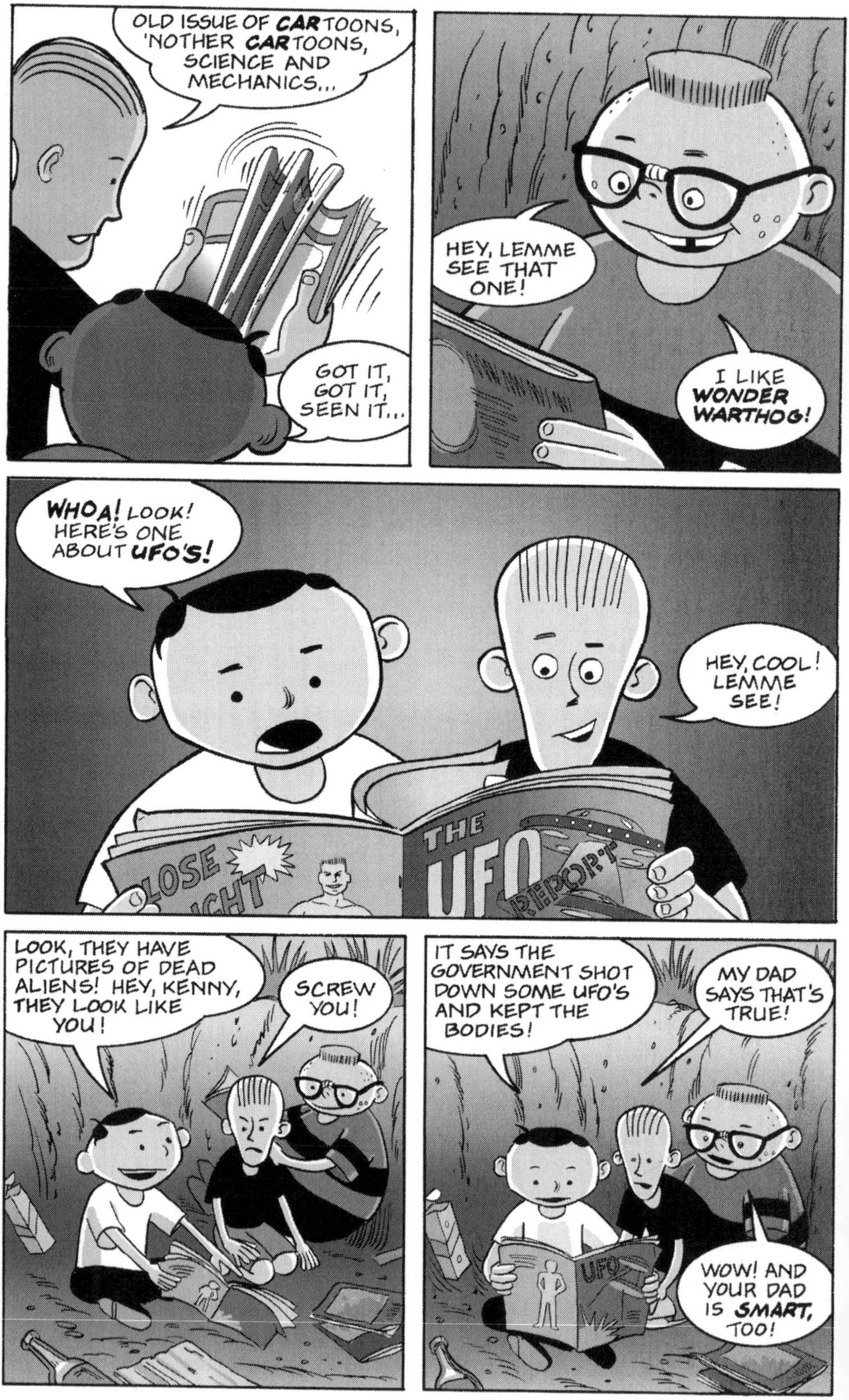

OLD ISSUE OF CARTOONS, 'NOTHER CARTOONS, SCIENCE AND MECHANICS...
GOT IT, GOT IT, SEEN IT...
HEY, LEMME SEE THAT ONE!
I LIKE WONDER WARTHOG!
WHOA! LOOK! HERE'S ONE ABOUT UFO'S!
HEY, COOL! LEMME SEE!
THE UFO REPORT
LOOK, THEY HAVE PICTURES OF DEAD ALIENS! HEY, KENNY, THEY LOOK LIKE YOU!
SCREW YOU!
IT SAYS THE GOVERNMENT SHOT DOWN SOME UFO'S AND KEPT THE BODIES!
MY DAD SAYS THAT'S TRUE!
WOW! AND YOUR DAD IS SMART, TOO!

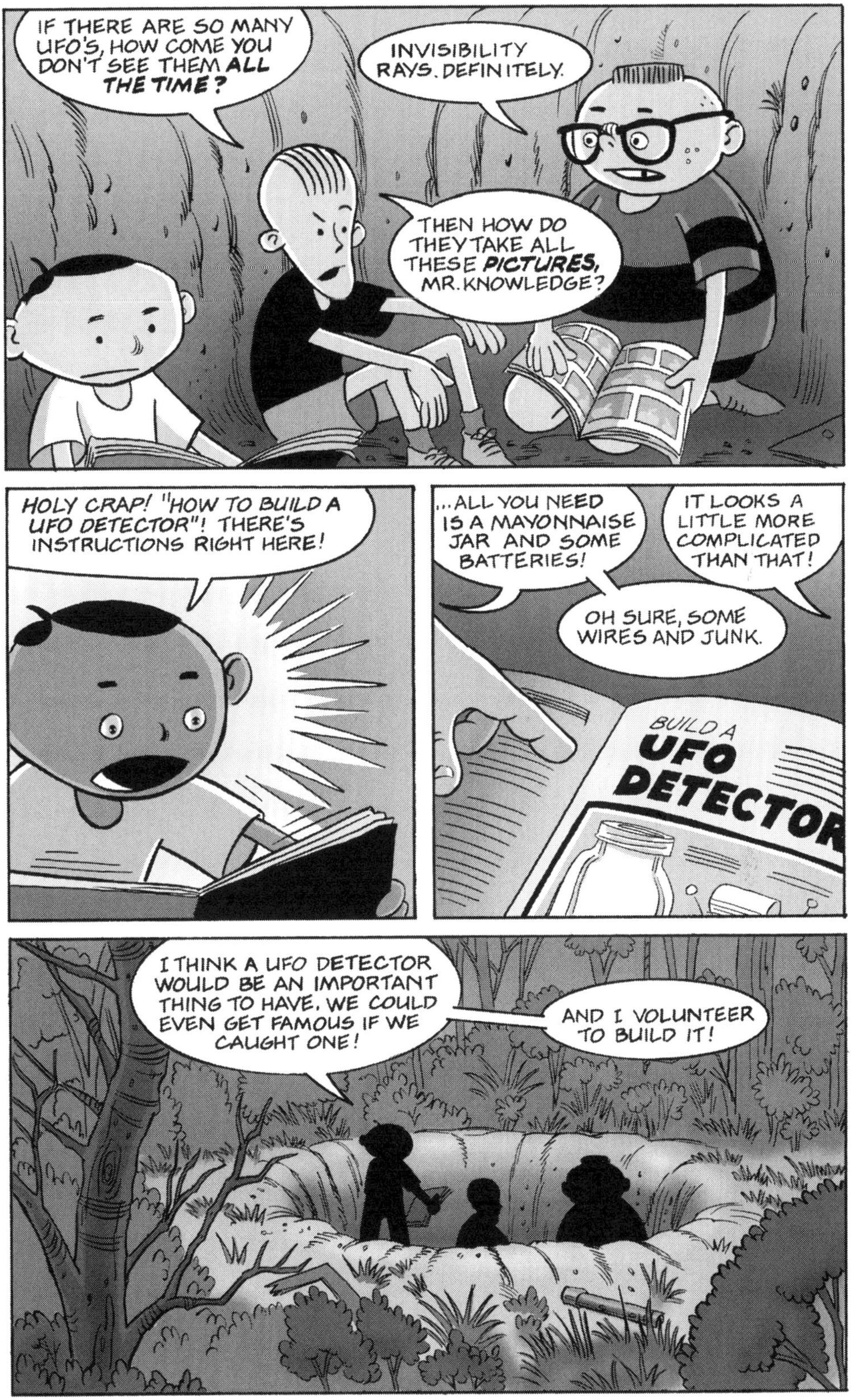
IF THERE ARE SO MANY UFO'S, HOW COME YOU DON'T SEE THEM **ALL THE TIME?**
INVISIBILITY RAYS. DEFINITELY.
THEN HOW DO THEY TAKE ALL THESE **PICTURES,** MR. KNOWLEDGE?
HOLY CRAP! "HOW TO BUILD A UFO DETECTOR"! THERE'S INSTRUCTIONS RIGHT HERE!
...ALL YOU NEED IS A MAYONNAISE JAR AND SOME BATTERIES!
IT LOOKS A LITTLE MORE COMPLICATED THAN THAT!
OH SURE, SOME WIRES AND JUNK.
BUILD A
UFO DETECTOR
I THINK A UFO DETECTOR WOULD BE AN IMPORTANT THING TO HAVE. WE COULD EVEN GET FAMOUS IF WE CAUGHT ONE!
AND I VOLUNTEER TO BUILD IT!

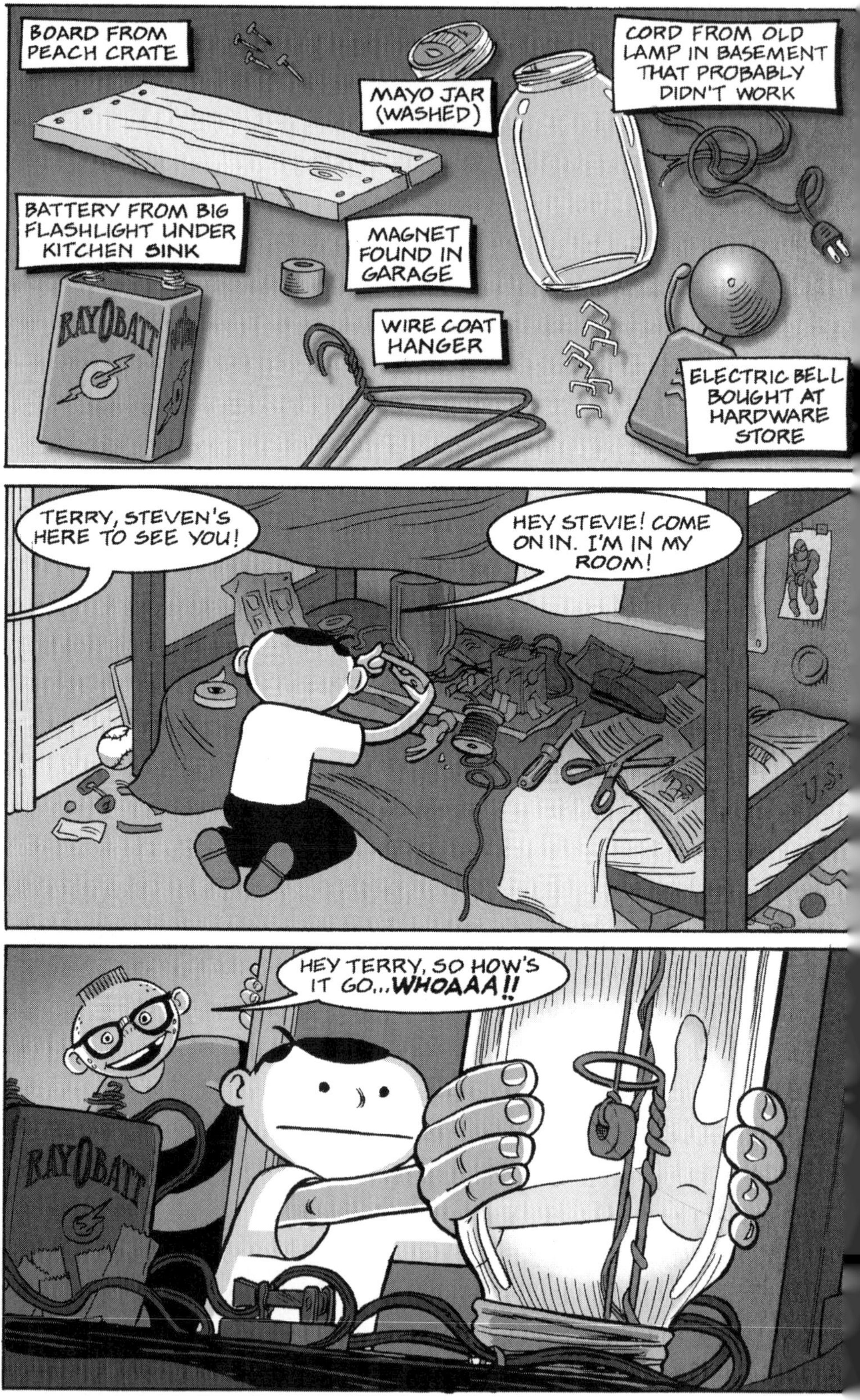
BOARD FROM PEACH CRATE
MAYO JAR (WASHED)
CORD FROM OLD LAMP IN BASEMENT THAT PROBABLY DIDN'T WORK
BATTERY FROM BIG FLASHLIGHT UNDER KITCHEN SINK
MAGNET FOUND IN GARAGE
RAYOBATT
WIRE COAT HANGER
ELECTRIC BELL BOUGHT AT HARDWARE STORE
TERRY, STEVEN'S HERE TO SEE YOU!
HEY STEVIE! COME ON IN. I'M IN MY ROOM!
U.S.
HEY TERRY, SO HOW'S IT GO... **WHOAAA!!**
RAYOBATT

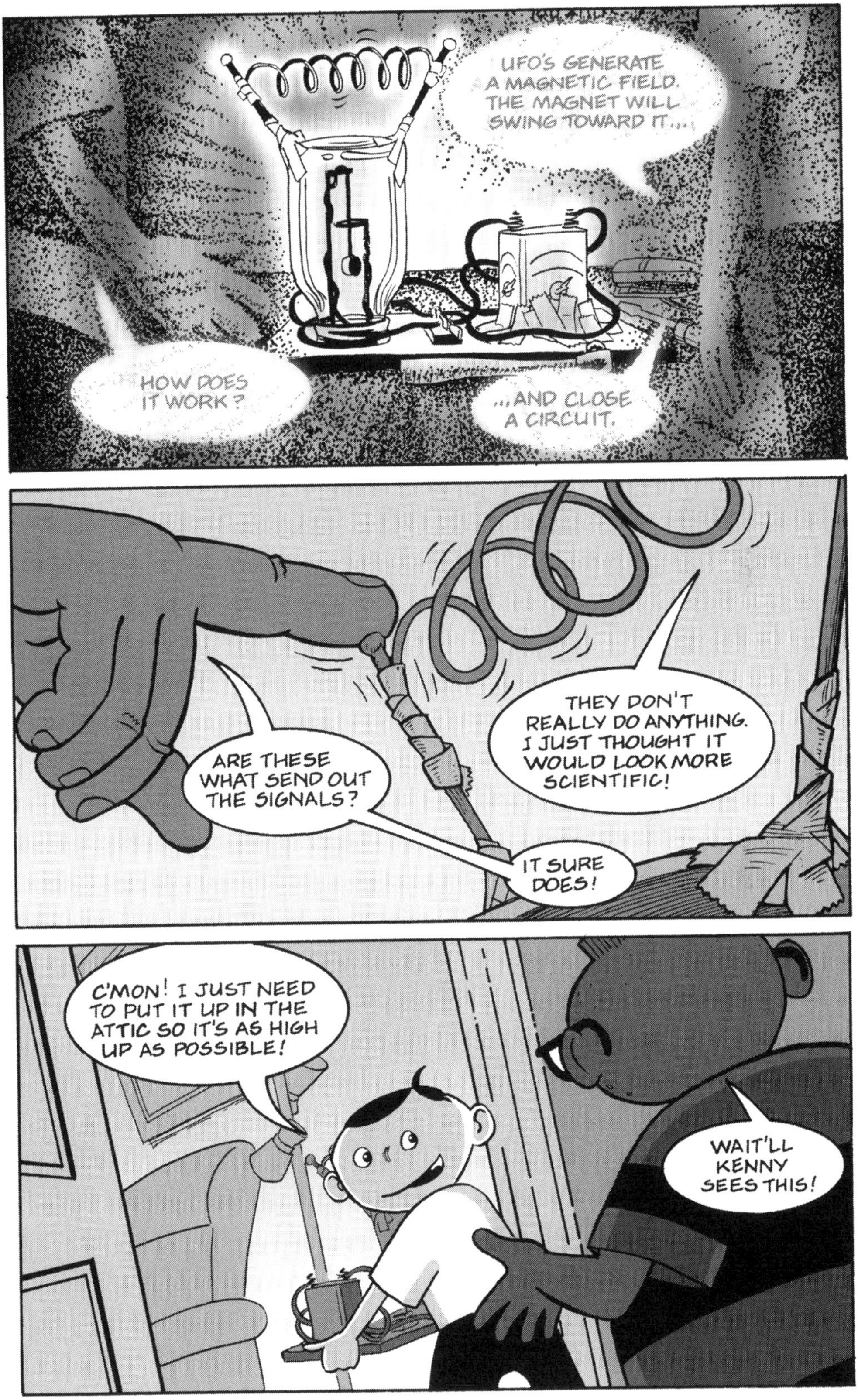
UFO'S GENERATE A MAGNETIC FIELD. THE MAGNET WILL SWING TOWARD IT...
HOW DOES IT WORK?
...AND CLOSE A CIRCUIT.
ARE THESE WHAT SEND OUT THE SIGNALS?
THEY DON'T REALLY DO ANYTHING. I JUST THOUGHT IT WOULD LOOK MORE SCIENTIFIC!
IT SURE DOES!
C'MON! I JUST NEED TO PUT IT UP IN THE ATTIC SO IT'S AS HIGH UP AS POSSIBLE!
WAIT'LL KENNY SEES THIS!

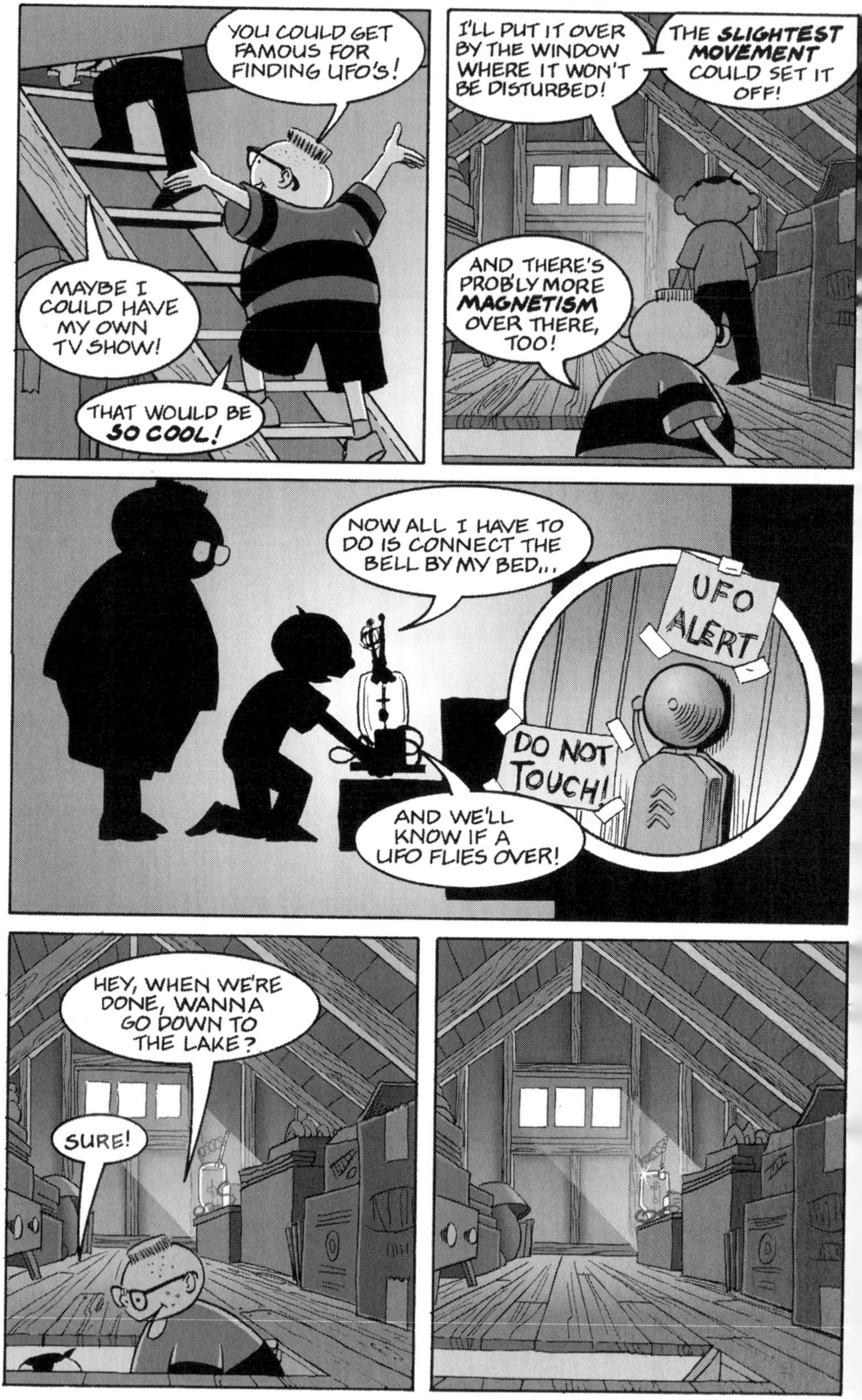
YOU COULD GET FAMOUS FOR FINDING UFO'S!
MAYBE I COULD HAVE MY OWN TV SHOW!
THAT WOULD BE SO COOL!
I'LL PUT IT OVER BY THE WINDOW WHERE IT WON'T BE DISTURBED!
THE SLIGHTEST MOVEMENT COULD SET IT OFF!
AND THERE'S PROB'LY MORE MAGNETISM OVER THERE, TOO!
NOW ALL I HAVE TO DO IS CONNECT THE BELL BY MY BED...
UFO ALERT
DO NOT TOUCH!
AND WE'LL KNOW IF A UFO FLIES OVER!
HEY, WHEN WE'RE DONE, WANNA GO DOWN TO THE LAKE?
SURE!

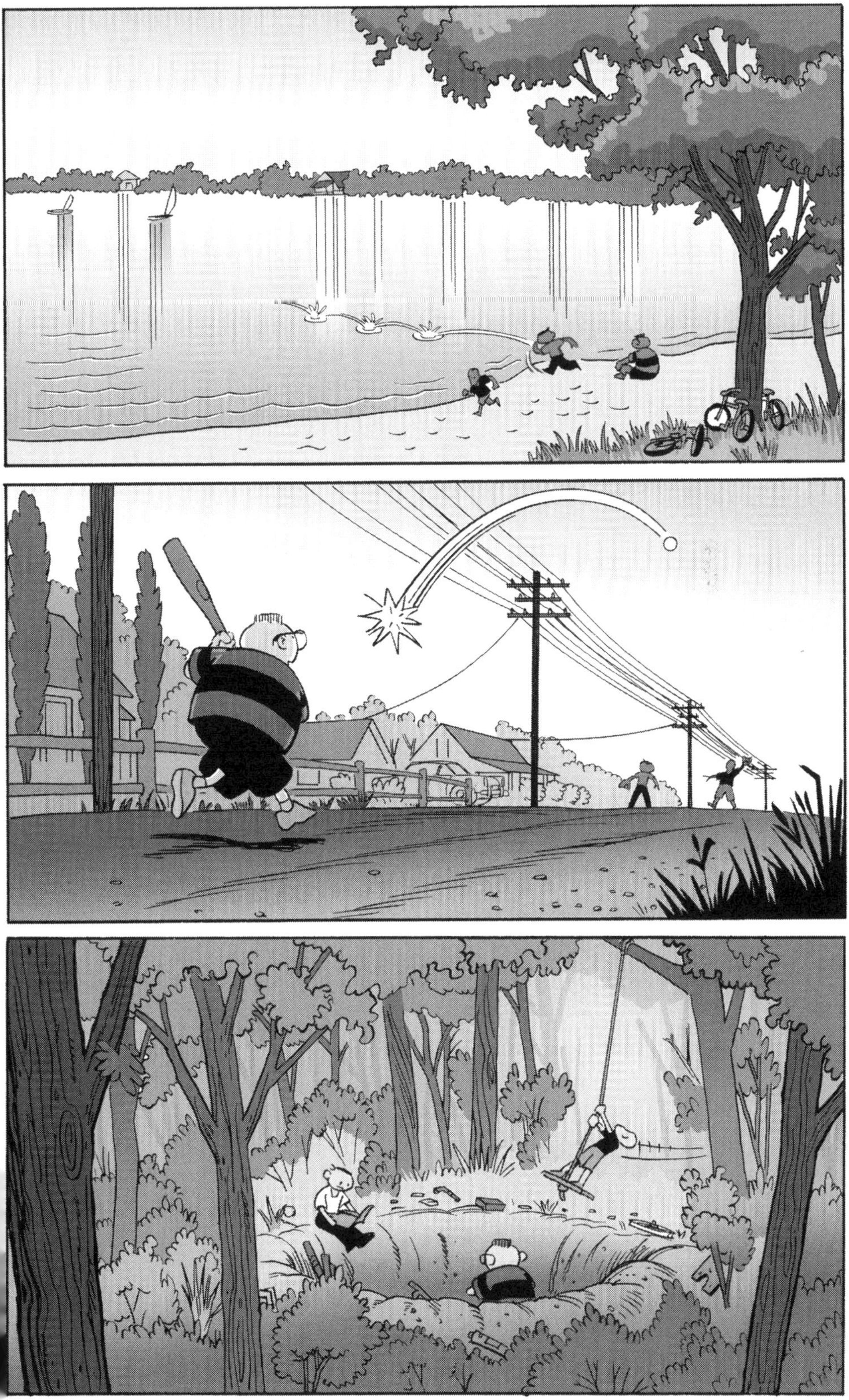

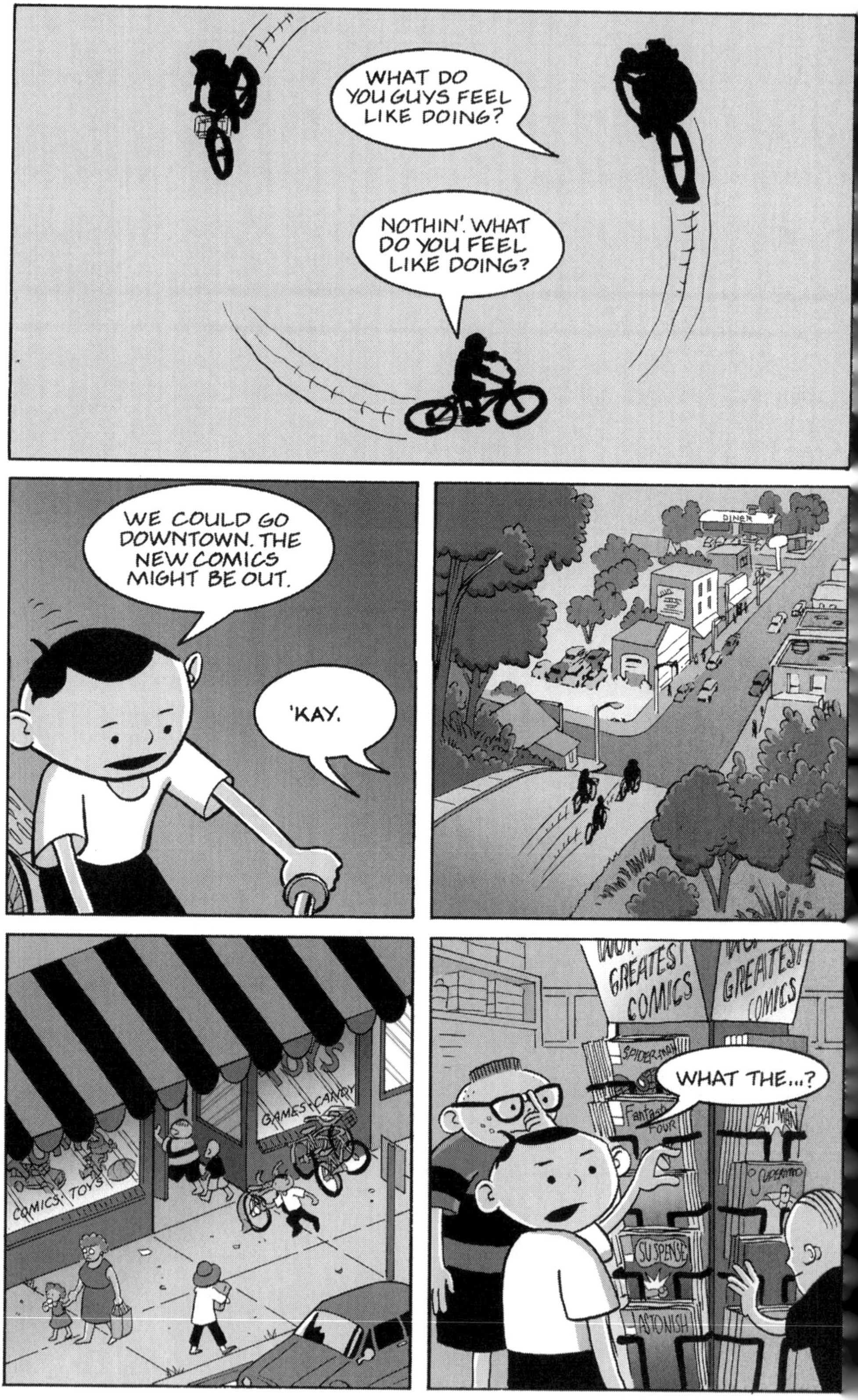
WHAT DO YOU GUYS FEEL LIKE DOING?
NOTHIN'. WHAT DO YOU FEEL LIKE DOING?
WE COULD GO DOWNTOWN. THE NEW COMICS MIGHT BE OUT.
'KAY.
DINER
GAMES CANDY
COMICS TOYS
GREATEST COMICS
GREATEST COMICS
SPIDER-MAN
WHAT THE...?
Fantastic FOUR
BATMAN
SUSPENSE
ASTONISH

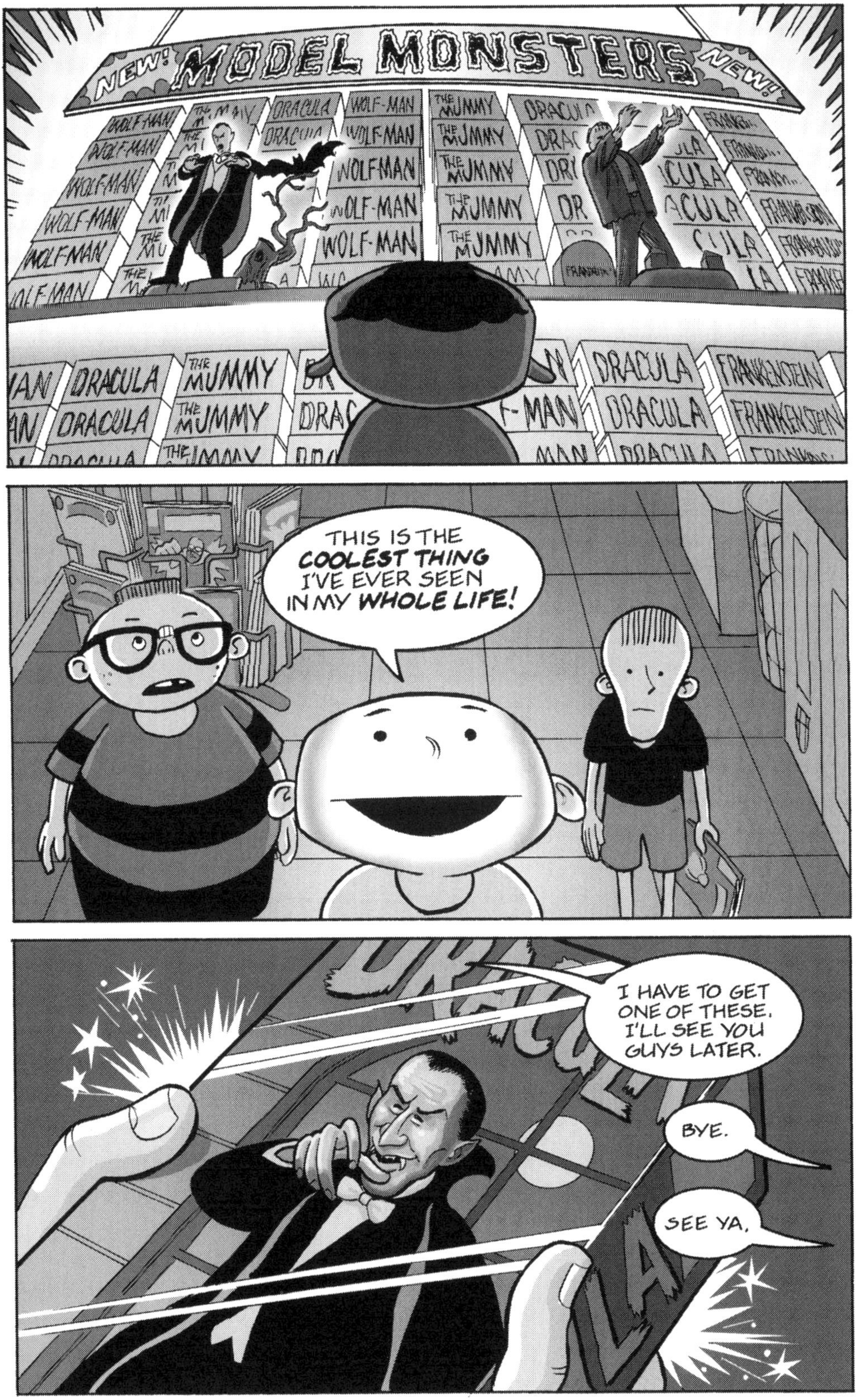
NEW! MODEL MONSTERS NEW!
THIS IS THE COOLEST THING I'VE EVER SEEN IN MY WHOLE LIFE!
I HAVE TO GET ONE OF THESE. I'LL SEE YOU GUYS LATER.
BYE.
SEE YA.

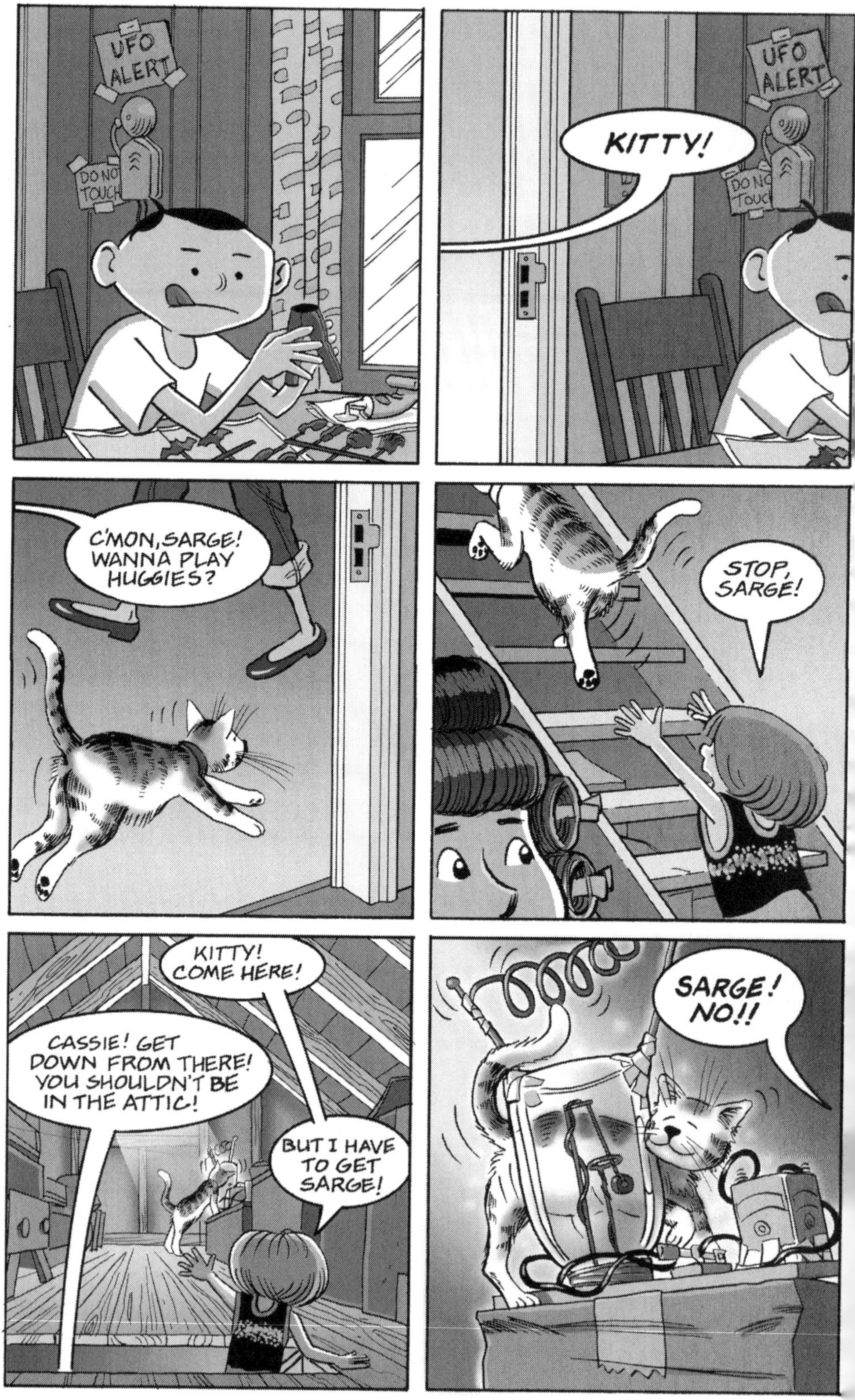
UFO ALERT
DO NOT TOUCH
KITTY!
C'MON, SARGE! WANNA PLAY HUGGIES?
STOP, SARGE!
KITTY! COME HERE!
CASSIE! GET DOWN FROM THERE! YOU SHOULDN'T BE IN THE ATTIC!
BUT I HAVE TO GET SARGE!
SARGE! NO!!

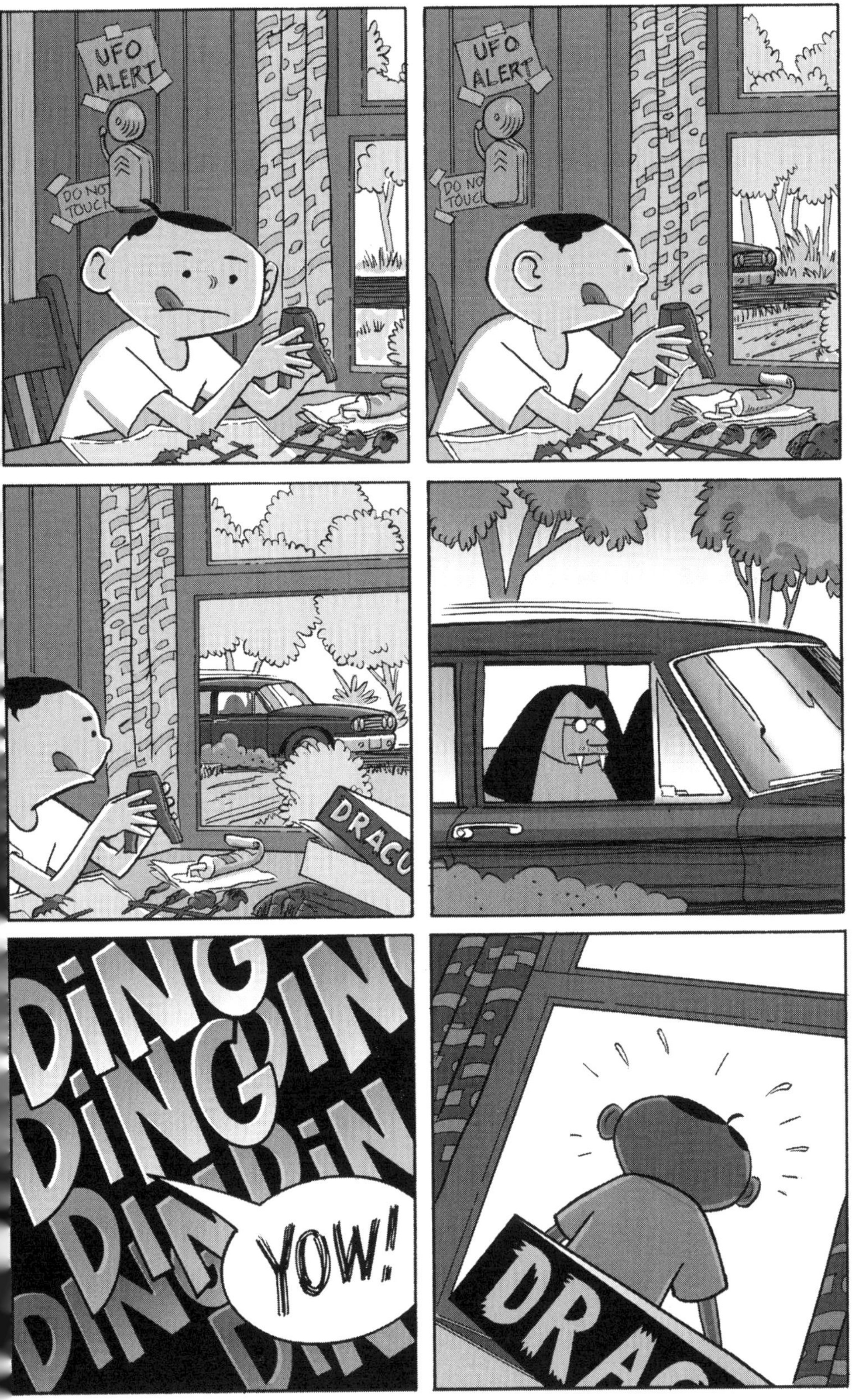
UFO ALERT
DO NO TOUCH
DRACU
DING DING DING
YOW!
DRA

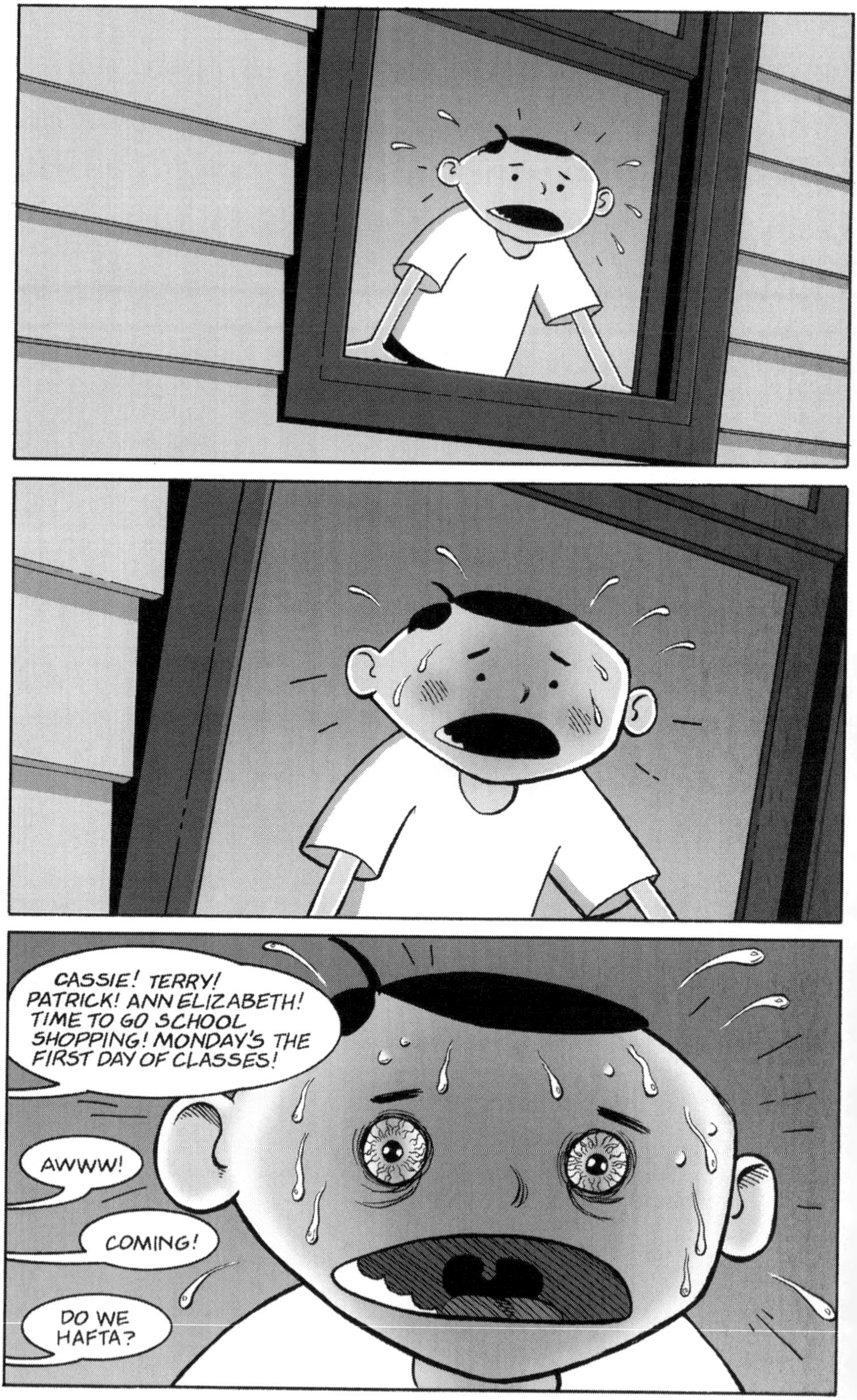
CASSIE! TERRY! PATRICK! ANN ELIZABETH! TIME TO GO SCHOOL SHOPPING! MONDAY'S THE FIRST DAY OF CLASSES!
AWWW!
COMING!
DO WE HAFTA?

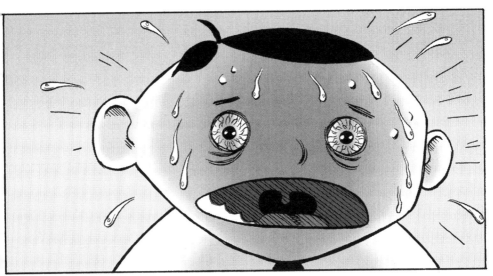

WELCOME BACK FOR ANOTHER WONDERFUL YEAR OF LEARNING, BOYS AND GIRLS! AT THE SOUND OF THE BELL, YOU WILL MARCH TO YOUR CLASSROOMS. AND *NO TALKING!*

BRRIINNG!

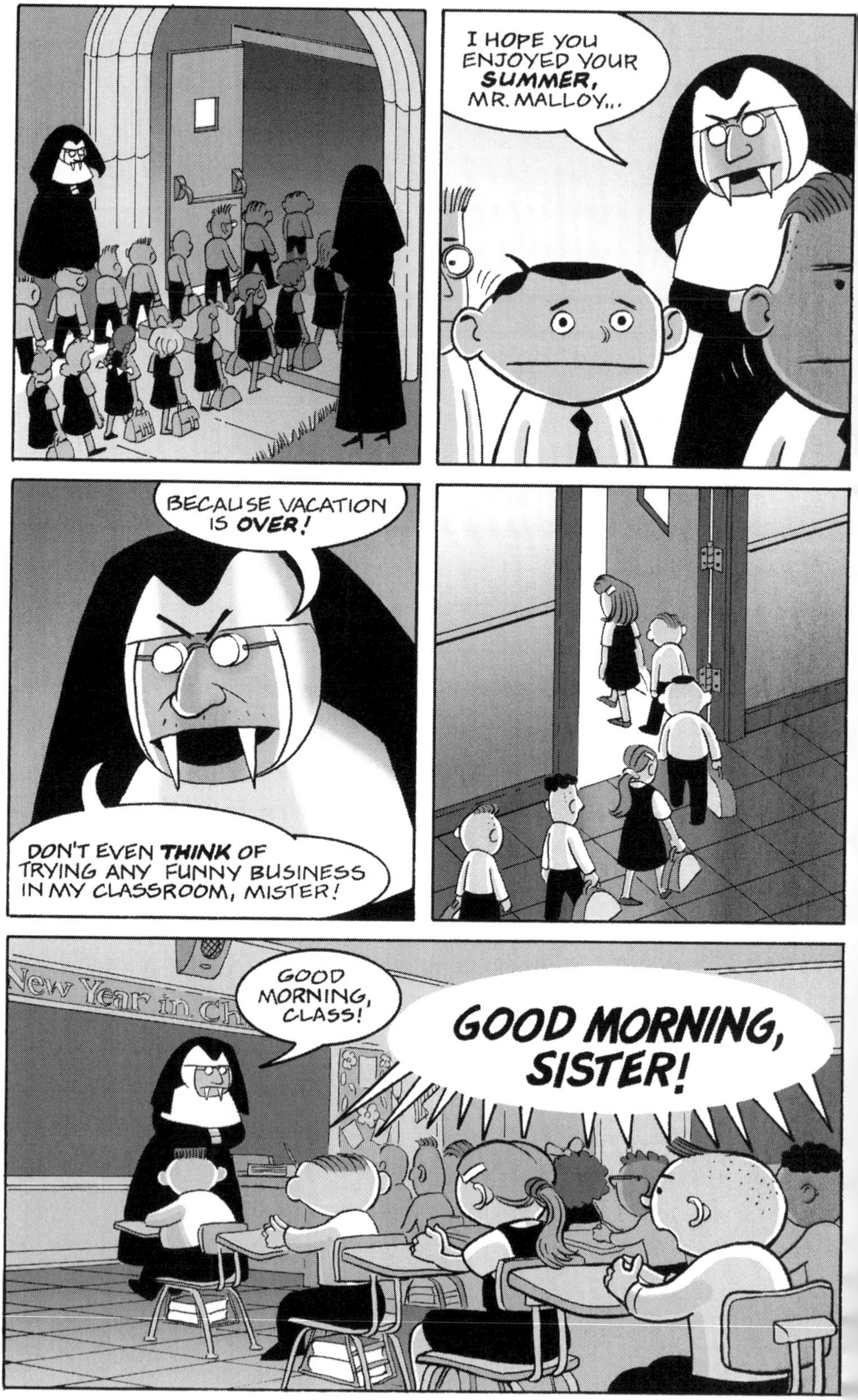
I HOPE YOU ENJOYED YOUR SUMMER, MR. MALLOY...
BECAUSE VACATION IS OVER!
DON'T EVEN THINK OF TRYING ANY FUNNY BUSINESS IN MY CLASSROOM, MISTER!
GOOD MORNING, CLASS!
GOOD MORNING, SISTER!

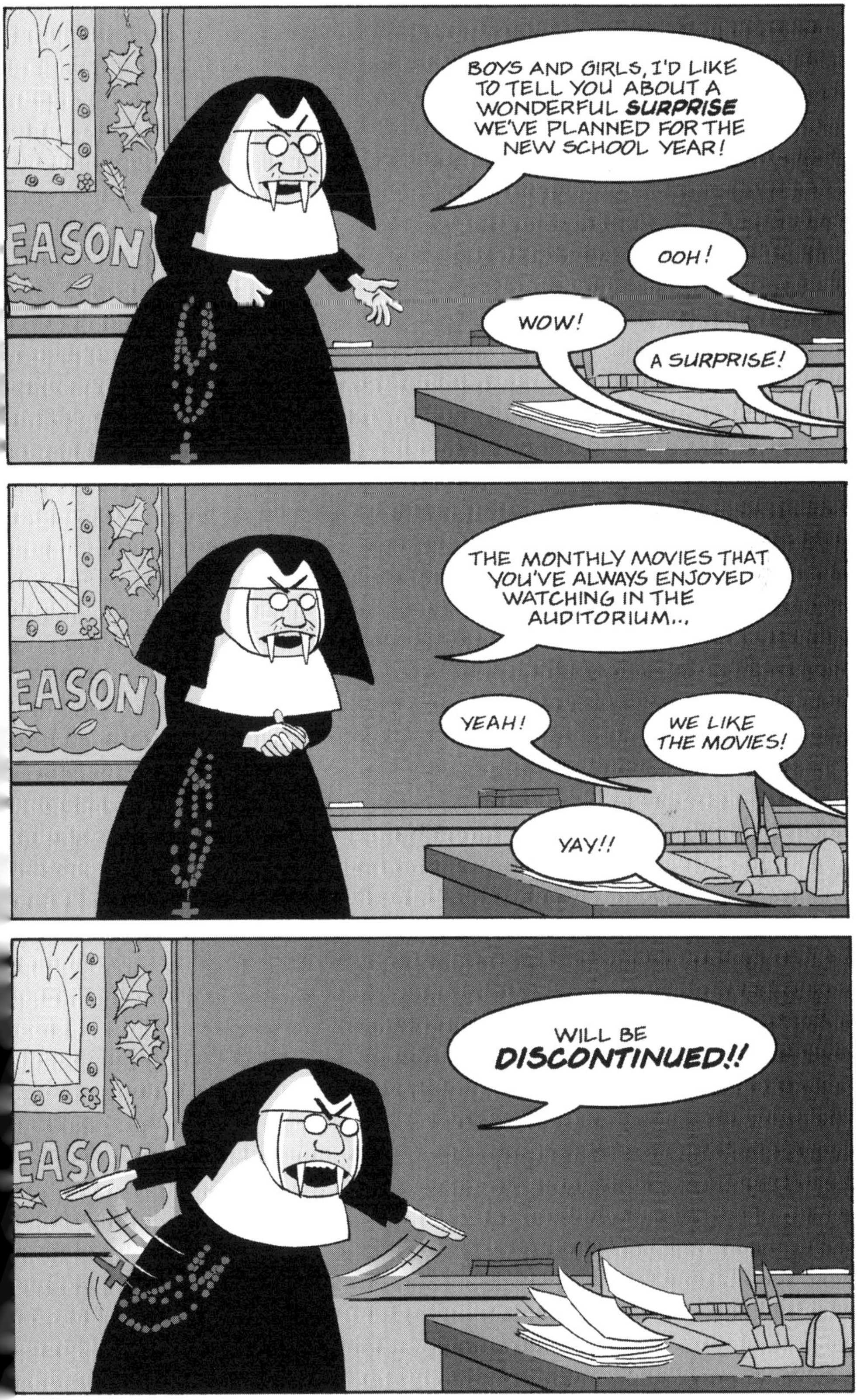

EASON
BOYS AND GIRLS, I'D LIKE TO TELL YOU ABOUT A WONDERFUL SURPRISE WE'VE PLANNED FOR THE NEW SCHOOL YEAR!
OOH!
WOW!
A SURPRISE!
EASON
THE MONTHLY MOVIES THAT YOU'VE ALWAYS ENJOYED WATCHING IN THE AUDITORIUM...
YEAH!
WE LIKE THE MOVIES!
YAY!!
WILL BE DISCONTINUED!!

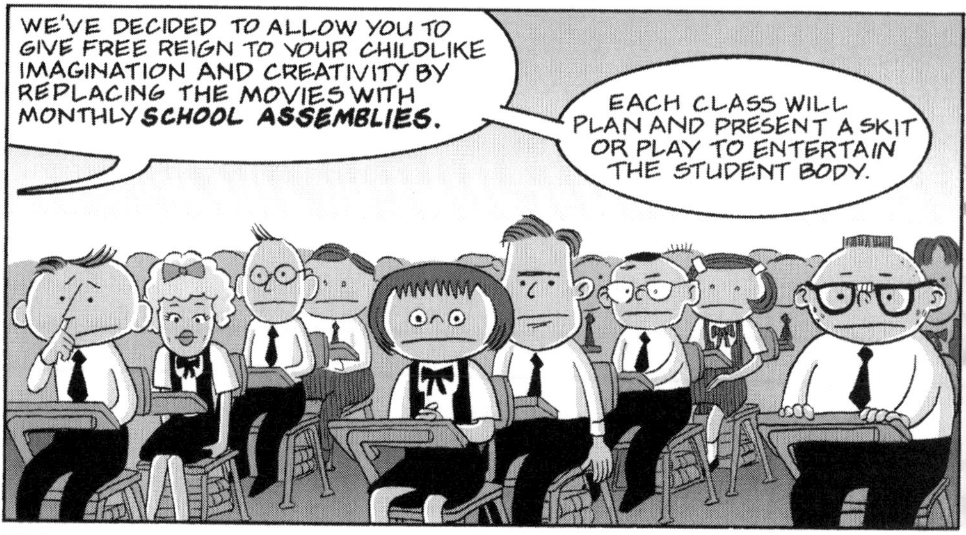
WE'VE DECIDED TO ALLOW YOU TO GIVE FREE REIGN TO YOUR CHILDLIKE IMAGINATION AND CREATIVITY BY REPLACING THE MOVIES WITH MONTHLY SCHOOL ASSEMBLIES.
EACH CLASS WILL PLAN AND PRESENT A SKIT OR PLAY TO ENTERTAIN THE STUDENT BODY.

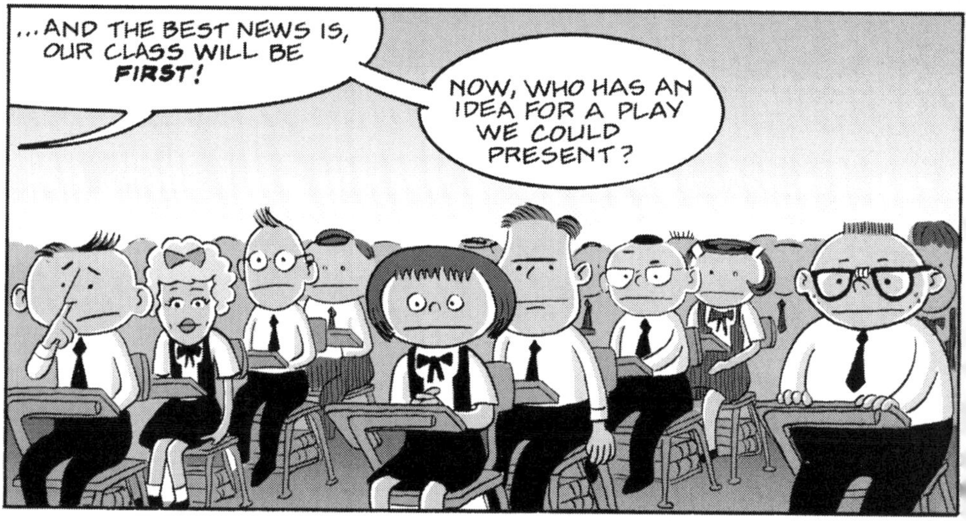
...AND THE BEST NEWS IS, OUR CLASS WILL BE FIRST!
NOW, WHO HAS AN IDEA FOR A PLAY WE COULD PRESENT?

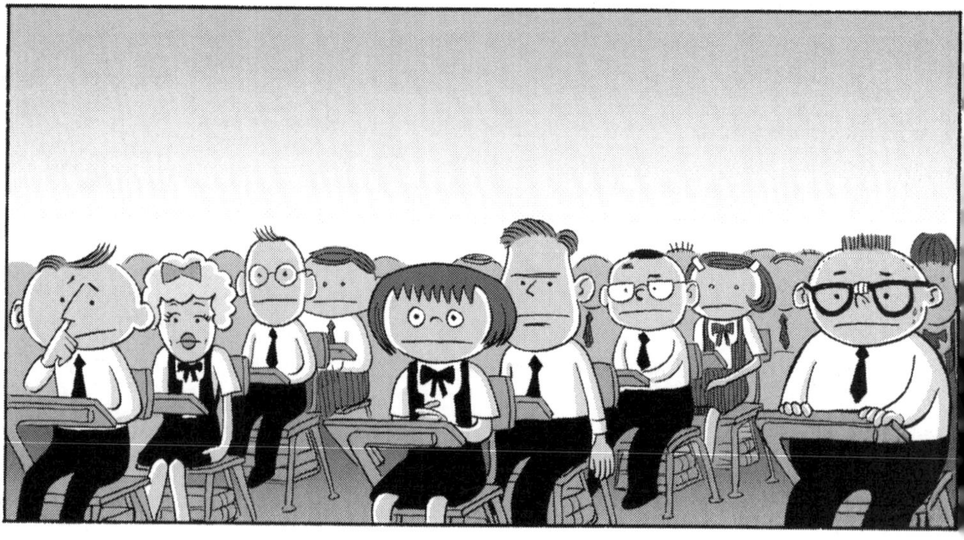

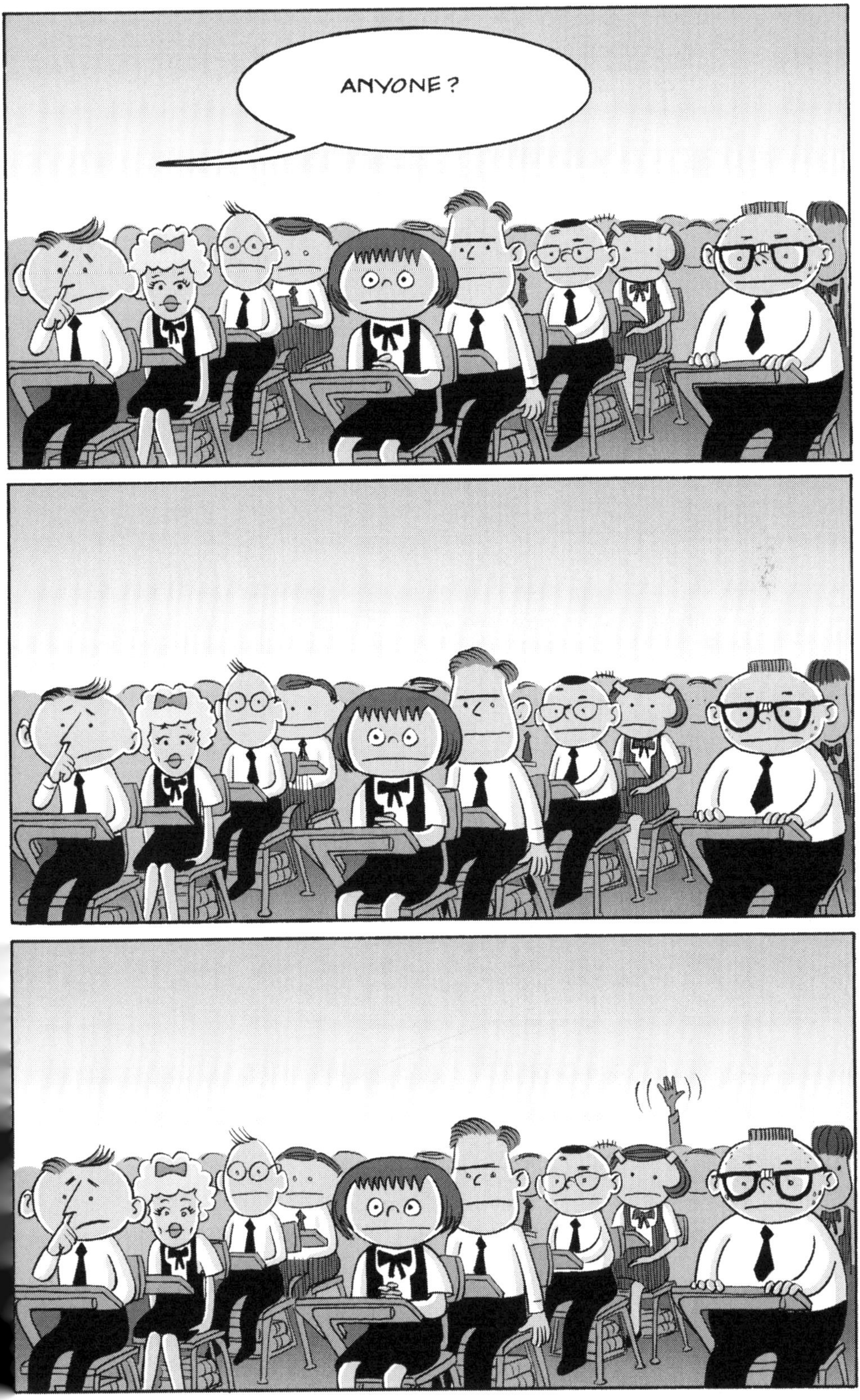
ANYONE?

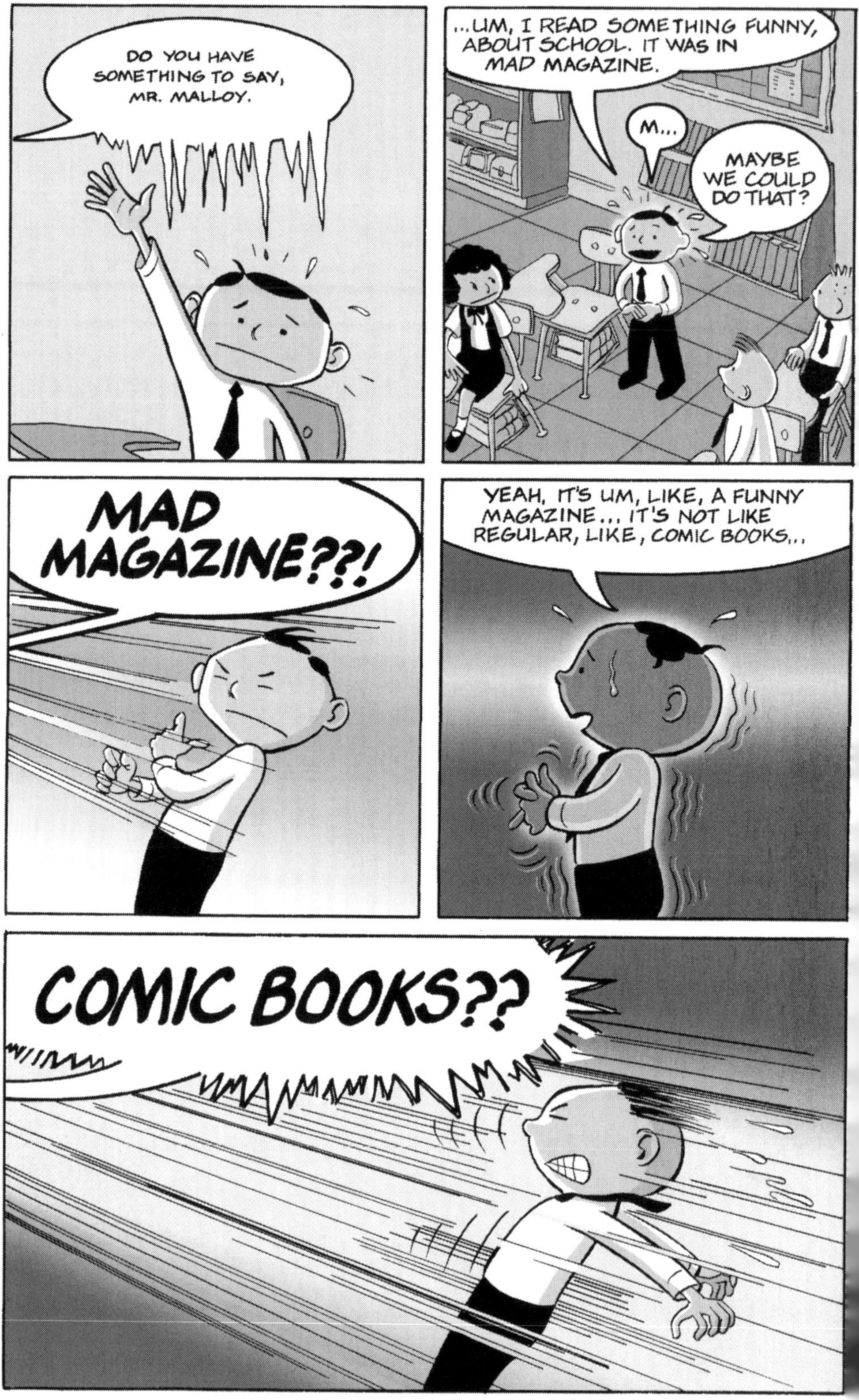
DO YOU HAVE SOMETHING TO SAY, MR. MALLOY.
...UM, I READ SOMETHING FUNNY, ABOUT SCHOOL. IT WAS IN MAD MAGAZINE.
M...
MAYBE WE COULD DO THAT?
MAD MAGAZINE??!
YEAH, IT'S UM, LIKE, A FUNNY MAGAZINE... IT'S NOT LIKE REGULAR, LIKE, COMIC BOOKS...
COMIC BOOKS??

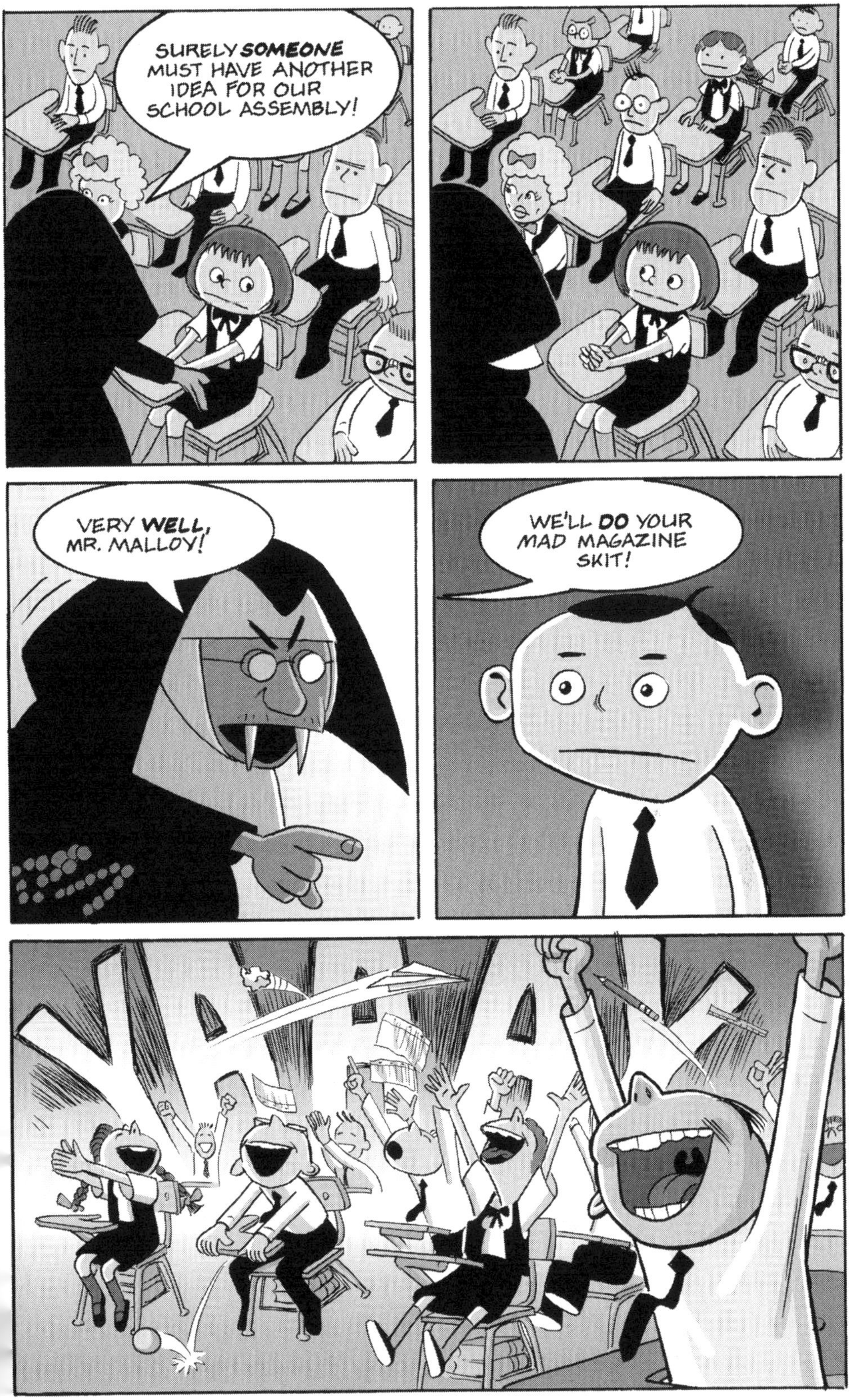
SURELY SOMEONE MUST HAVE ANOTHER IDEA FOR OUR SCHOOL ASSEMBLY!
VERY WELL, MR. MALLOY!
WE'LL DO YOUR MAD MAGAZINE SKIT!

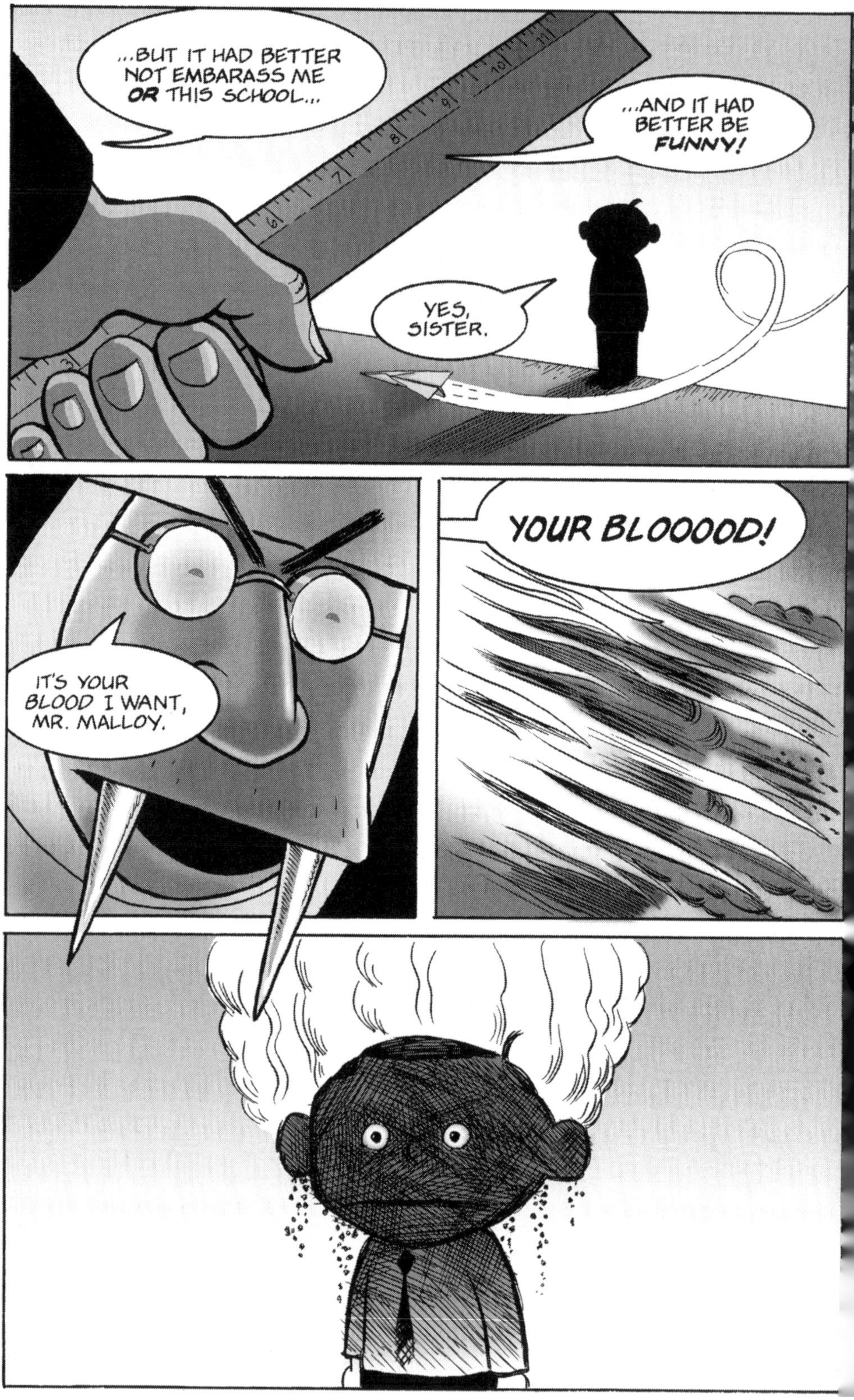
...BUT IT HAD BETTER NOT EMBARASS ME OR THIS SCHOOL...
...AND IT HAD BETTER BE FUNNY!
YES, SISTER.
IT'S YOUR BLOOD I WANT, MR. MALLOY.
YOUR BLOOOOD!

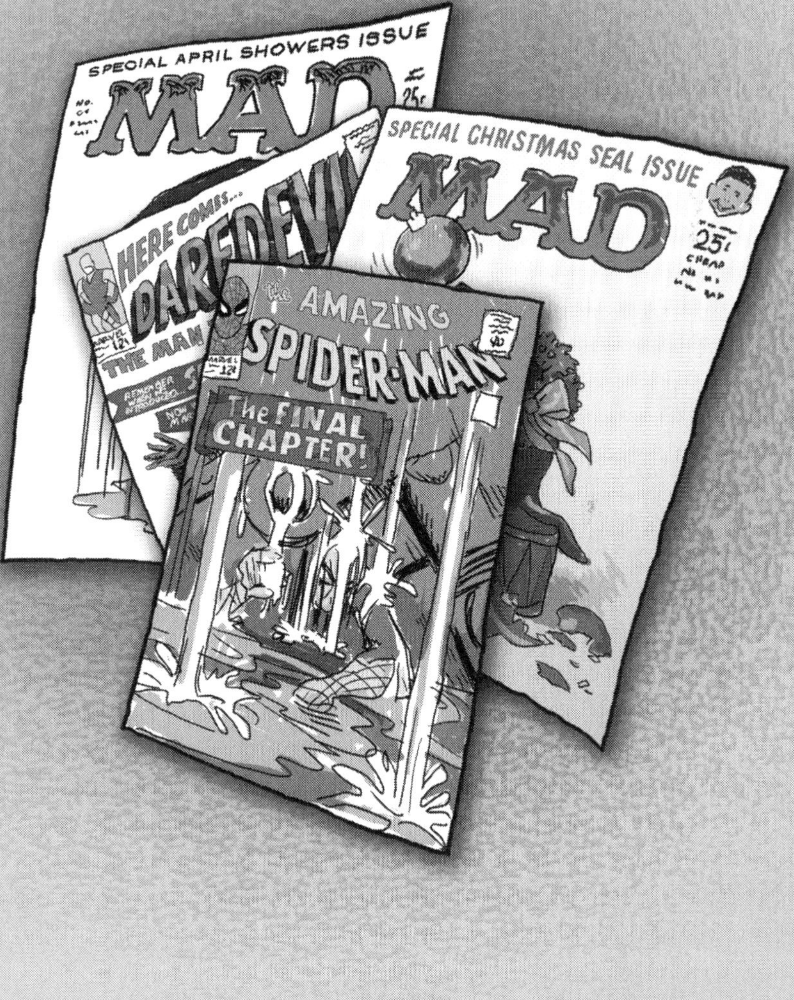
SPECIAL APRIL SHOWERS ISSUE
MAD
25¢
SPECIAL CHRISTMAS SEAL ISSUE
MAD
25¢
HERE COMES...
The AMAZING
SPIDER-MAN
The FINAL CHAPTER!

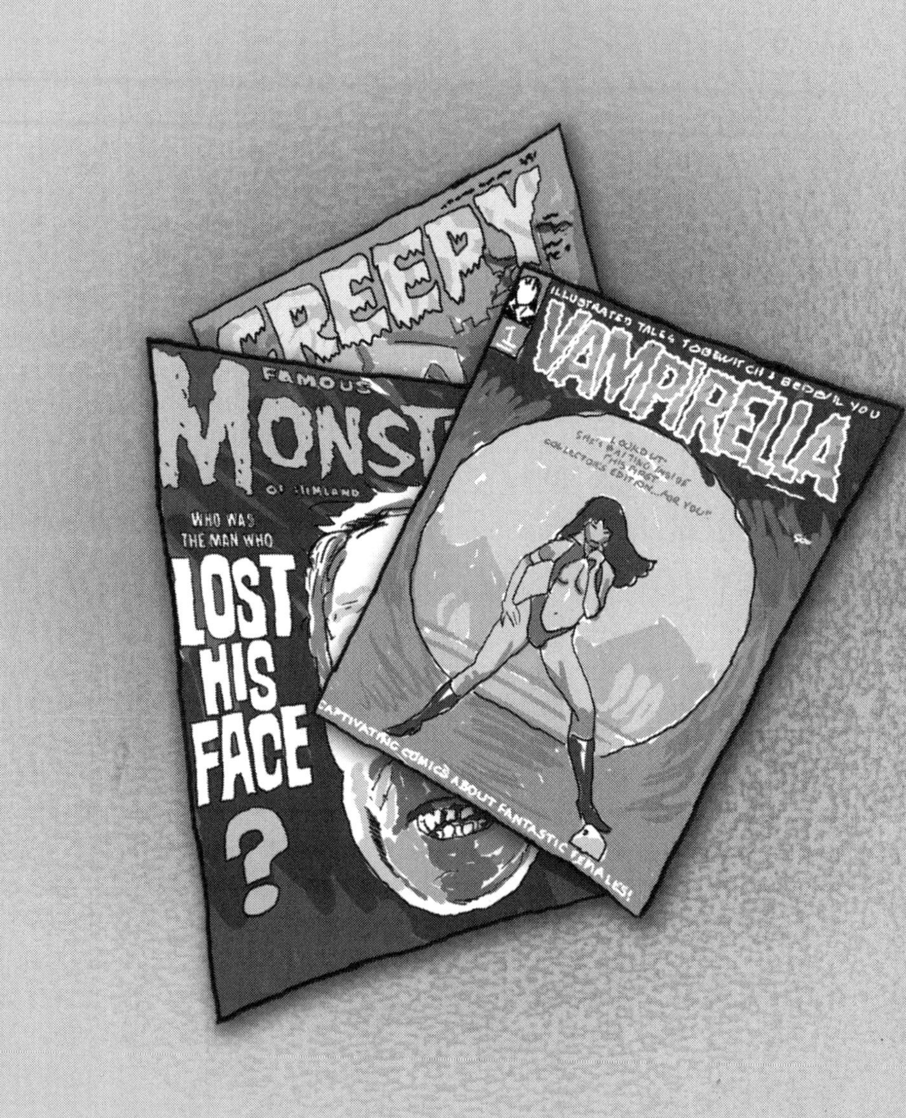
CREEPY
FAMOUS
MONST
WHO WAS
THE MAN WHO
LOST
HIS
FACE
?
1
VAMPIRELLA
CAPTIVATING COMICS ABOUT FANTASTIC FEMALES!

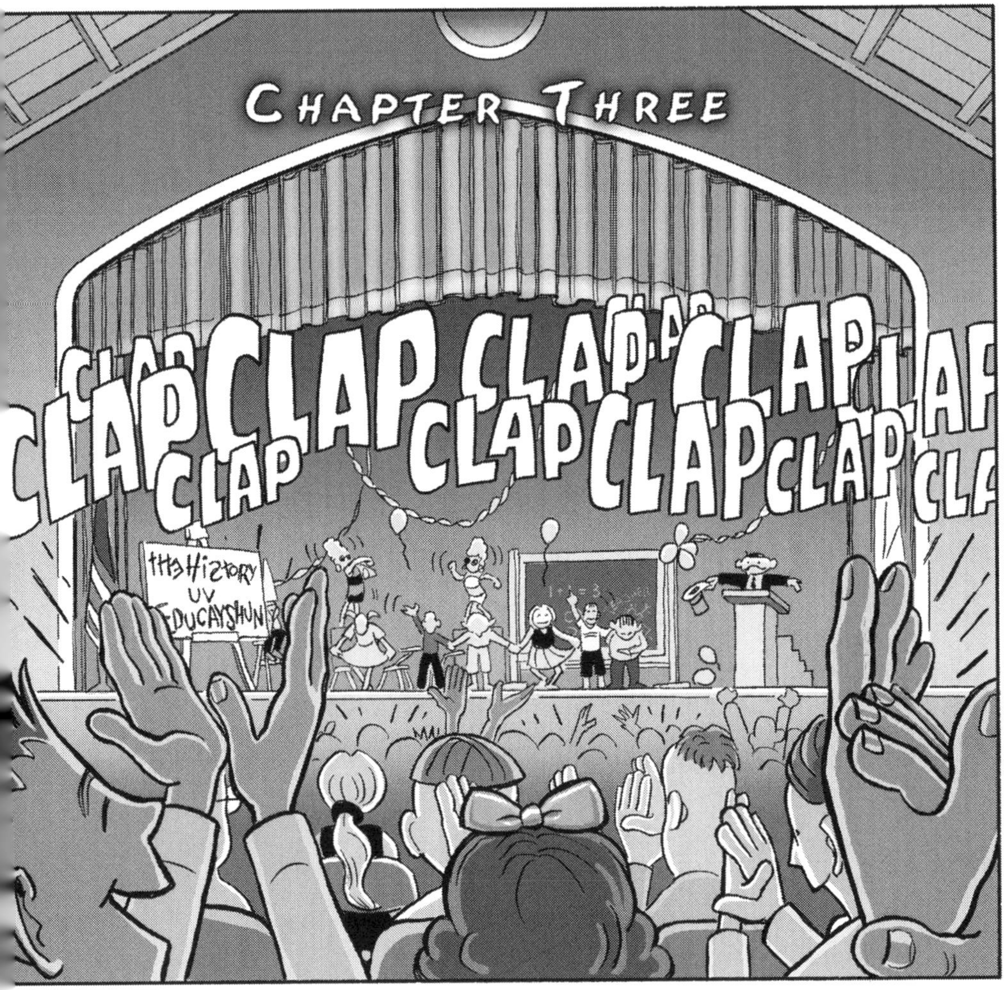
CHAPTER THREE
CLAP CLAP CLAP CLAP CLAP CLAP CLAP CLAP CLAP CLAP CLAP CLAP
tHe HiSTORY UV EDUCAYSHUN

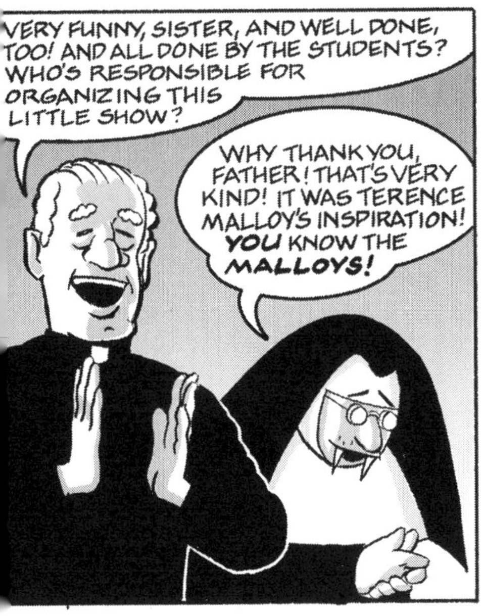
VERY FUNNY, SISTER, AND WELL DONE, TOO! AND ALL DONE BY THE STUDENTS? WHO'S RESPONSIBLE FOR ORGANIZING THIS LITTLE SHOW?
WHY THANK YOU, FATHER! THAT'S VERY KIND! IT WAS TERENCE MALLOY'S INSPIRATION! **YOU** KNOW THE **MALLOYS!**

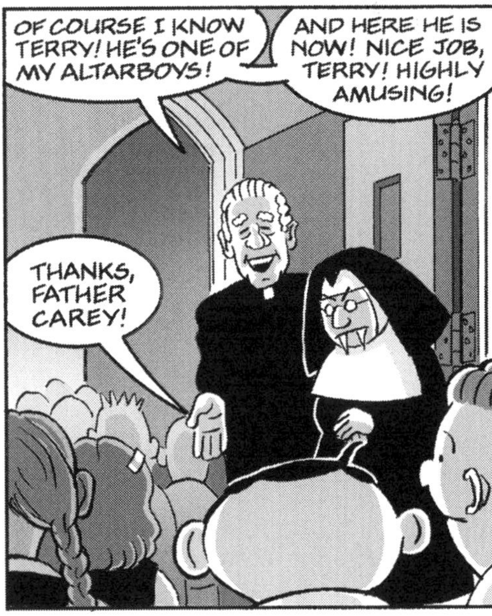
OF COURSE I KNOW TERRY! HE'S ONE OF MY ALTARBOYS!
AND HERE HE IS NOW! NICE JOB, TERRY! HIGHLY AMUSING!
THANKS, FATHER CAREY!

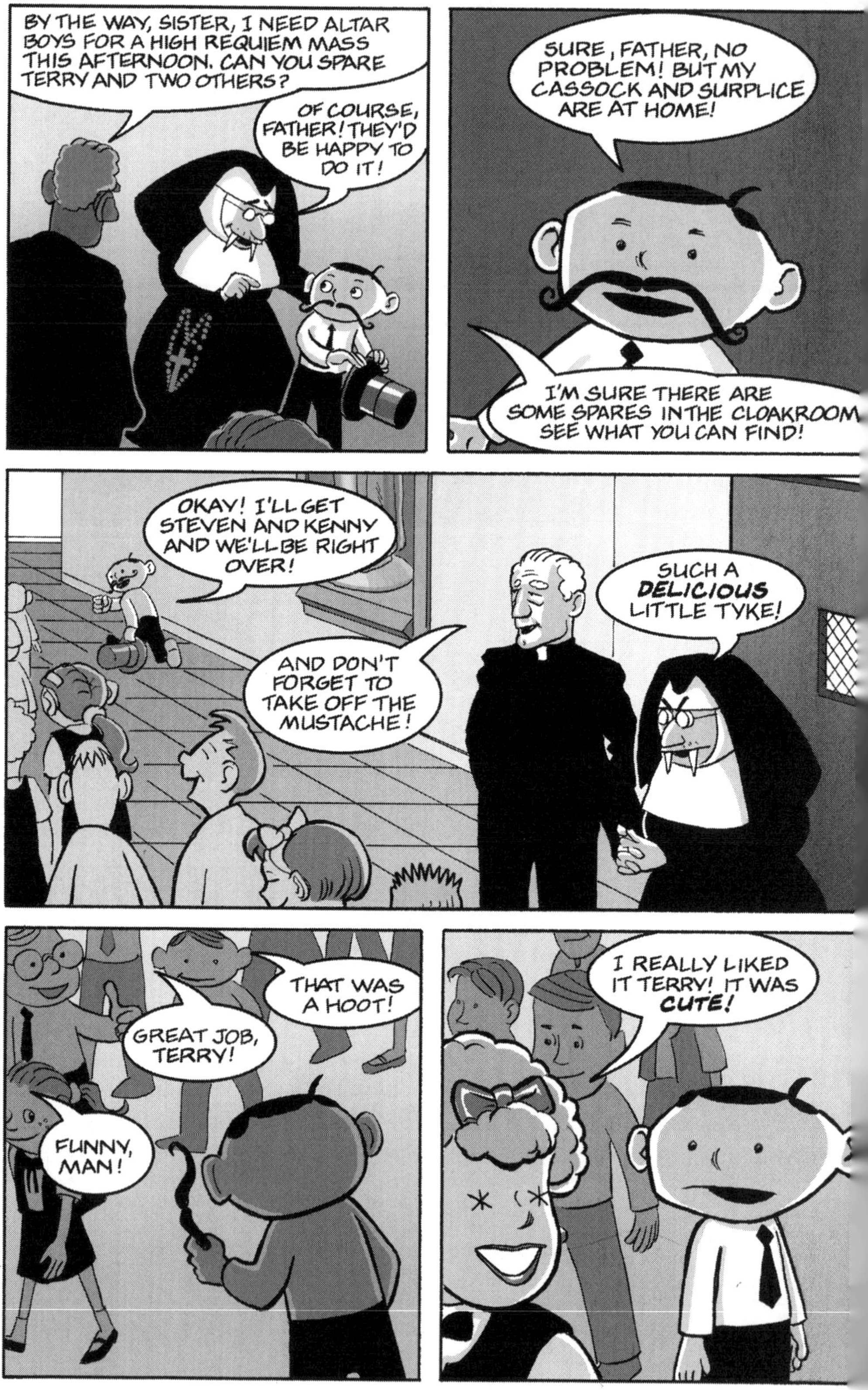
BY THE WAY, SISTER, I NEED ALTAR BOYS FOR A HIGH REQUIEM MASS THIS AFTERNOON. CAN YOU SPARE TERRY AND TWO OTHERS?
OF COURSE, FATHER! THEY'D BE HAPPY TO DO IT!
SURE, FATHER, NO PROBLEM! BUT MY CASSOCK AND SURPLICE ARE AT HOME!
I'M SURE THERE ARE SOME SPARES IN THE CLOAKROOM. SEE WHAT YOU CAN FIND!
OKAY! I'LL GET STEVEN AND KENNY AND WE'LL BE RIGHT OVER!
AND DON'T FORGET TO TAKE OFF THE MUSTACHE!
SUCH A **DELICIOUS** LITTLE TYKE!
THAT WAS A HOOT!
GREAT JOB, TERRY!
FUNNY, MAN!
I REALLY LIKED IT TERRY! IT WAS **CUTE!**

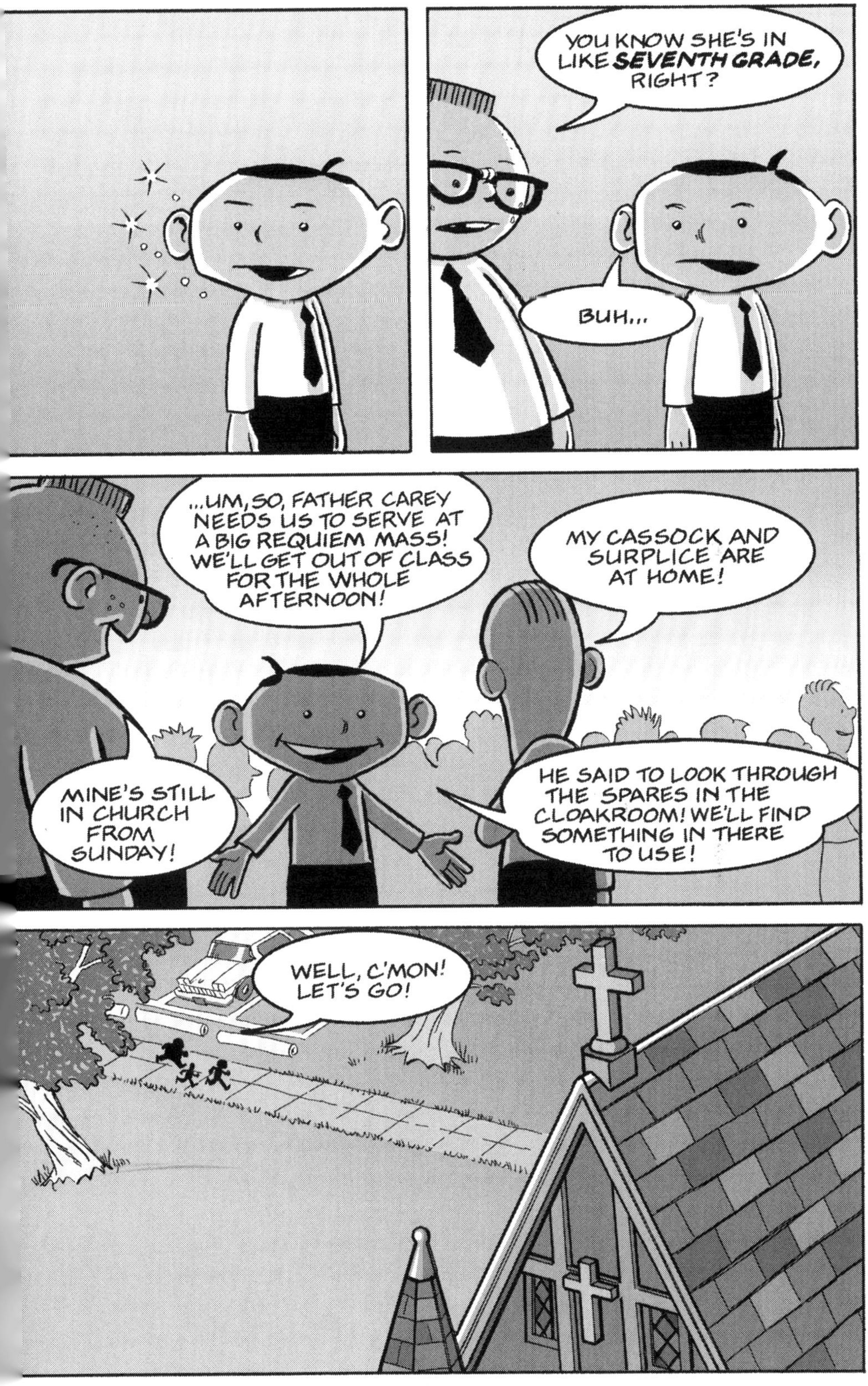
YOU KNOW SHE'S IN LIKE SEVENTH GRADE, RIGHT?
BUH...
...UM, SO, FATHER CAREY NEEDS US TO SERVE AT A BIG REQUIEM MASS! WE'LL GET OUT OF CLASS FOR THE WHOLE AFTERNOON!
MY CASSOCK AND SURPLICE ARE AT HOME!
MINE'S STILL IN CHURCH FROM SUNDAY!
HE SAID TO LOOK THROUGH THE SPARES IN THE CLOAKROOM! WE'LL FIND SOMETHING IN THERE TO USE!
WELL, C'MON! LET'S GO!

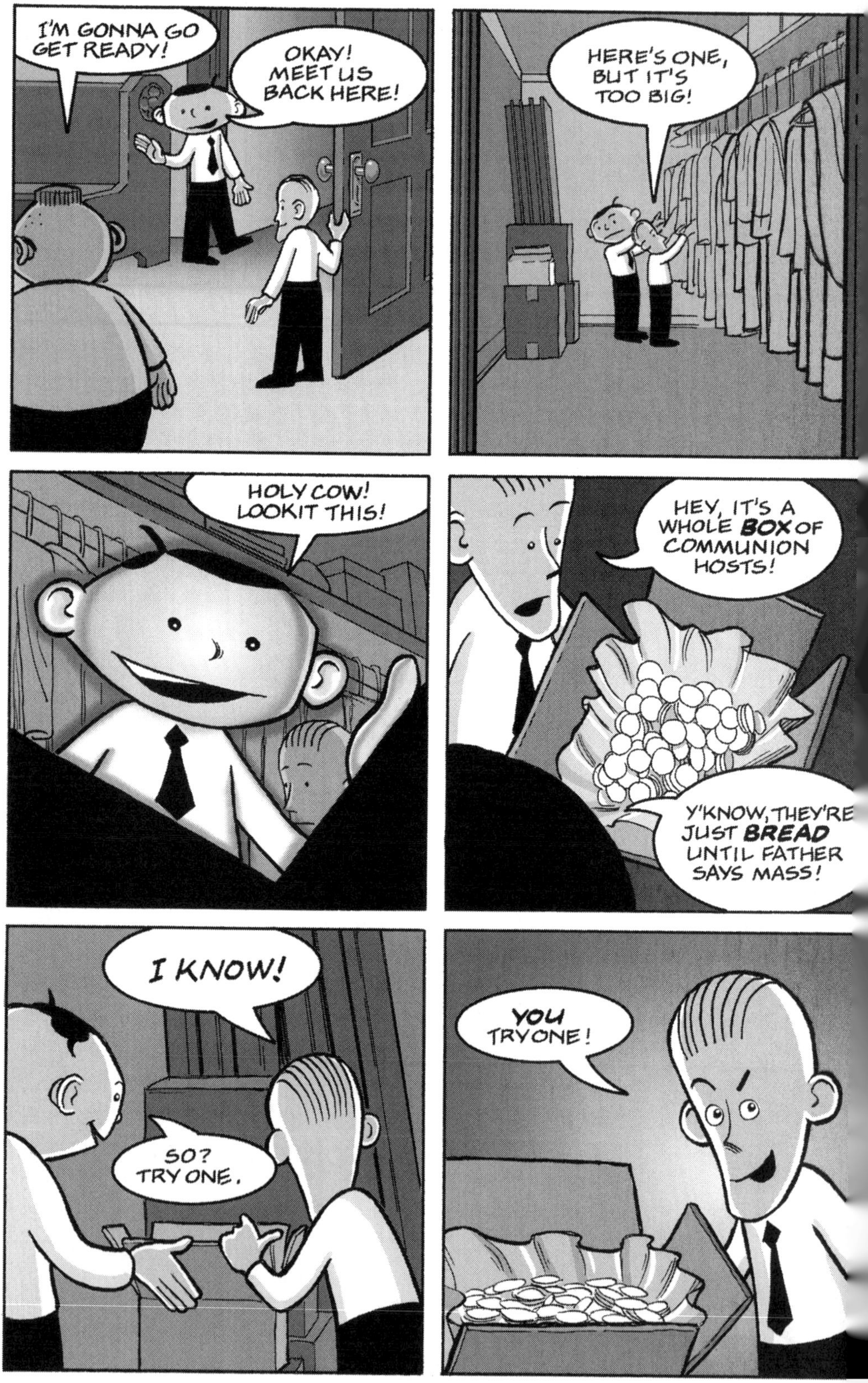

I'M GONNA GO GET READY!
OKAY! MEET US BACK HERE!
HERE'S ONE, BUT IT'S TOO BIG!
HOLY COW! LOOKIT THIS!
HEY, IT'S A WHOLE BOX OF COMMUNION HOSTS!
Y'KNOW, THEY'RE JUST BREAD UNTIL FATHER SAYS MASS!
I KNOW!
SO? TRY ONE.
YOU TRY ONE!

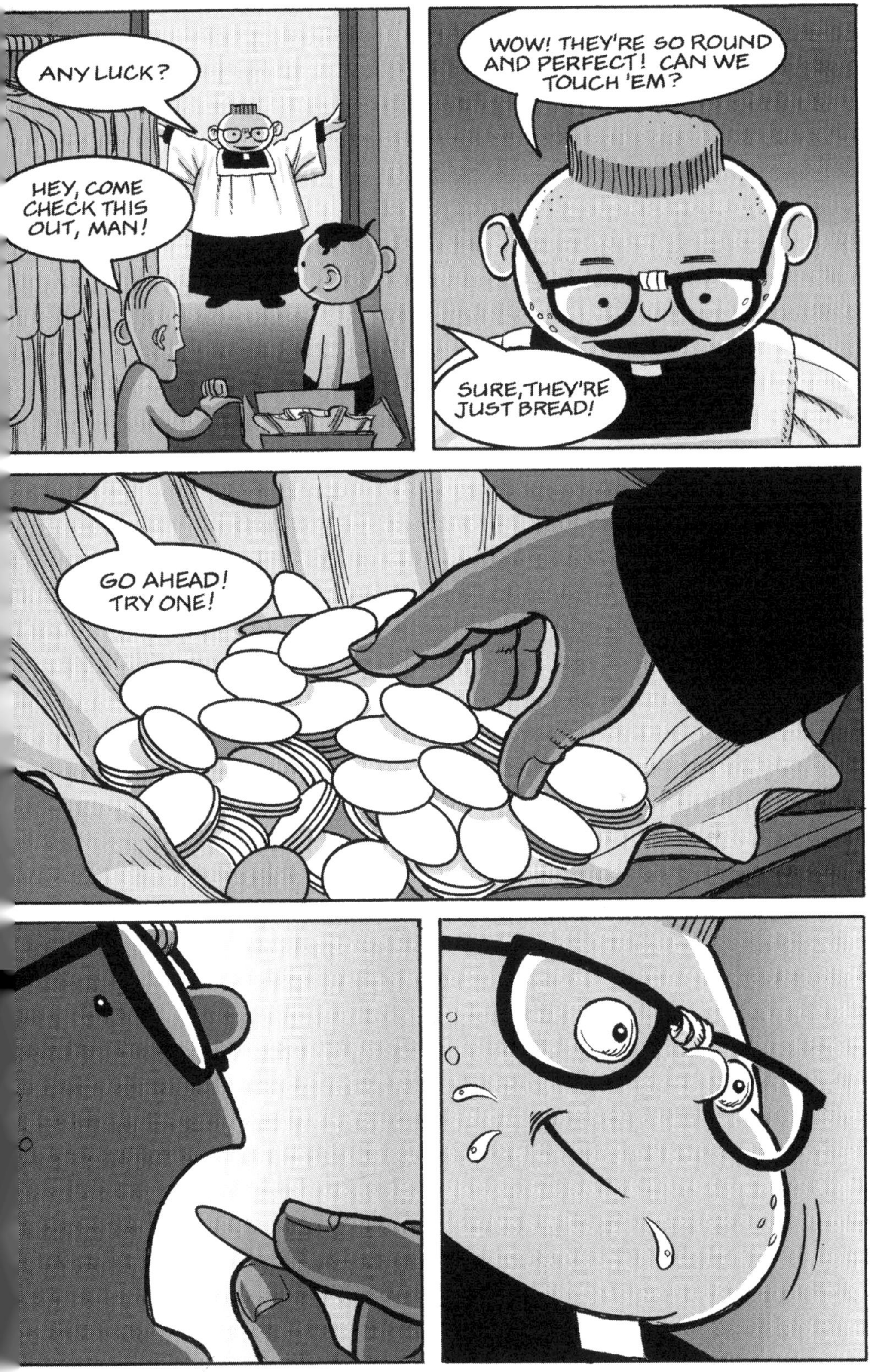
ANY LUCK?
HEY, COME CHECK THIS OUT, MAN!
WOW! THEY'RE SO ROUND AND PERFECT! CAN WE TOUCH 'EM?
SURE, THEY'RE JUST BREAD!
GO AHEAD! TRY ONE!

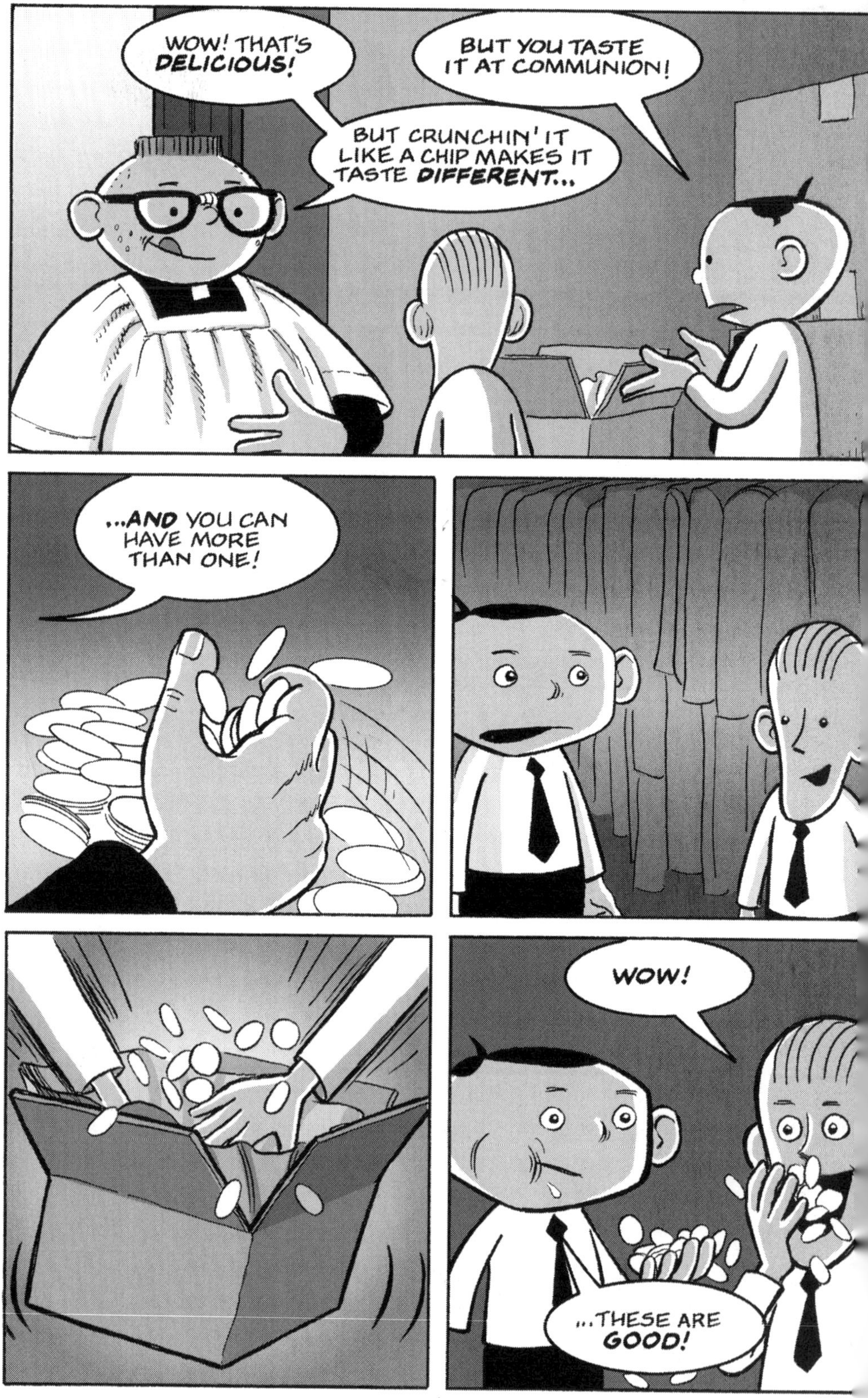
WOW! THAT'S DELICIOUS!
BUT YOU TASTE IT AT COMMUNION!
BUT CRUNCHIN' IT LIKE A CHIP MAKES IT TASTE DIFFERENT...
...AND YOU CAN HAVE MORE THAN ONE!
WOW!
...THESE ARE GOOD!

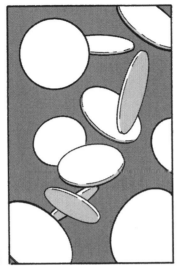

SNAP!

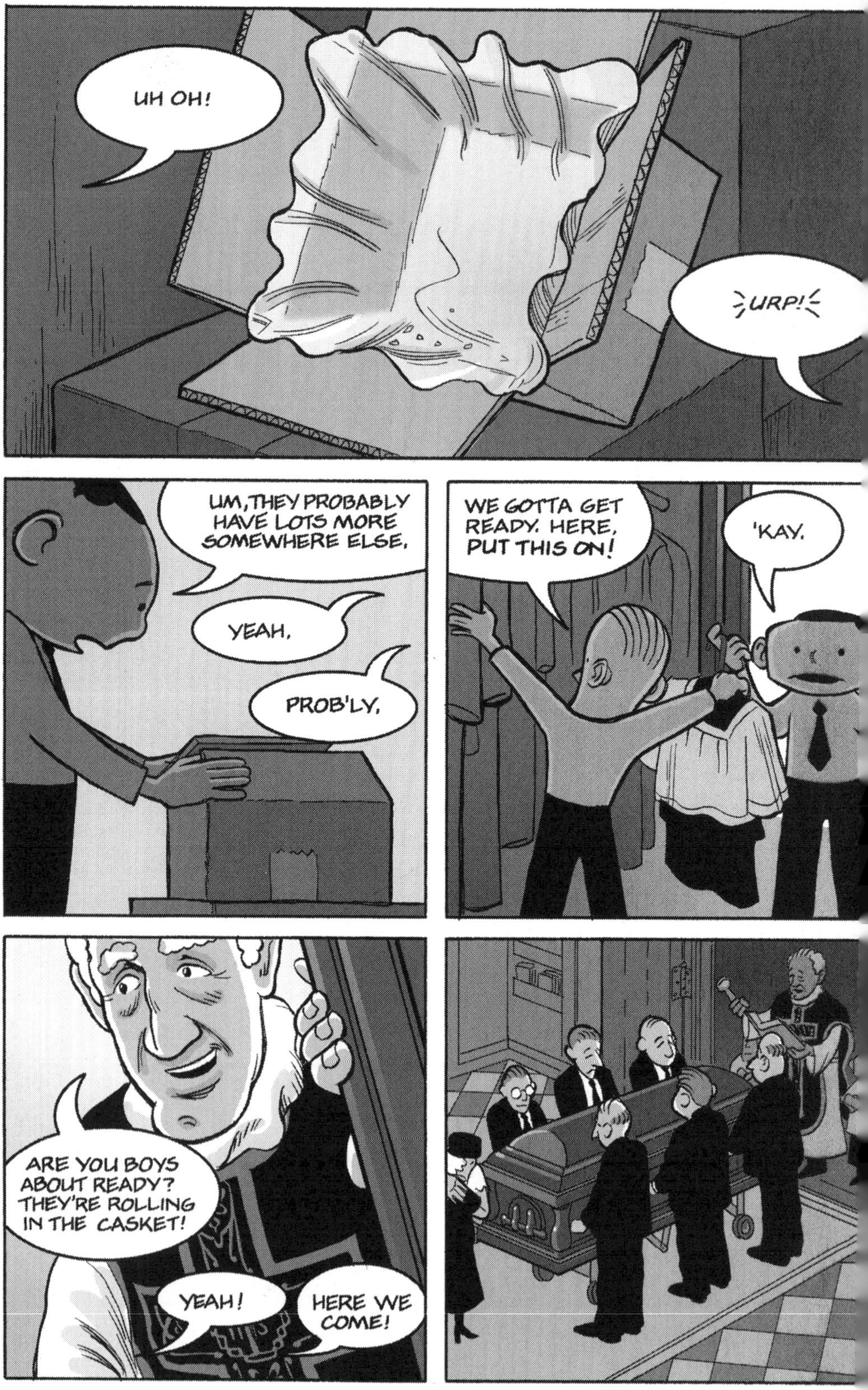
UH OH!
URP!
UM, THEY PROBABLY HAVE LOTS MORE SOMEWHERE ELSE.
YEAH.
PROB'LY.
WE GOTTA GET READY. HERE, PUT THIS ON!
'KAY.
ARE YOU BOYS ABOUT READY? THEY'RE ROLLING IN THE CASKET!
YEAH!
HERE WE COME!

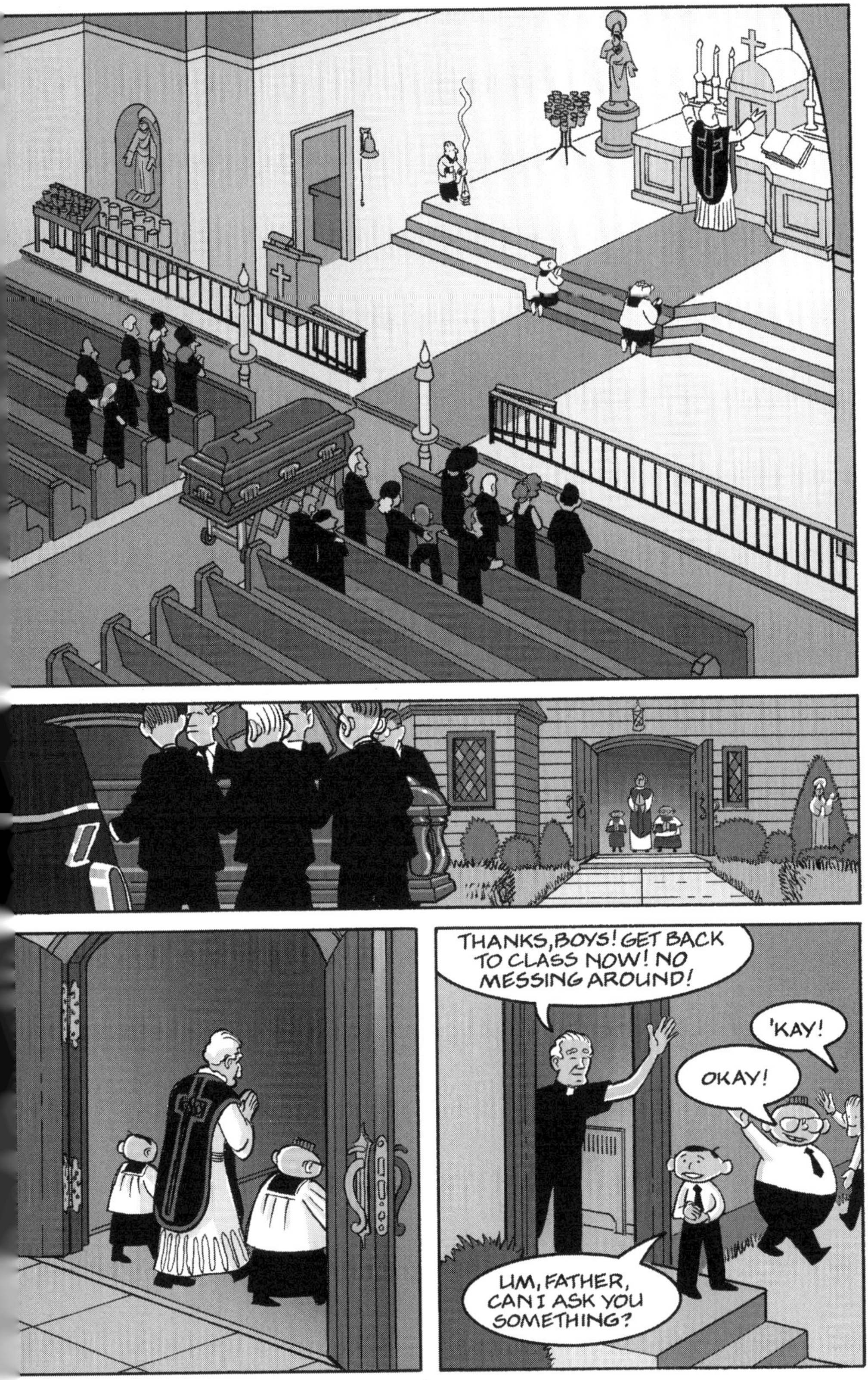
THANKS, BOYS! GET BACK TO CLASS NOW! NO MESSING AROUND!
'KAY!
OKAY!
UM, FATHER, CAN I ASK YOU SOMETHING?

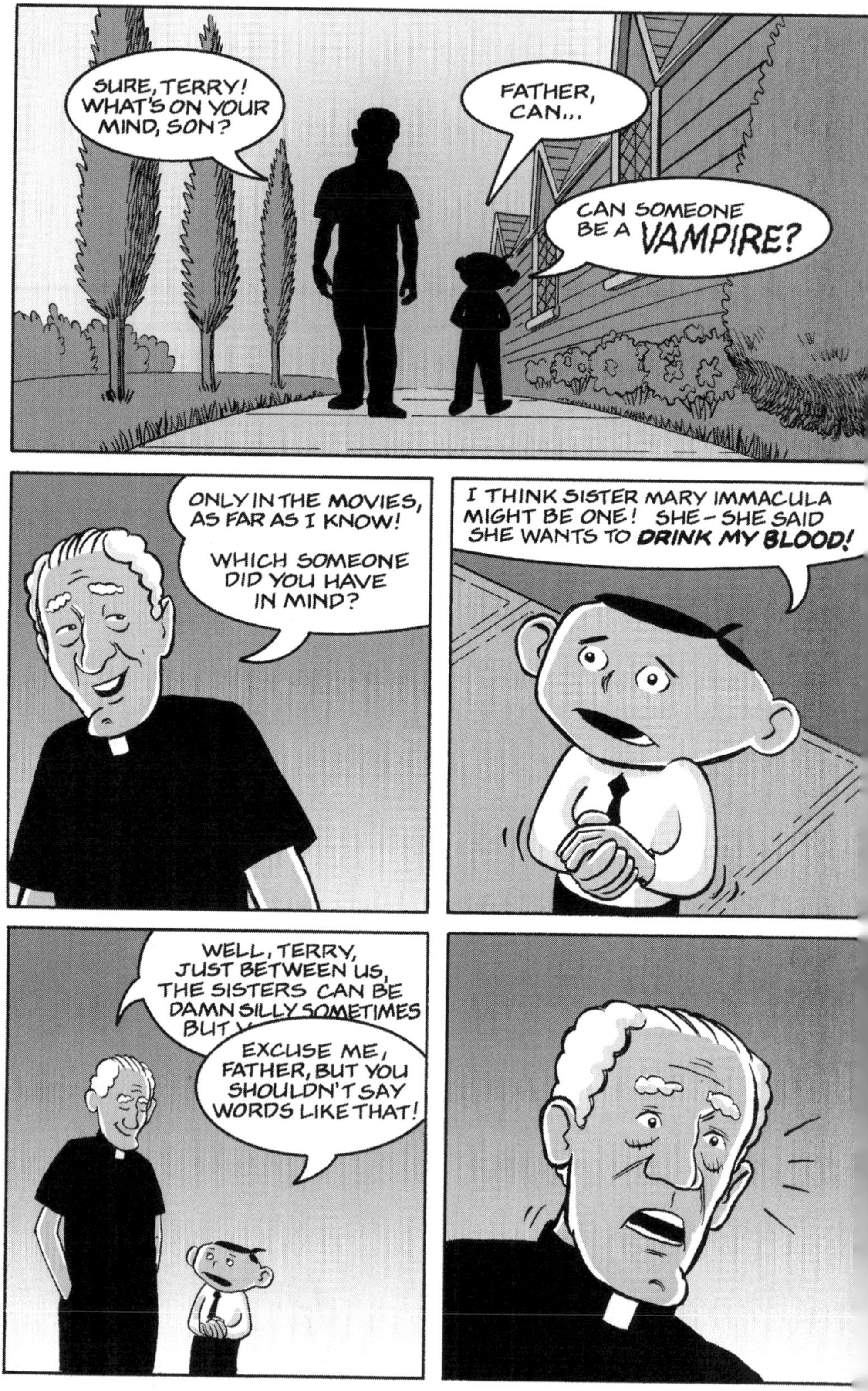
SURE, TERRY! WHAT'S ON YOUR MIND, SON?
FATHER, CAN...
CAN SOMEONE BE A **VAMPIRE?**
ONLY IN THE MOVIES, AS FAR AS I KNOW!
WHICH SOMEONE DID YOU HAVE IN MIND?
I THINK SISTER MARY IMMACULA MIGHT BE ONE! SHE - SHE SAID SHE WANTS TO ***DRINK MY BLOOD!***
WELL, TERRY, JUST BETWEEN US, THE SISTERS CAN BE DAMN SILLY SOMETIMES BUT
EXCUSE ME, FATHER, BUT YOU SHOULDN'T SAY WORDS LIKE THAT!

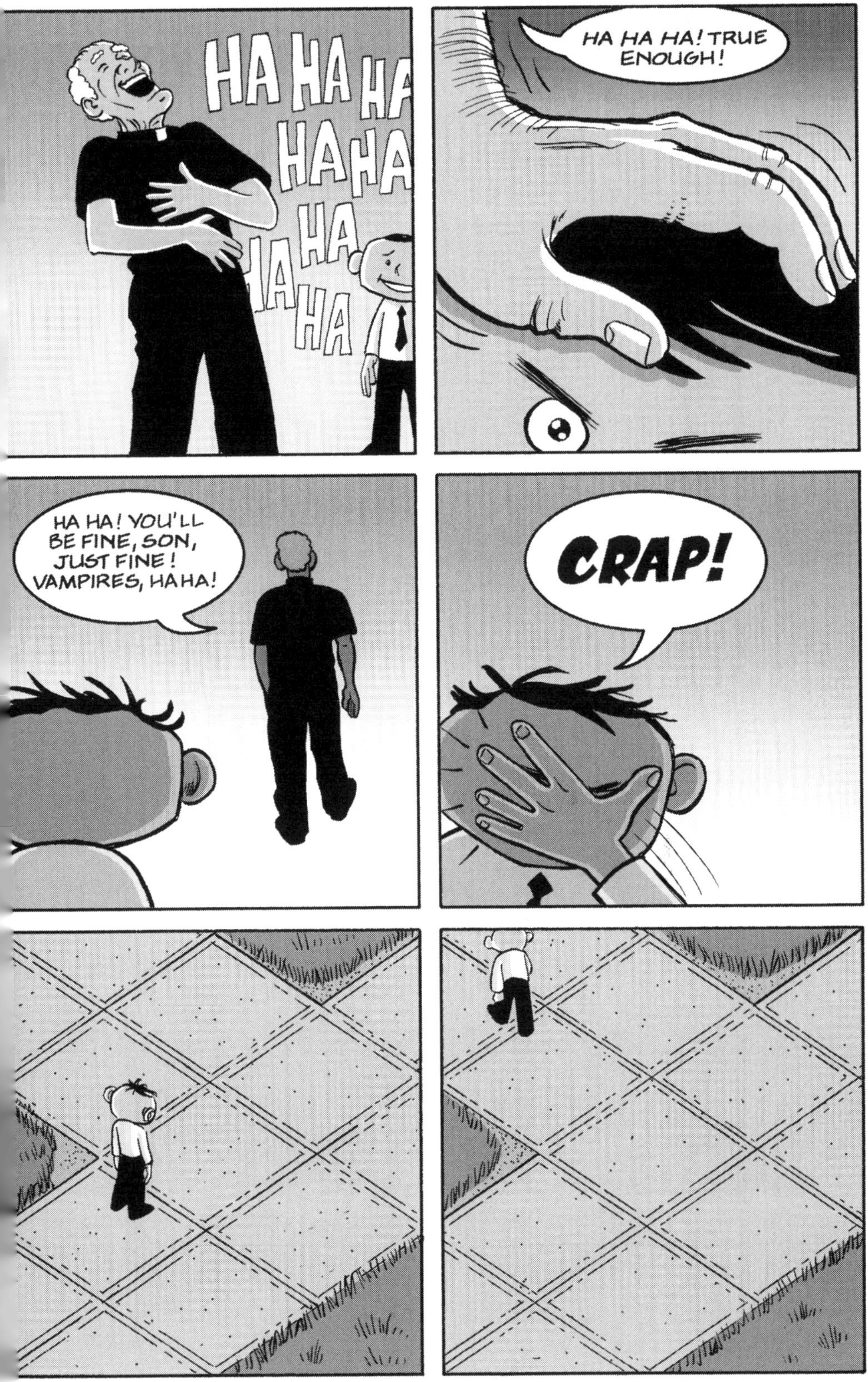
HA HA HA HA HA HA HA HA HA HA HA
HA HA HA! TRUE ENOUGH!
HA HA! YOU'LL BE FINE, SON, JUST FINE! VAMPIRES, HA HA!
CRAP!

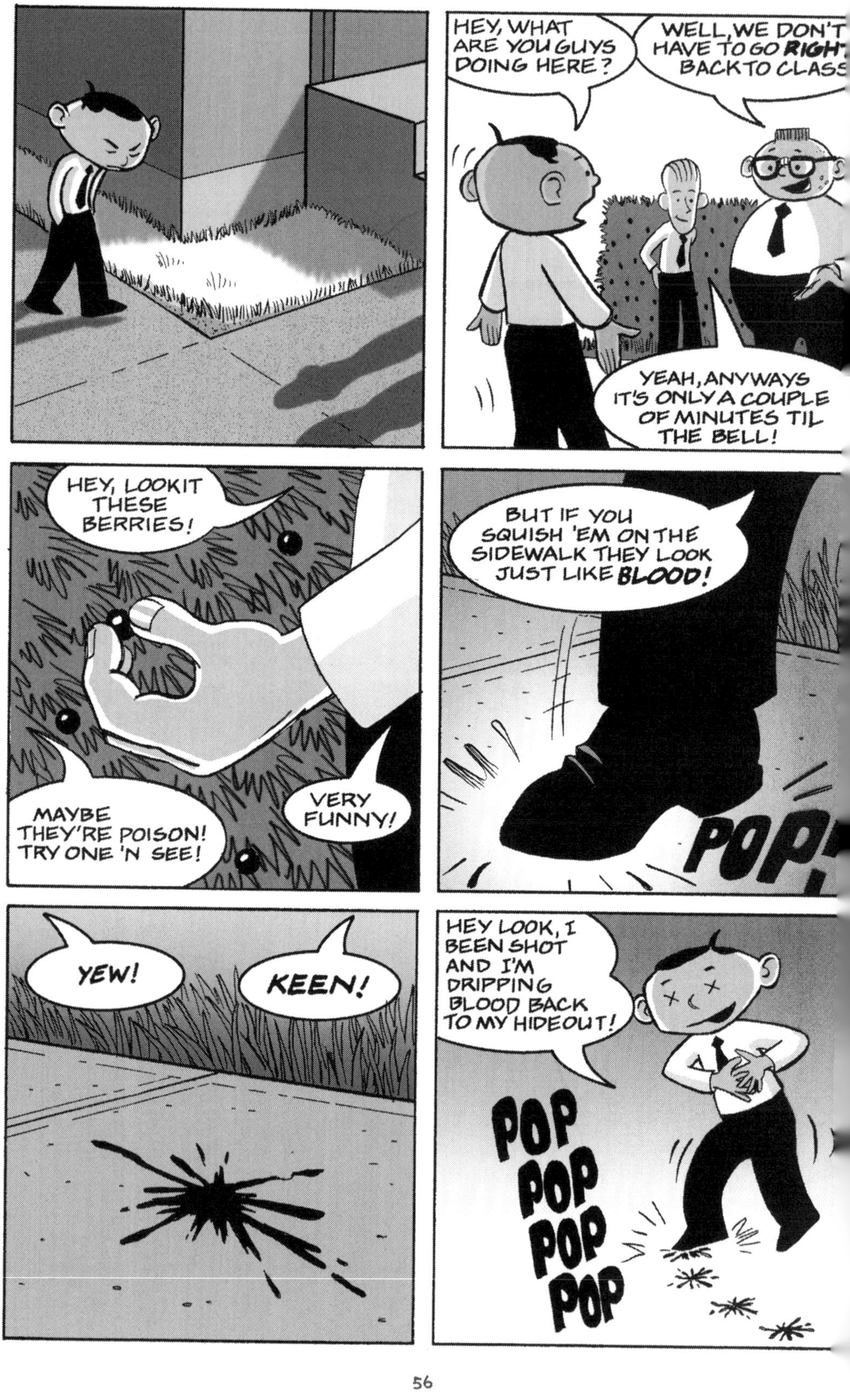
HEY, WHAT ARE YOU GUYS DOING HERE?
WELL, WE DON'T HAVE TO GO RIGH BACK TO CLAS
YEAH, ANYWAYS IT'S ONLY A COUPLE OF MINUTES TIL THE BELL!
HEY, LOOKIT THESE BERRIES!
MAYBE THEY'RE POISON! TRY ONE 'N SEE!
VERY FUNNY!
BUT IF YOU SQUISH 'EM ON THE SIDEWALK THEY LOOK JUST LIKE BLOOD!
POP
YEW!
KEEN!
HEY LOOK, I BEEN SHOT AND I'M DRIPPING BLOOD BACK TO MY HIDEOUT!
POP POP POP POP POP

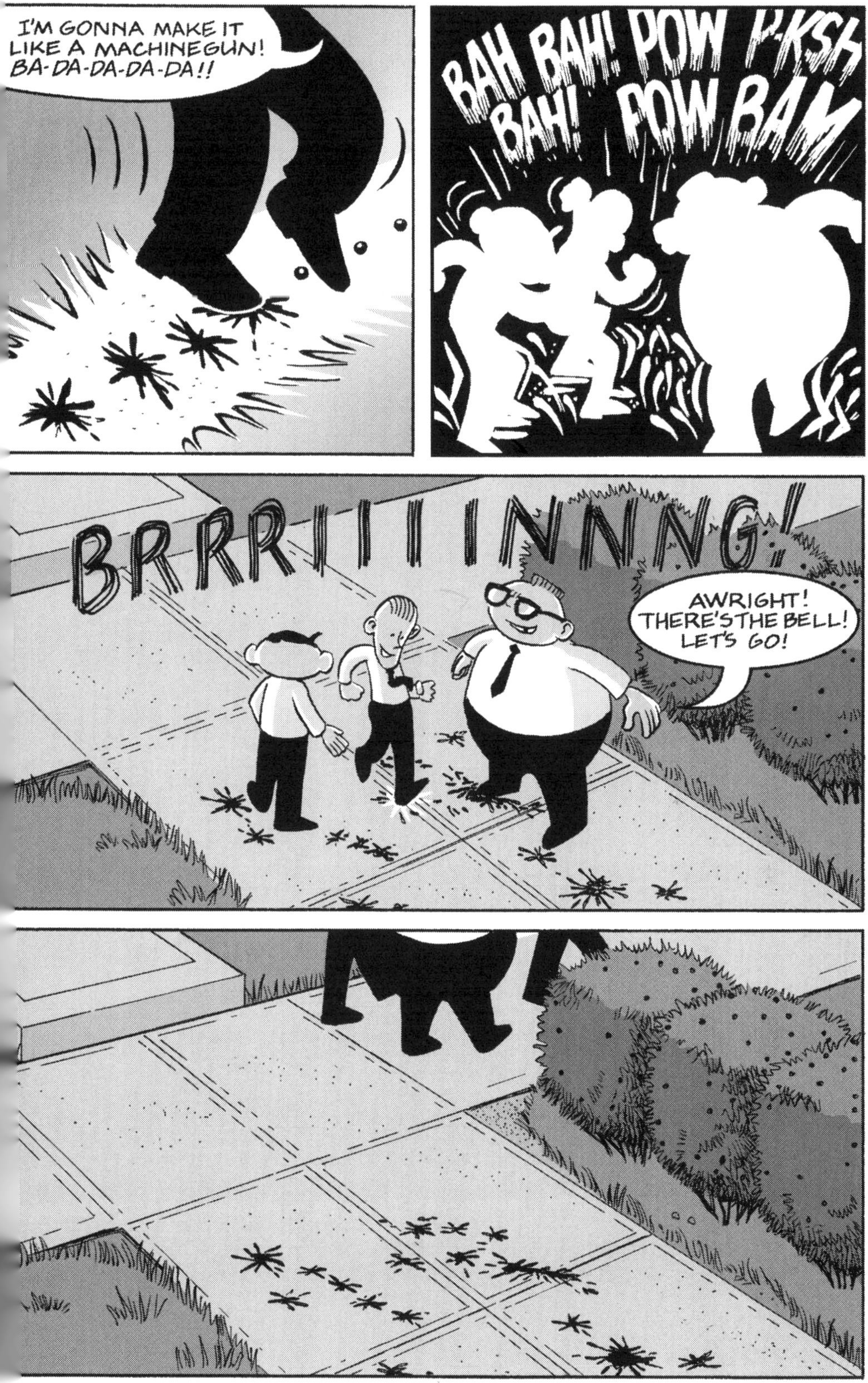
I'M GONNA MAKE IT LIKE A MACHINEGUN! BA-DA-DA-DA-DA!!
BAH BAH! POW P-KSH
BAH! POW BAM
BRRRIIIINNNG!
AWRIGHT! THERE'S THE BELL! LET'S GO!

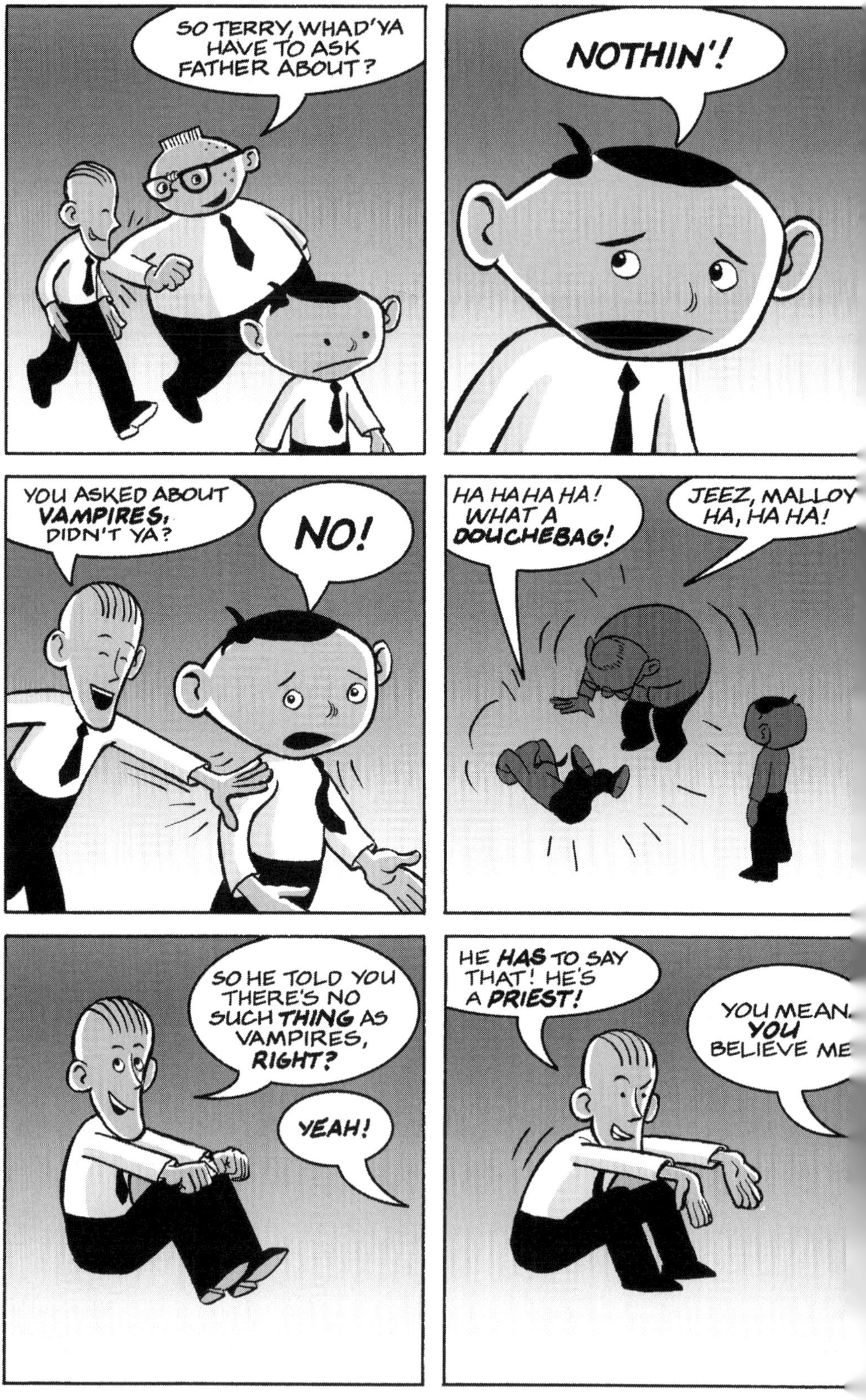
SO TERRY, WHAD'YA HAVE TO ASK FATHER ABOUT?
NOTHIN'!
YOU ASKED ABOUT **VAMPIRES**, DIDN'T YA?
NO!
HA HA HA HA! WHAT A **DOUCHEBAG**!
JEEZ, MALLOY HA, HA HA!
SO HE TOLD YOU THERE'S NO SUCH **THING** AS VAMPIRES, **RIGHT?**
YEAH!
HE **HAS** TO SAY THAT! HE'S A **PRIEST**!
YOU MEAN **YOU** BELIEVE ME

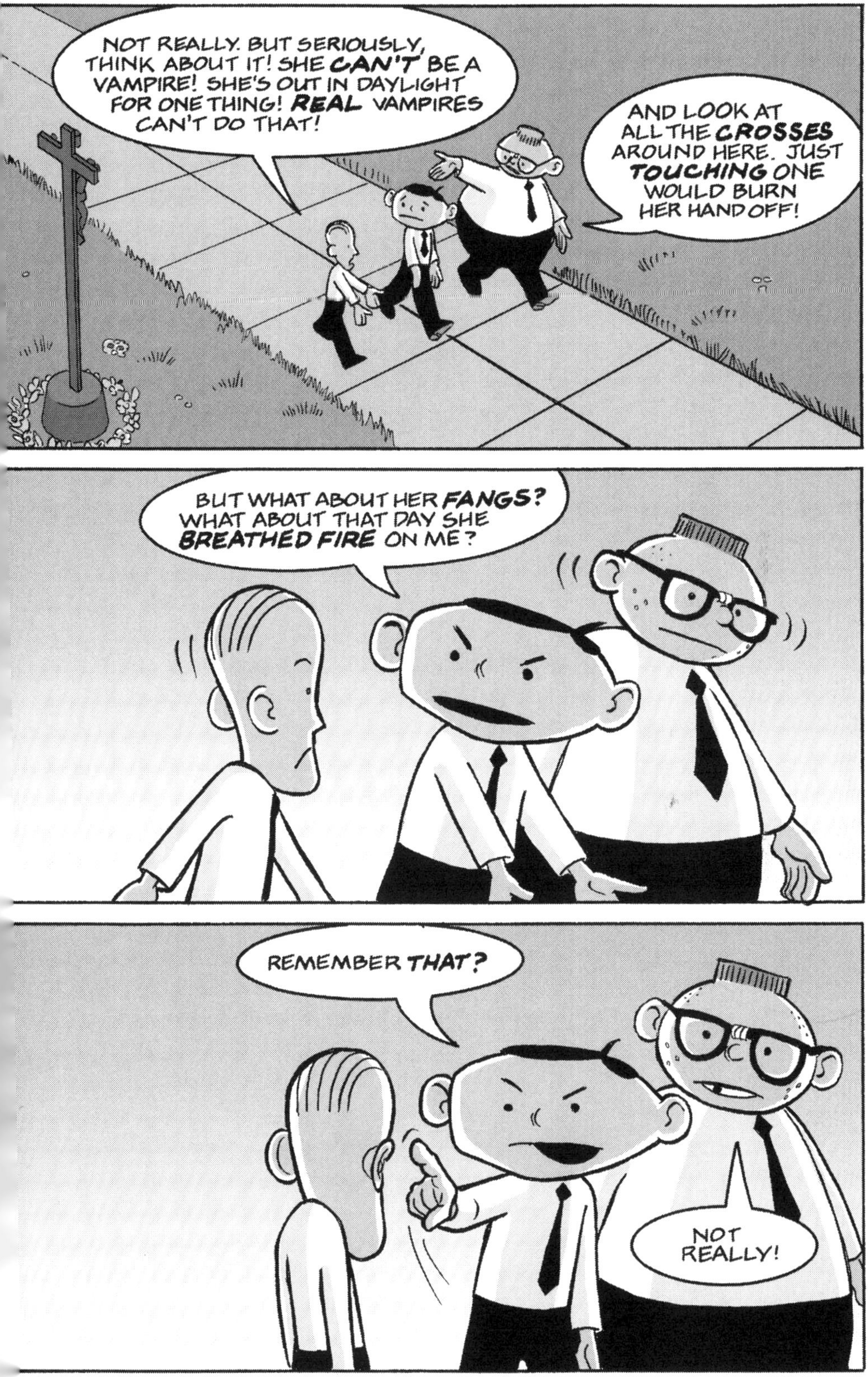
NOT REALLY. BUT SERIOUSLY, THINK ABOUT IT! SHE CAN'T BE A VAMPIRE! SHE'S OUT IN DAYLIGHT FOR ONE THING! REAL VAMPIRES CAN'T DO THAT!
AND LOOK AT ALL THE CROSSES AROUND HERE. JUST TOUCHING ONE WOULD BURN HER HAND OFF!
BUT WHAT ABOUT HER FANGS? WHAT ABOUT THAT DAY SHE BREATHED FIRE ON ME?
REMEMBER THAT?
NOT REALLY!

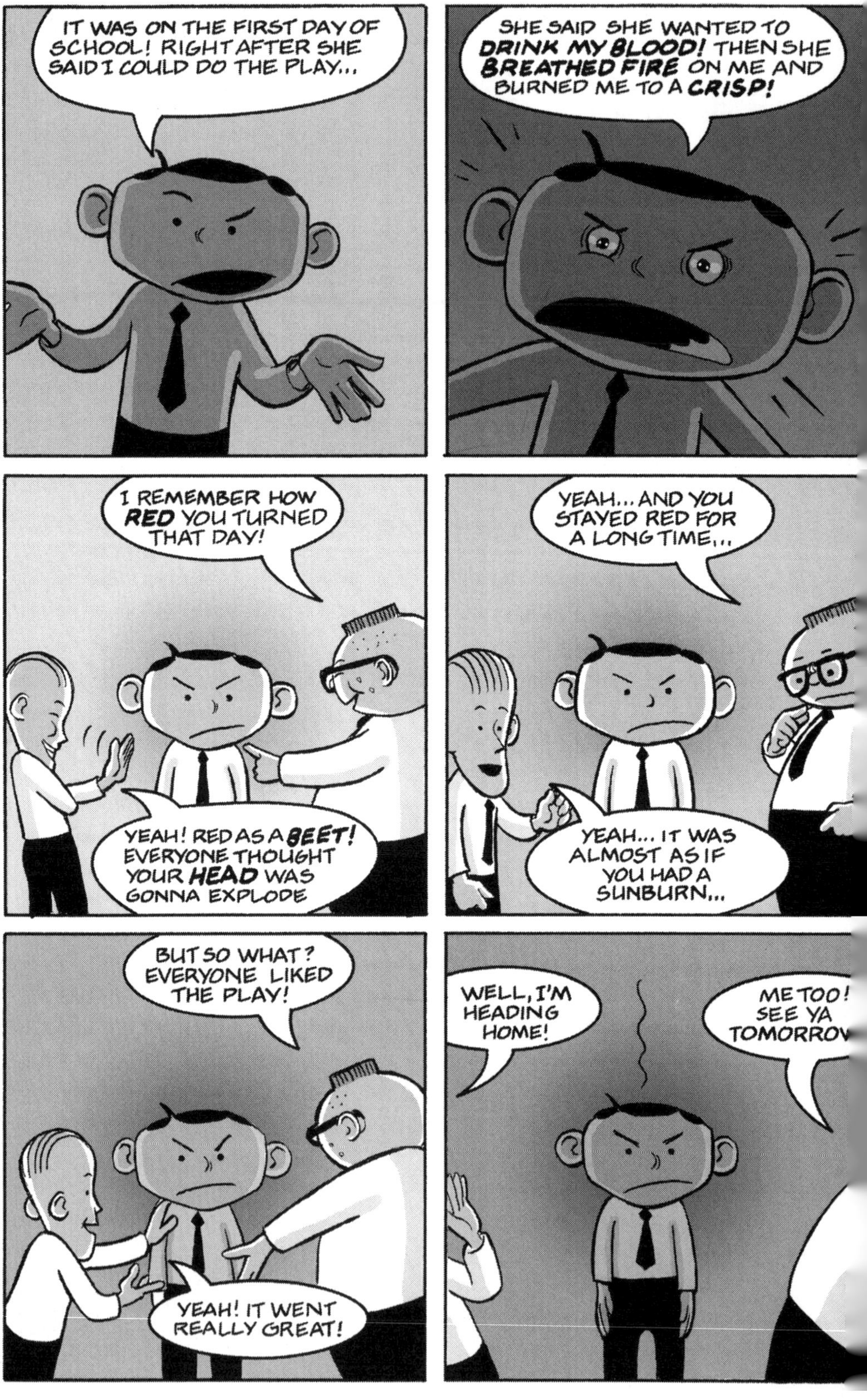
IT WAS ON THE FIRST DAY OF SCHOOL! RIGHT AFTER SHE SAID I COULD DO THE PLAY...
SHE SAID SHE WANTED TO DRINK MY BLOOD! THEN SHE BREATHED FIRE ON ME AND BURNED ME TO A CRISP!
I REMEMBER HOW RED YOU TURNED THAT DAY!
YEAH! RED AS A BEET! EVERYONE THOUGHT YOUR HEAD WAS GONNA EXPLODE
YEAH... AND YOU STAYED RED FOR A LONG TIME...
YEAH... IT WAS ALMOST AS IF YOU HAD A SUNBURN...
BUT SO WHAT? EVERYONE LIKED THE PLAY!
YEAH! IT WENT REALLY GREAT!
WELL, I'M HEADING HOME!
ME TOO! SEE YA TOMORROW

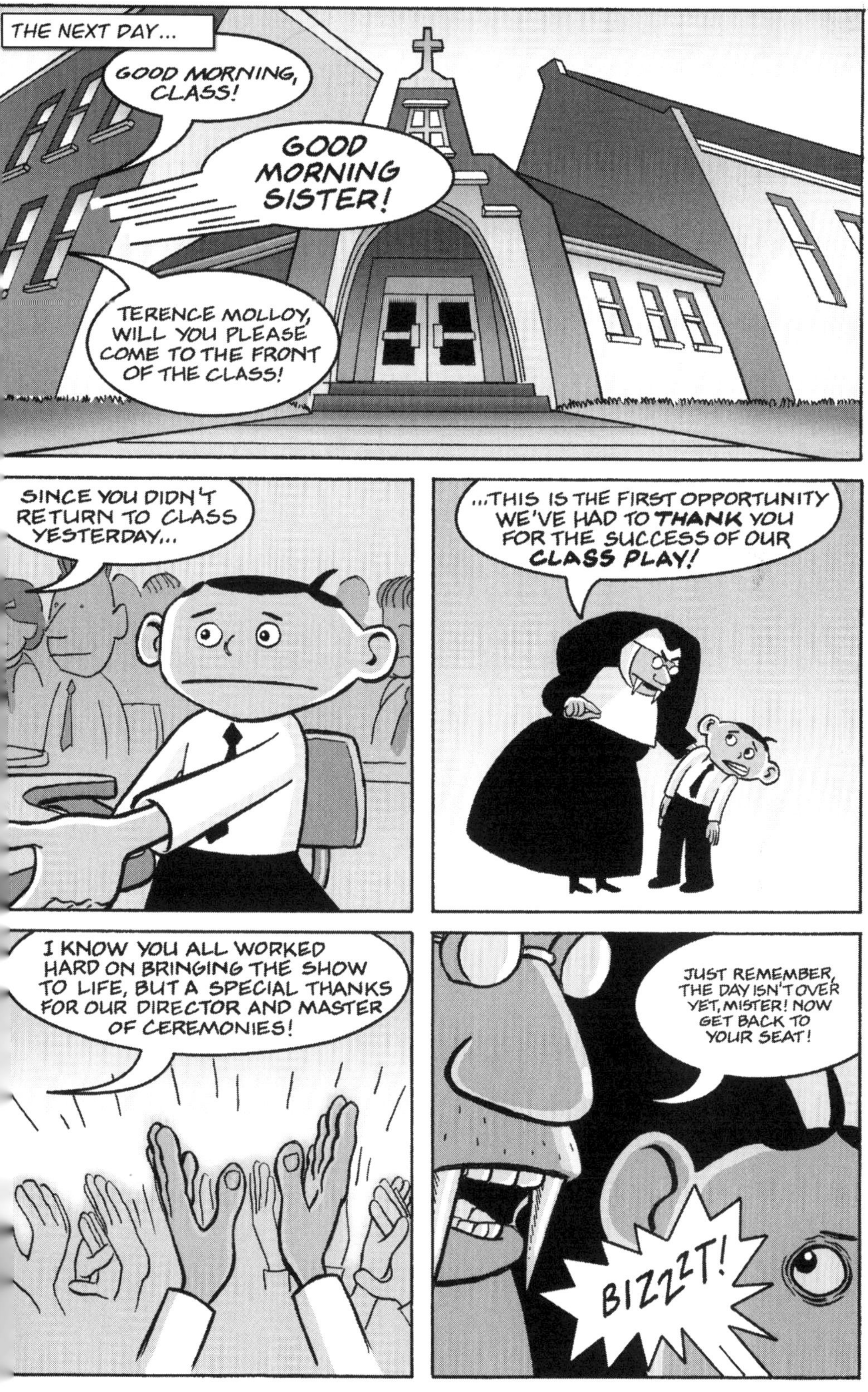
THE NEXT DAY...
GOOD MORNING, CLASS!
GOOD MORNING SISTER!
TERENCE MOLLOY, WILL YOU PLEASE COME TO THE FRONT OF THE CLASS!
SINCE YOU DIDN'T RETURN TO CLASS YESTERDAY...
...THIS IS THE FIRST OPPORTUNITY WE'VE HAD TO THANK YOU FOR THE SUCCESS OF OUR CLASS PLAY!
I KNOW YOU ALL WORKED HARD ON BRINGING THE SHOW TO LIFE, BUT A SPECIAL THANKS FOR OUR DIRECTOR AND MASTER OF CEREMONIES!
JUST REMEMBER, THE DAY ISN'T OVER YET, MISTER! NOW GET BACK TO YOUR SEAT!
BIZZZT!

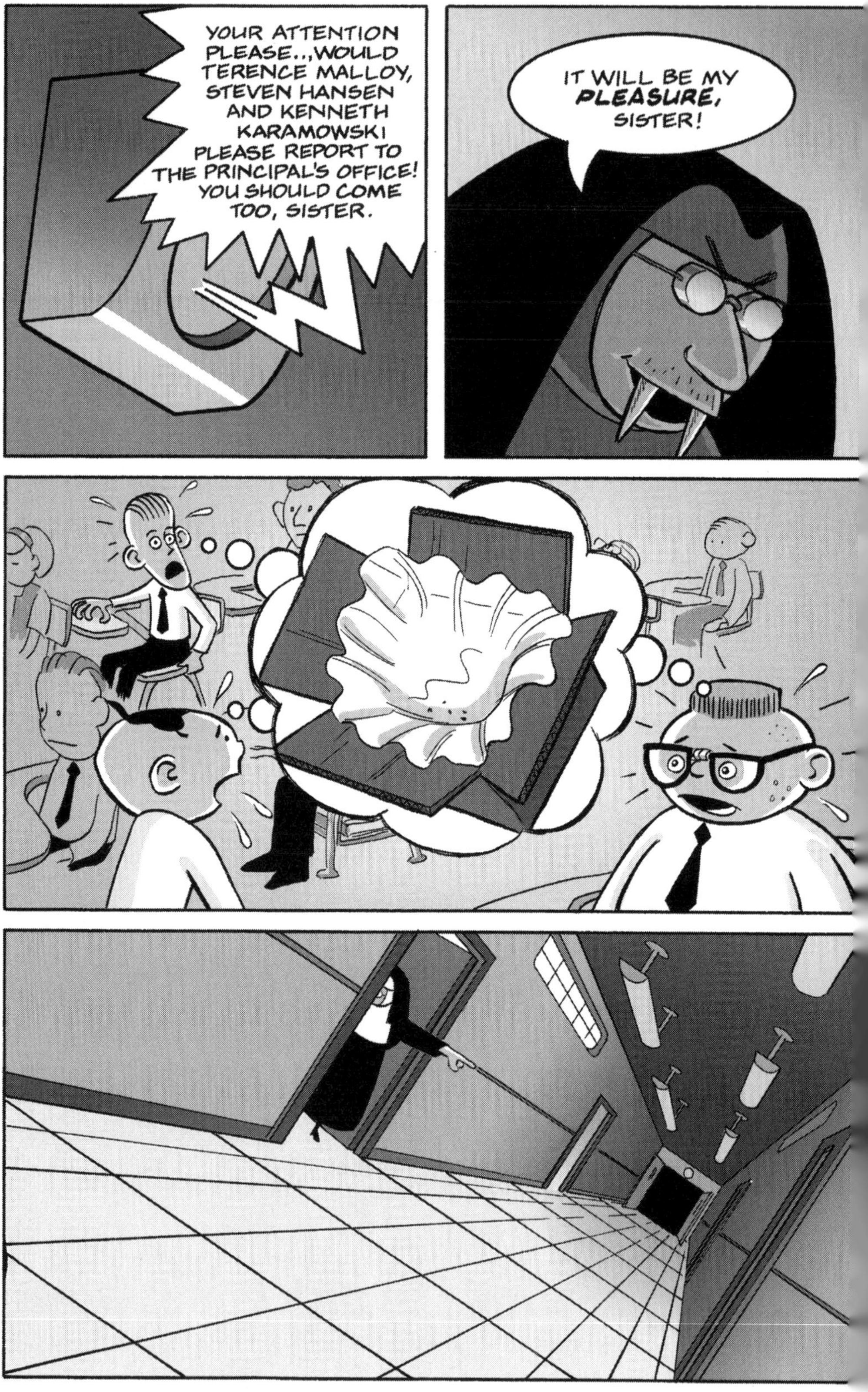
YOUR ATTENTION PLEASE..,WOULD TERENCE MALLOY, STEVEN HANSEN AND KENNETH KARAMOWSKI PLEASE REPORT TO THE PRINCIPAL'S OFFICE! YOU SHOULD COME TOO, SISTER.
IT WILL BE MY **PLEASURE,** SISTER!

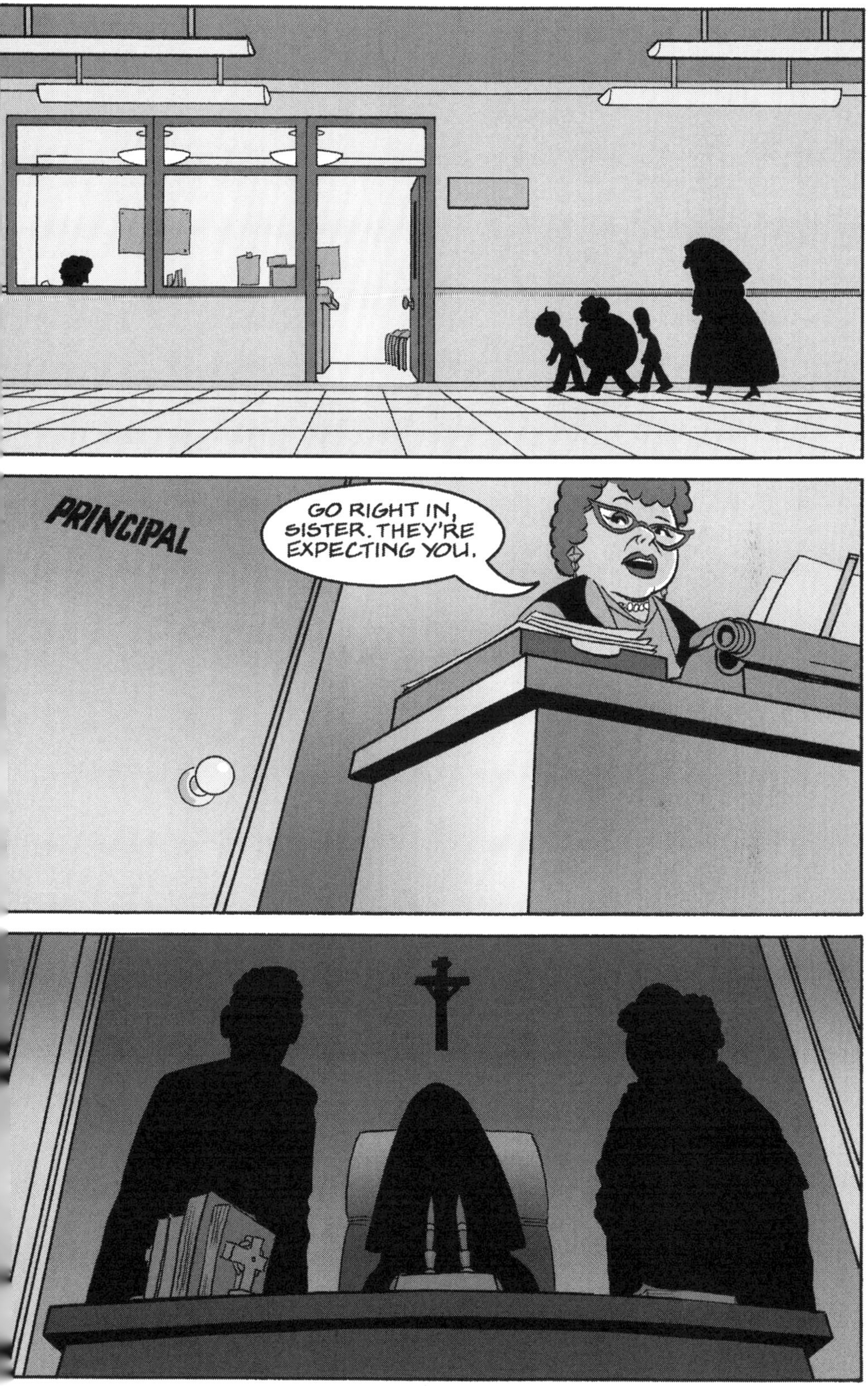
PRINCIPAL
GO RIGHT IN, SISTER. THEY'RE EXPECTING YOU.

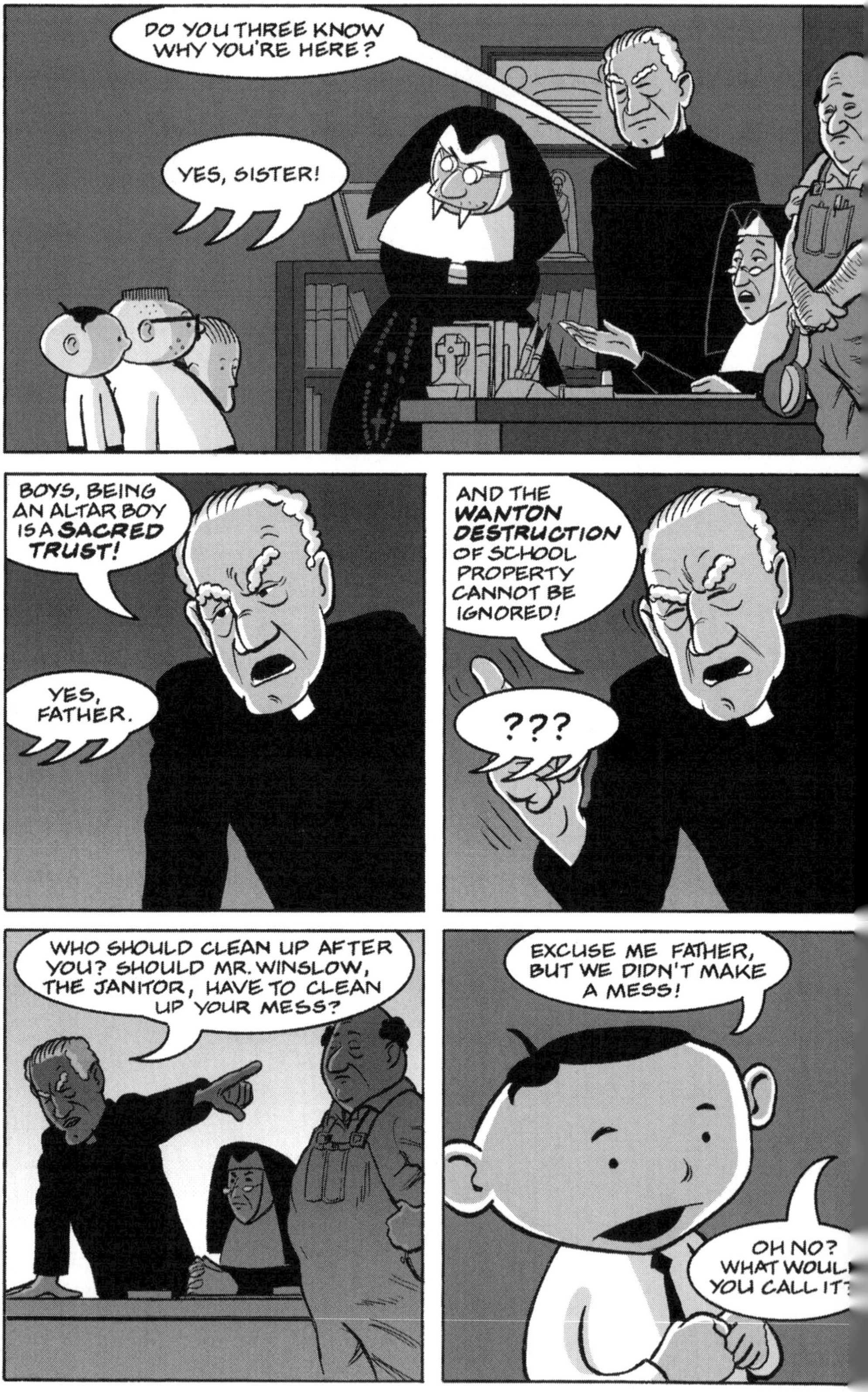
DO YOU THREE KNOW WHY YOU'RE HERE?
YES, SISTER!
BOYS, BEING AN ALTAR BOY IS A **SACRED TRUST!**
YES, FATHER.
AND THE **WANTON DESTRUCTION** OF SCHOOL PROPERTY CANNOT BE IGNORED!
???
WHO SHOULD CLEAN UP AFTER YOU? SHOULD MR. WINSLOW, THE JANITOR, HAVE TO CLEAN UP YOUR MESS?
EXCUSE ME FATHER, BUT WE DIDN'T MAKE A MESS!
OH NO? WHAT WOUL YOU CALL IT?

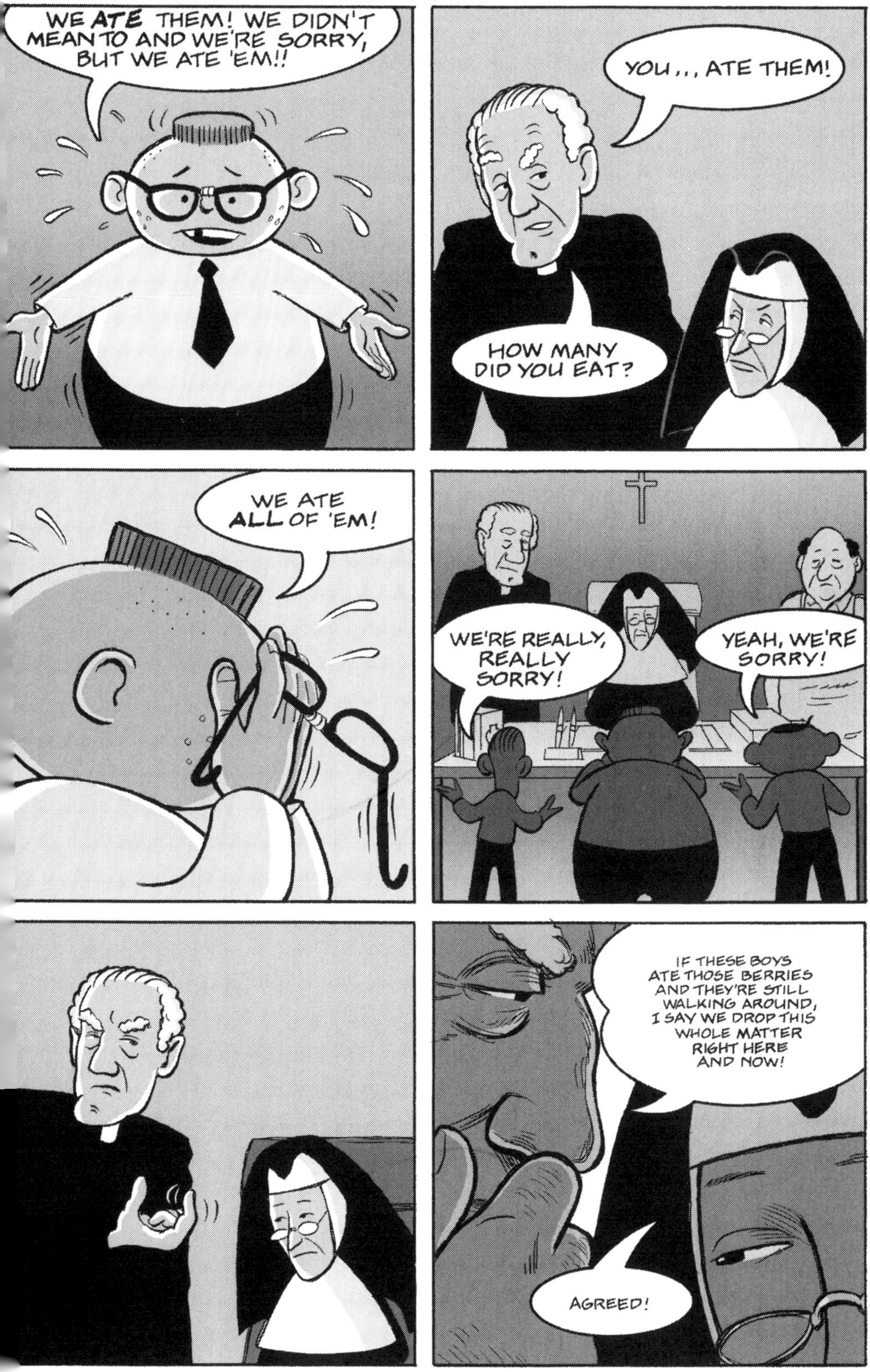
WE ATE THEM! WE DIDN'T MEAN TO AND WE'RE SORRY, BUT WE ATE 'EM!!
YOU... ATE THEM!
HOW MANY DID YOU EAT?
WE ATE ALL OF 'EM!
WE'RE REALLY, REALLY SORRY!
YEAH, WE'RE SORRY!
IF THESE BOYS ATE THOSE BERRIES AND THEY'RE STILL WALKING AROUND, I SAY WE DROP THIS WHOLE MATTER RIGHT HERE AND NOW!
AGREED!

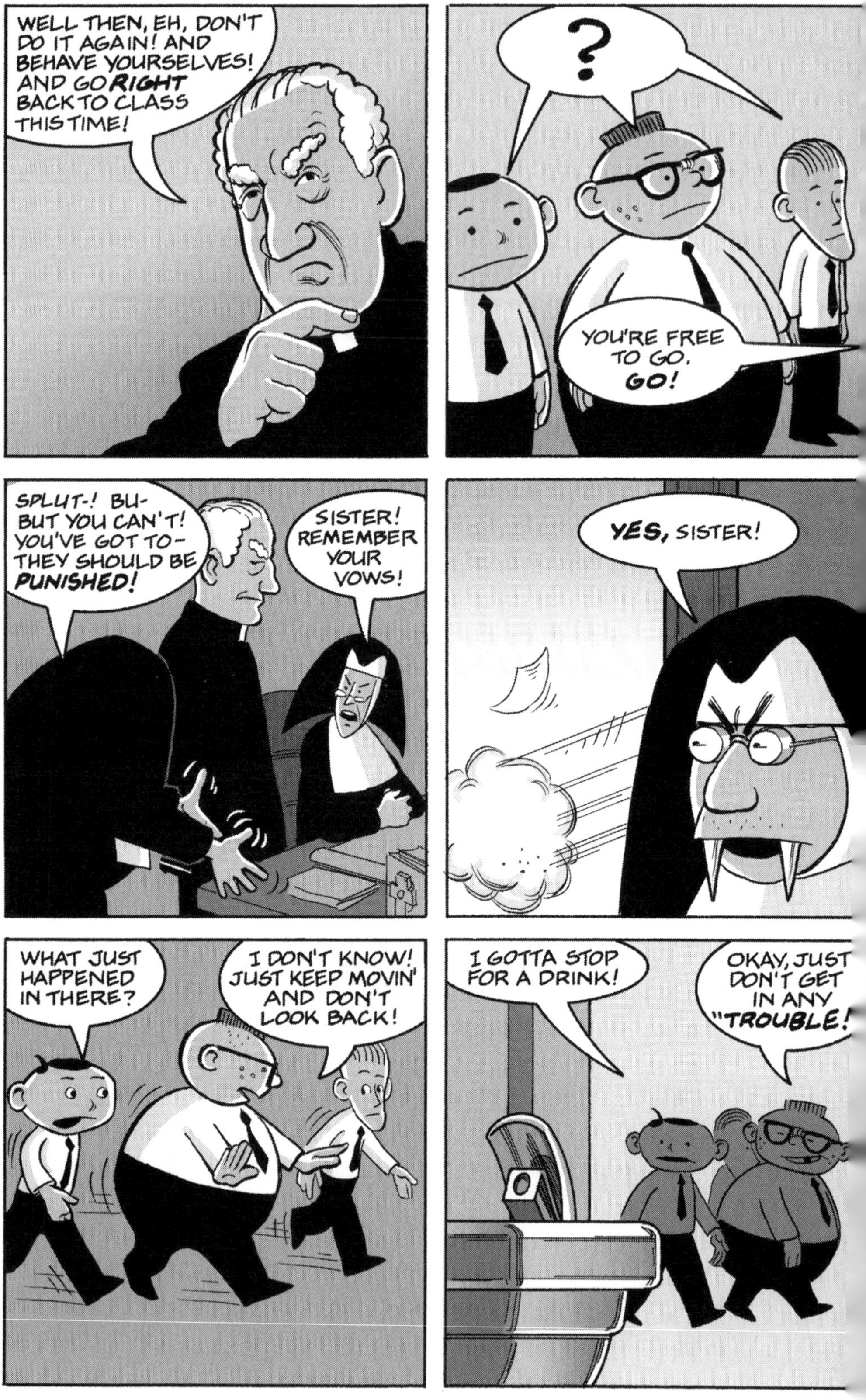
WELL THEN, EH, DON'T DO IT AGAIN! AND BEHAVE YOURSELVES! AND GO RIGHT BACK TO CLASS THIS TIME!
?
YOU'RE FREE TO GO. GO!
SPLUT-! BU-BUT YOU CAN'T! YOU'VE GOT TO- THEY SHOULD BE PUNISHED!
SISTER! REMEMBER YOUR VOWS!
YES, SISTER!
WHAT JUST HAPPENED IN THERE?
I DON'T KNOW! JUST KEEP MOVIN' AND DON'T LOOK BACK!
I GOTTA STOP FOR A DRINK!
OKAY, JUST DON'T GET IN ANY "TROUBLE!"

YEAH, *"TROUBLE"*! HA HA!

HA HA HA HA!!

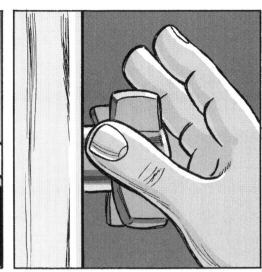

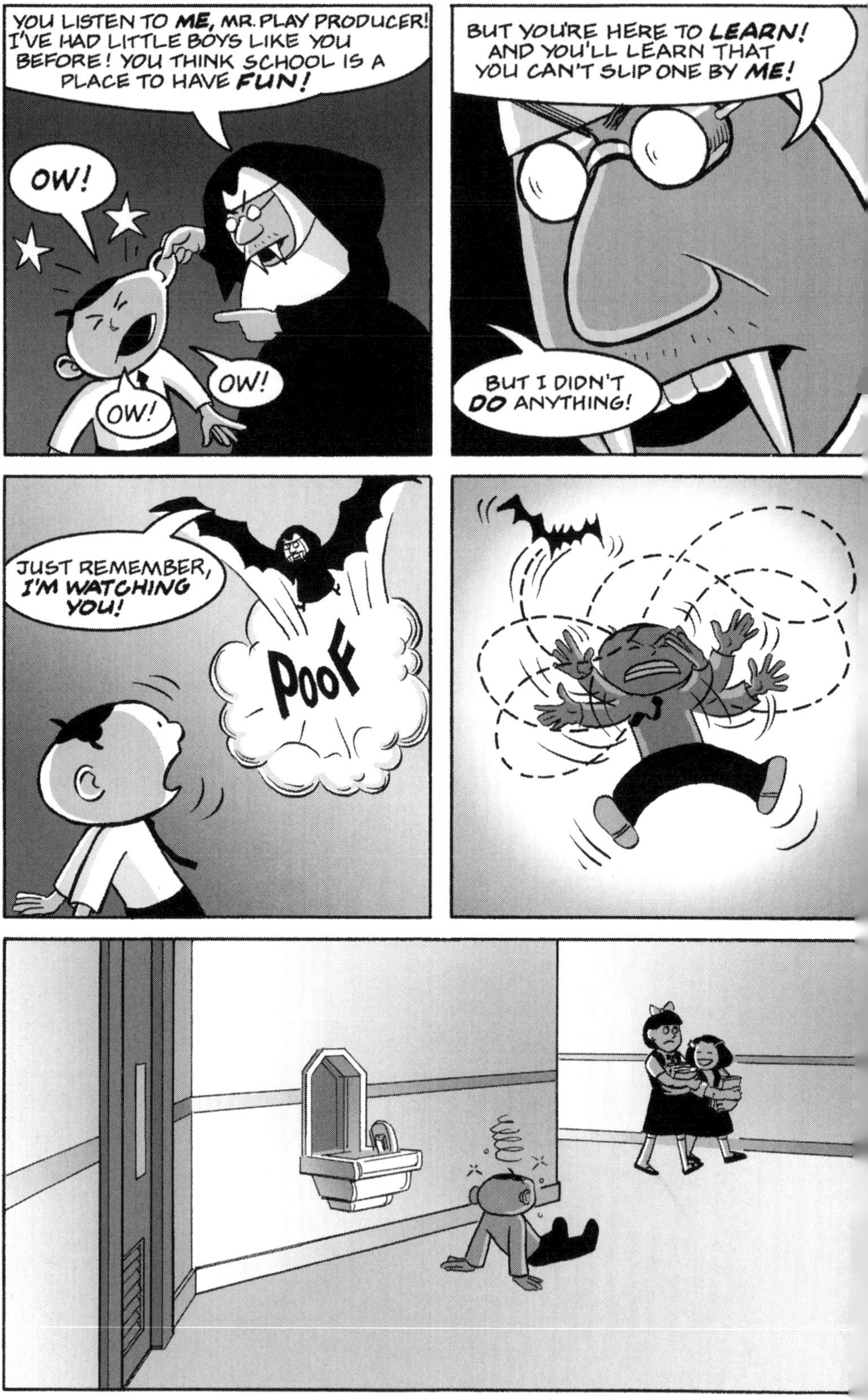
YOU LISTEN TO ME, MR. PLAY PRODUCER! I'VE HAD LITTLE BOYS LIKE YOU BEFORE! YOU THINK SCHOOL IS A PLACE TO HAVE FUN!
OW!
OW!
OW!
BUT YOU'RE HERE TO LEARN! AND YOU'LL LEARN THAT YOU CAN'T SLIP ONE BY ME!
BUT I DIDN'T DO ANYTHING!
JUST REMEMBER, I'M WATCHING YOU!
POOF

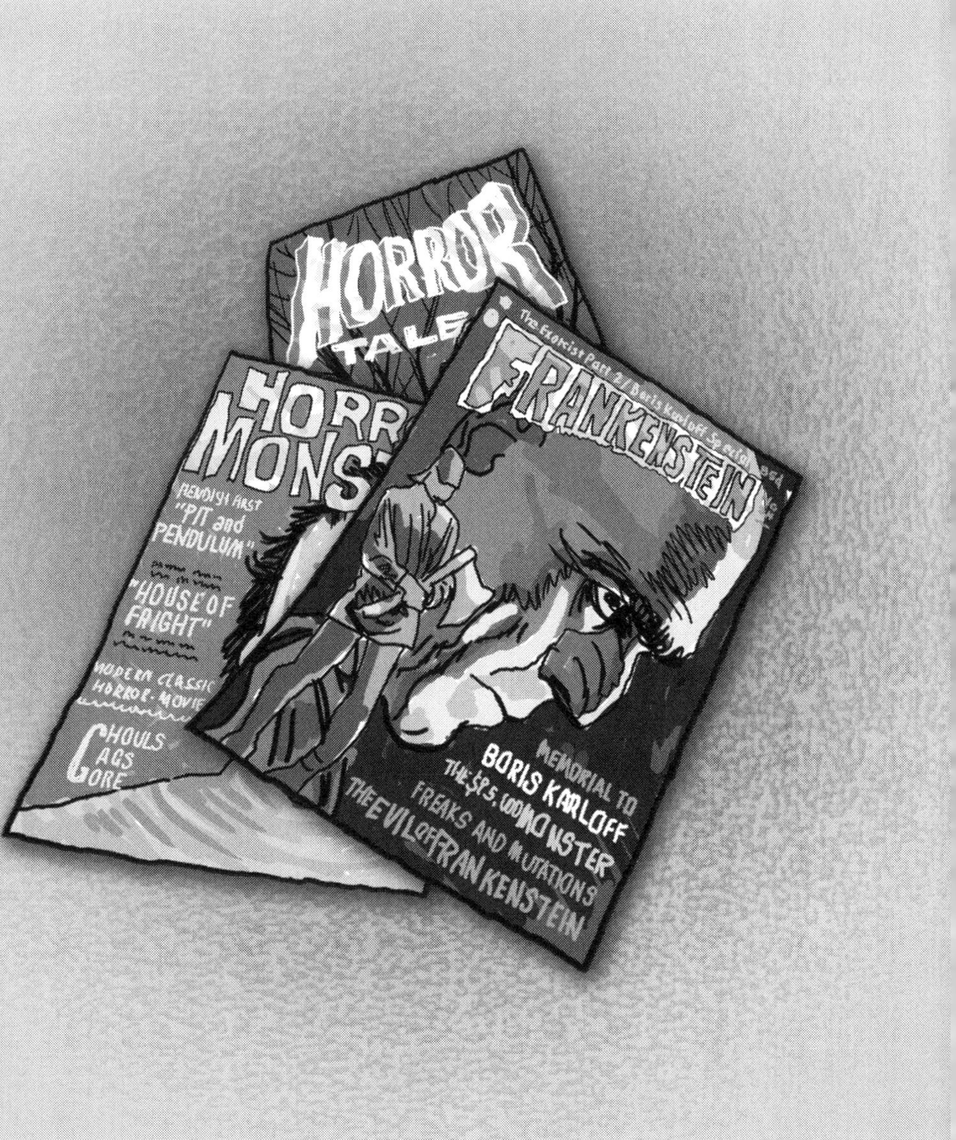
HORROR
FRANKENSTEIN
FIENDISH FIRST
"PIT and PENDULUM"
"HOUSE OF FRIGHT"
MODERN CLASSIC
HORROR-MOVIE
GHOULS
GAGS
GORE
MEMORIAL TO
BORIS KARLOFF
FREAKS AND MUTATIONS
THE EVIL OF FRANKENSTEIN

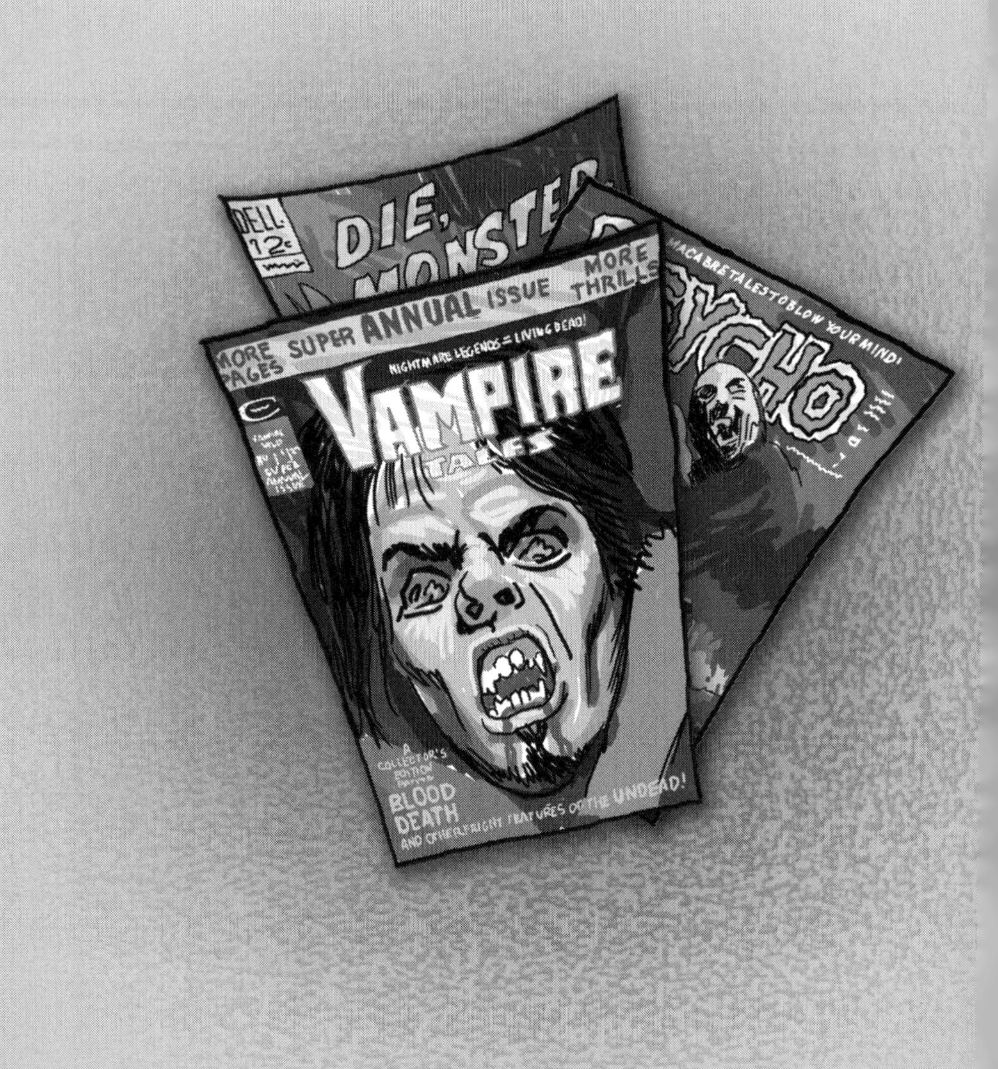
DELL 12¢
DIE,
MACABRE TALES TO BLOW YOUR MIND!
MORE PAGES
SUPER ANNUAL ISSUE
MORE THRILLS
NIGHTMARE LEGENDS = LIVING DEAD!
VAMPIRE
TALES
A COLLECTOR'S EDITION
BLOOD
DEATH
AND OTHER FRIGHT FEATURES OF THE UNDEAD!

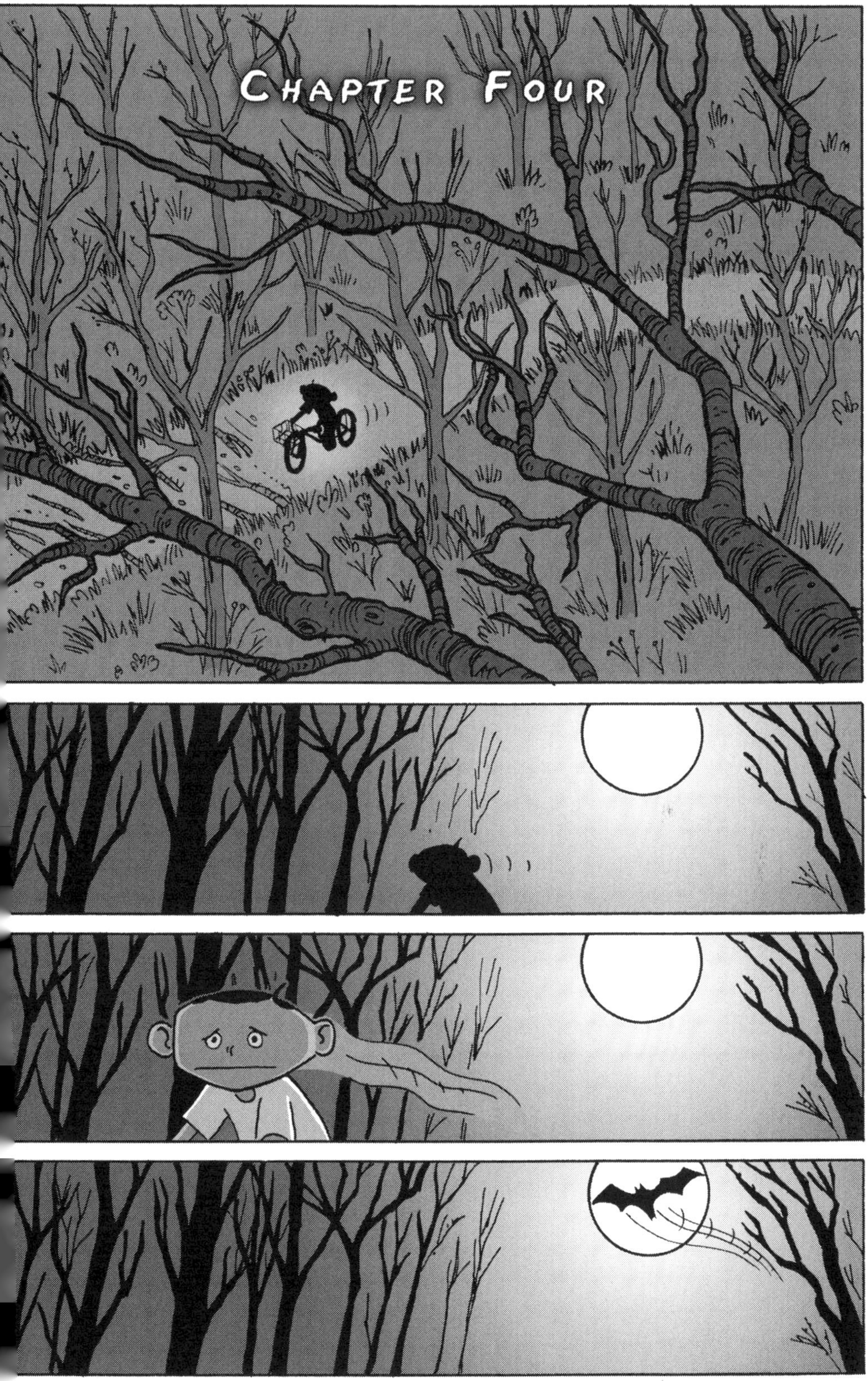
CHAPTER FOUR

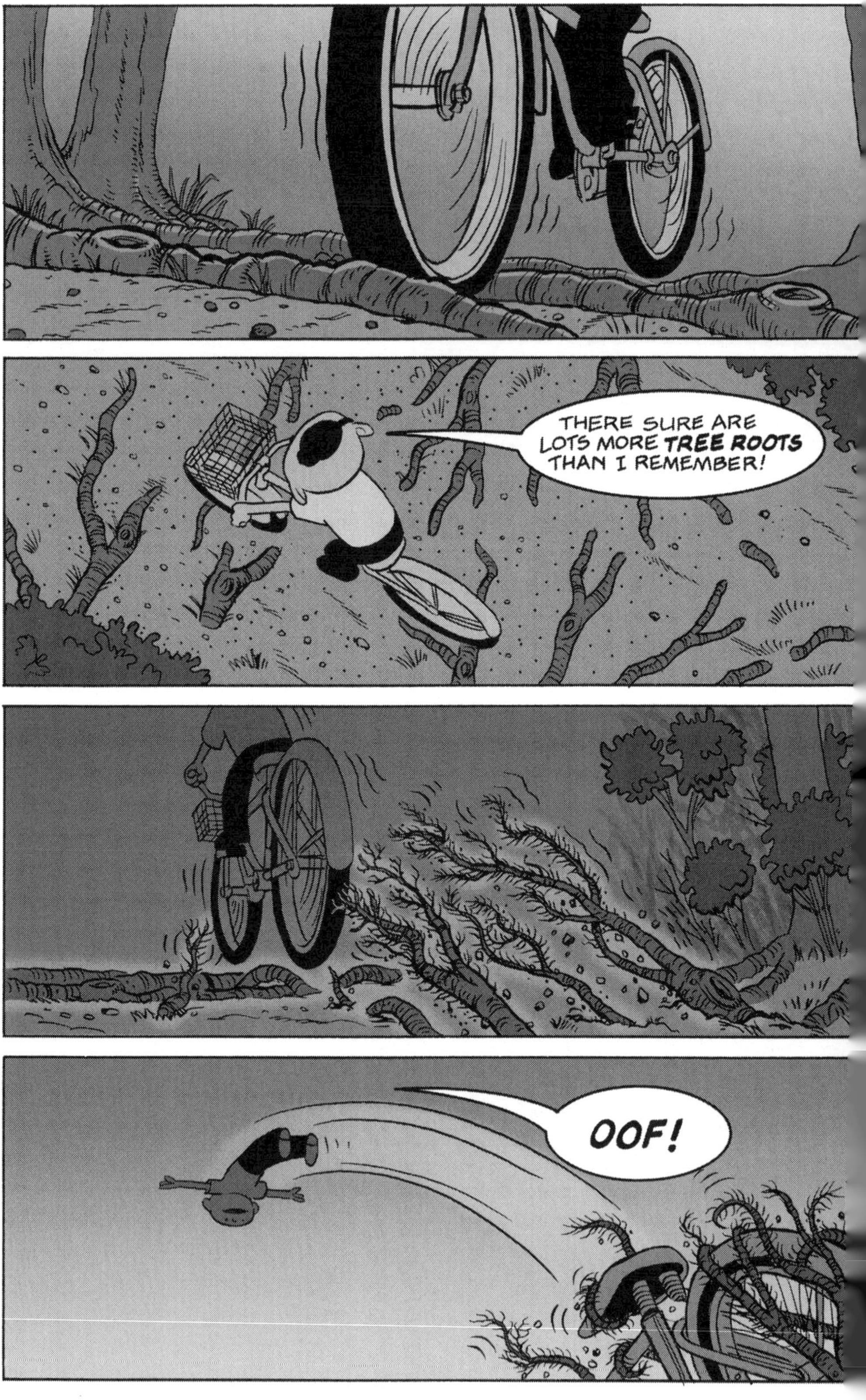
THERE SURE ARE LOTS MORE TREE ROOTS THAN I REMEMBER!
OOF!

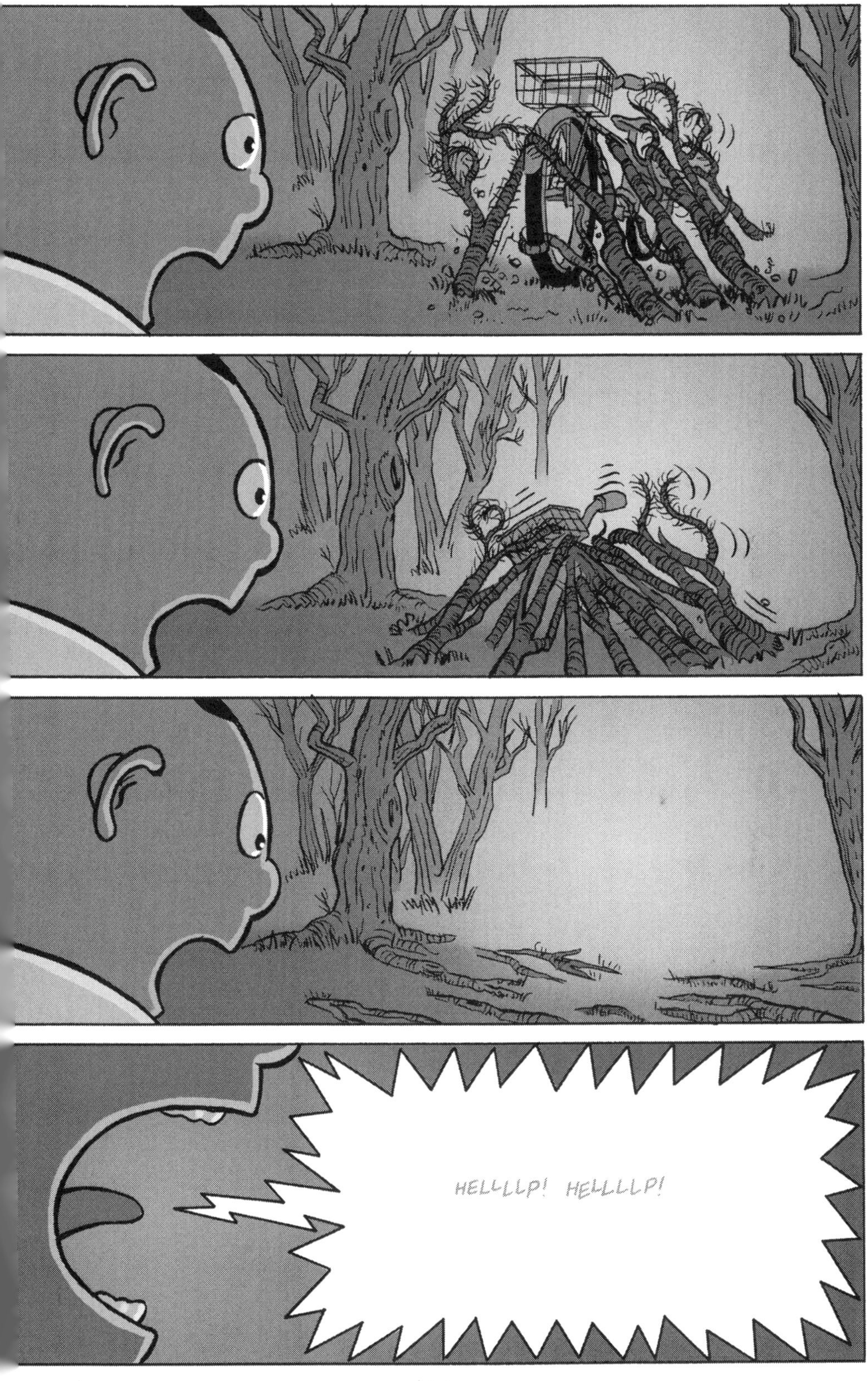
HELLLLP! HELLLLP!

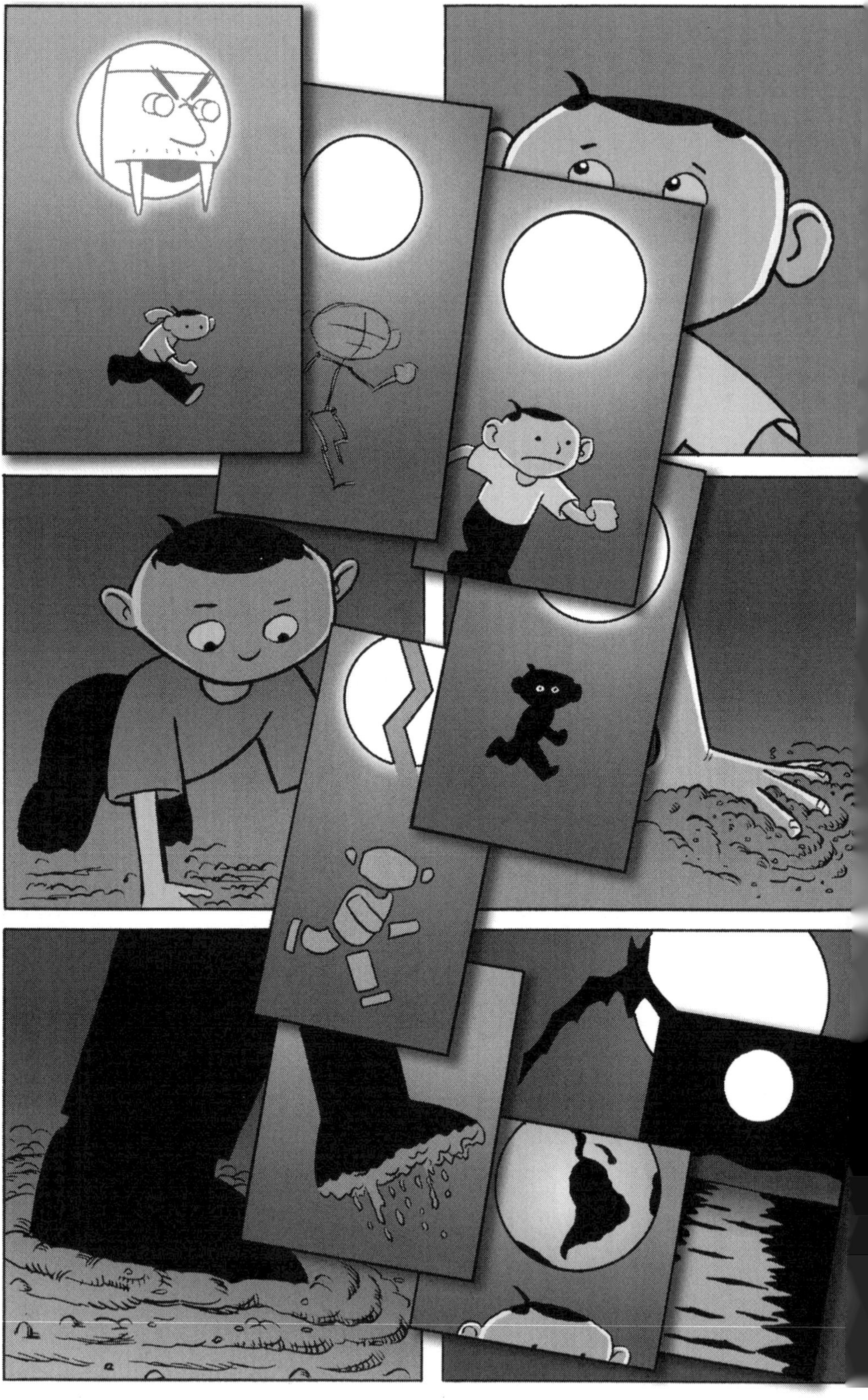

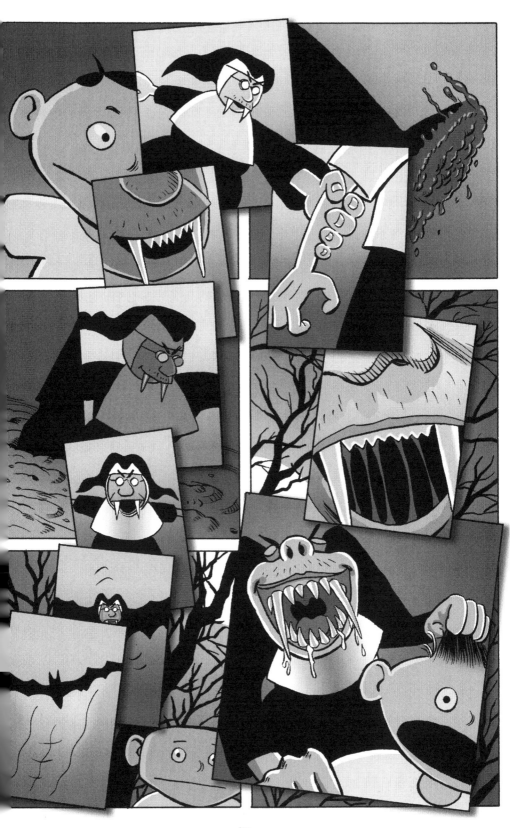

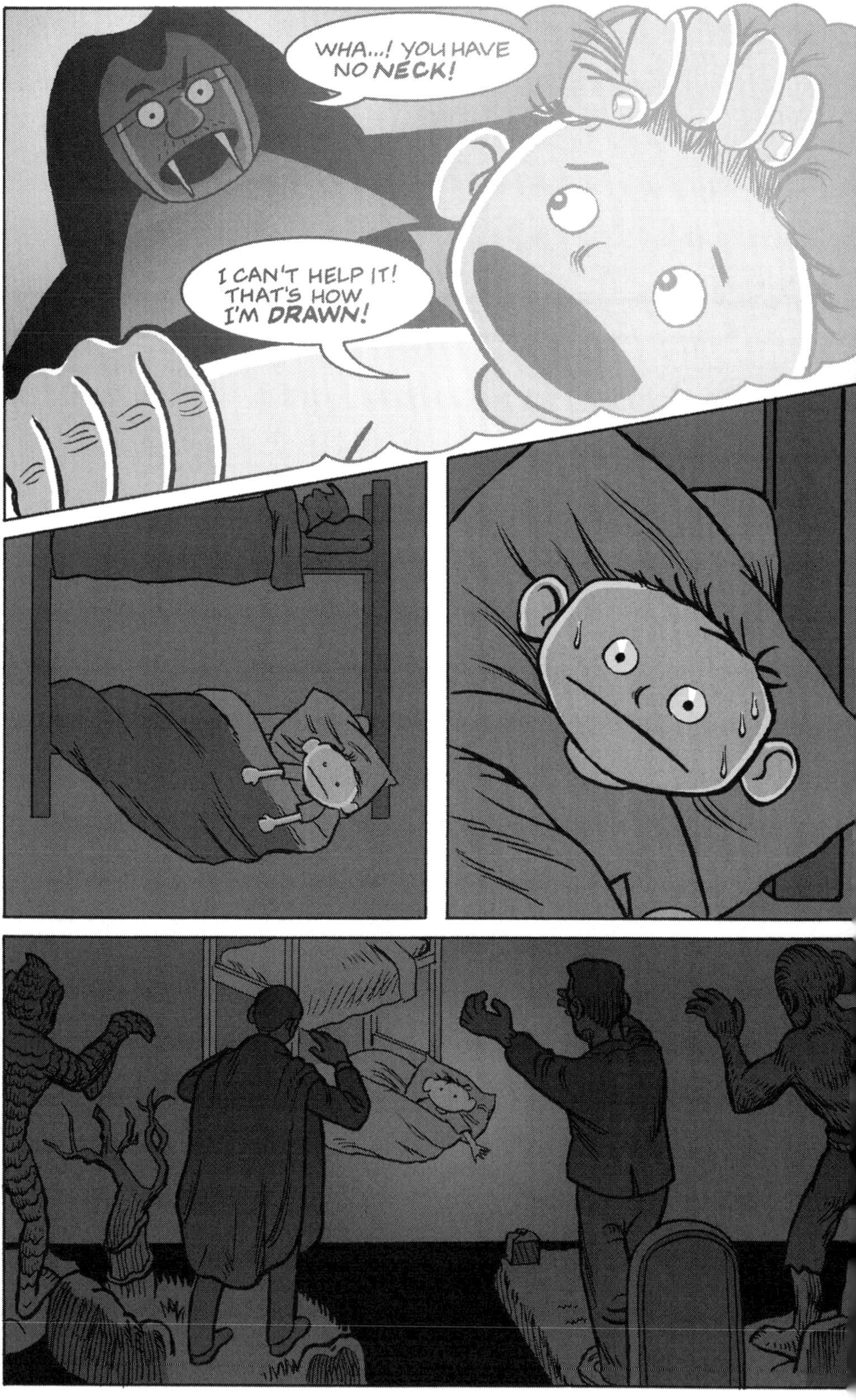
WHA...! YOU HAVE NO NECK!
I CAN'T HELP IT! THAT'S HOW I'M DRAWN!

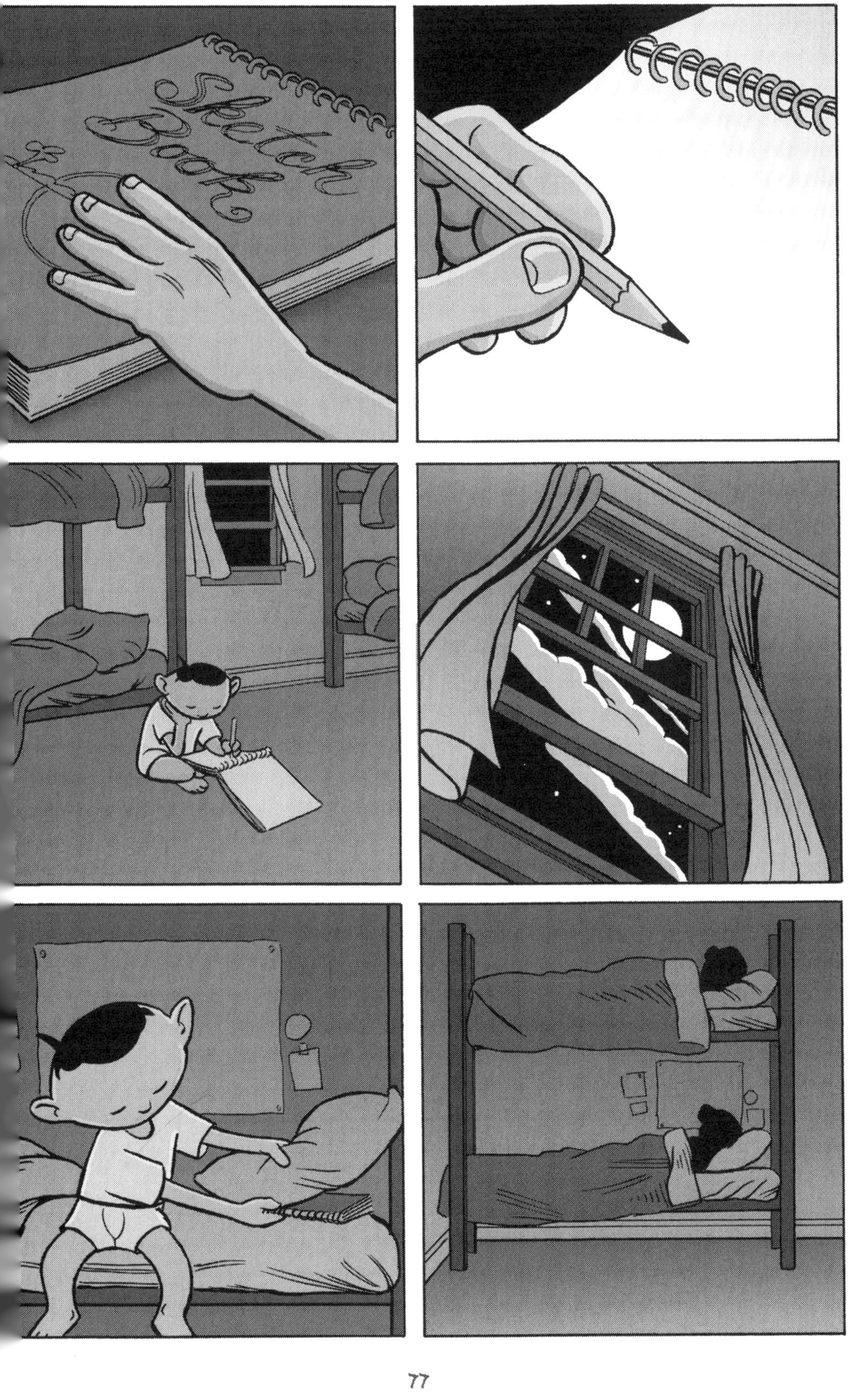
Sketch Book

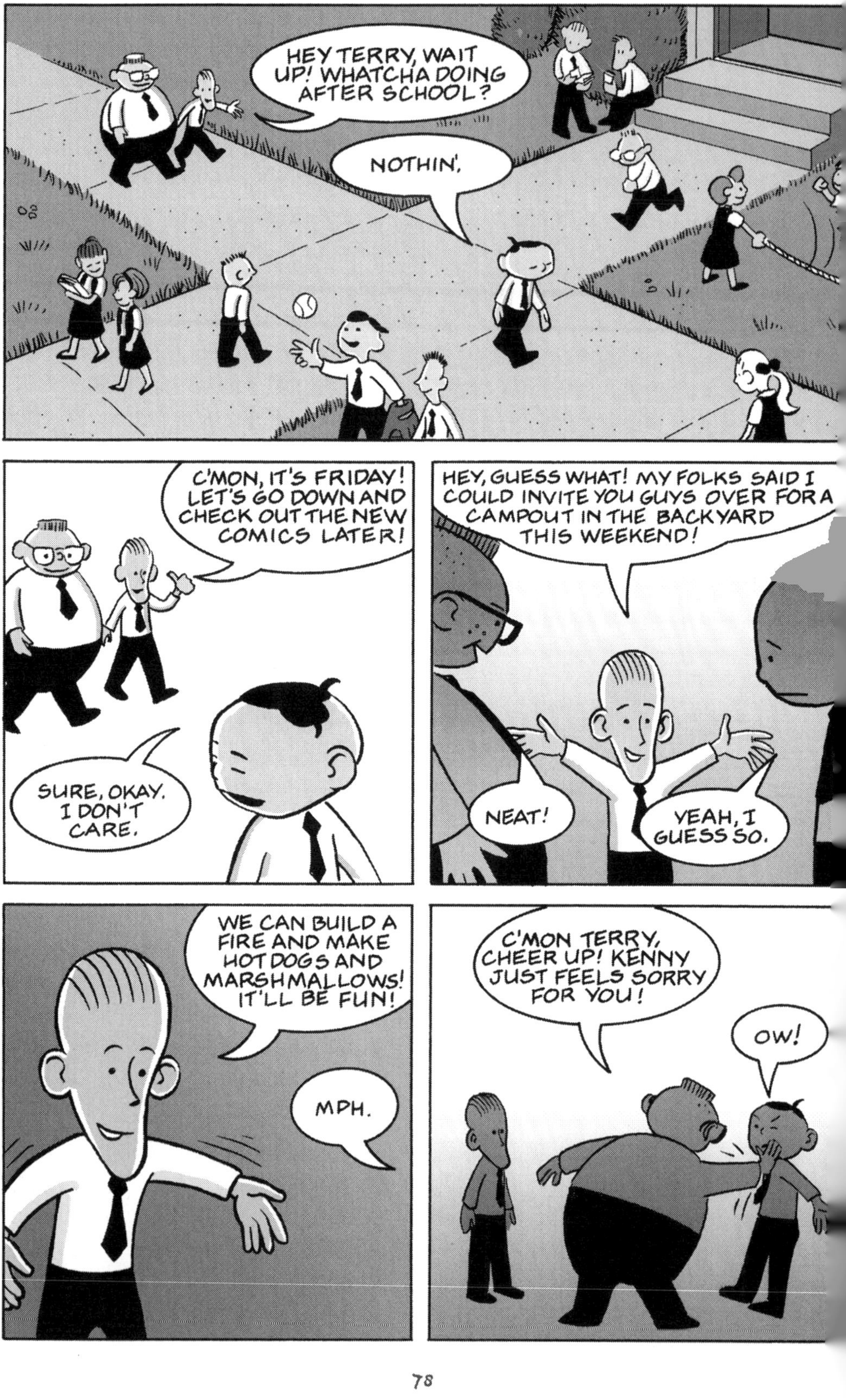
HEY TERRY, WAIT UP! WHATCHA DOING AFTER SCHOOL?
NOTHIN'.
C'MON, IT'S FRIDAY! LET'S GO DOWN AND CHECK OUT THE NEW COMICS LATER!
SURE, OKAY. I DON'T CARE.
HEY, GUESS WHAT! MY FOLKS SAID I COULD INVITE YOU GUYS OVER FOR A CAMPOUT IN THE BACKYARD THIS WEEKEND!
NEAT!
YEAH, I GUESS SO.
WE CAN BUILD A FIRE AND MAKE HOT DOGS AND MARSHMALLOWS! IT'LL BE FUN!
MPH.
C'MON TERRY, CHEER UP! KENNY JUST FEELS SORRY FOR YOU!
OW!

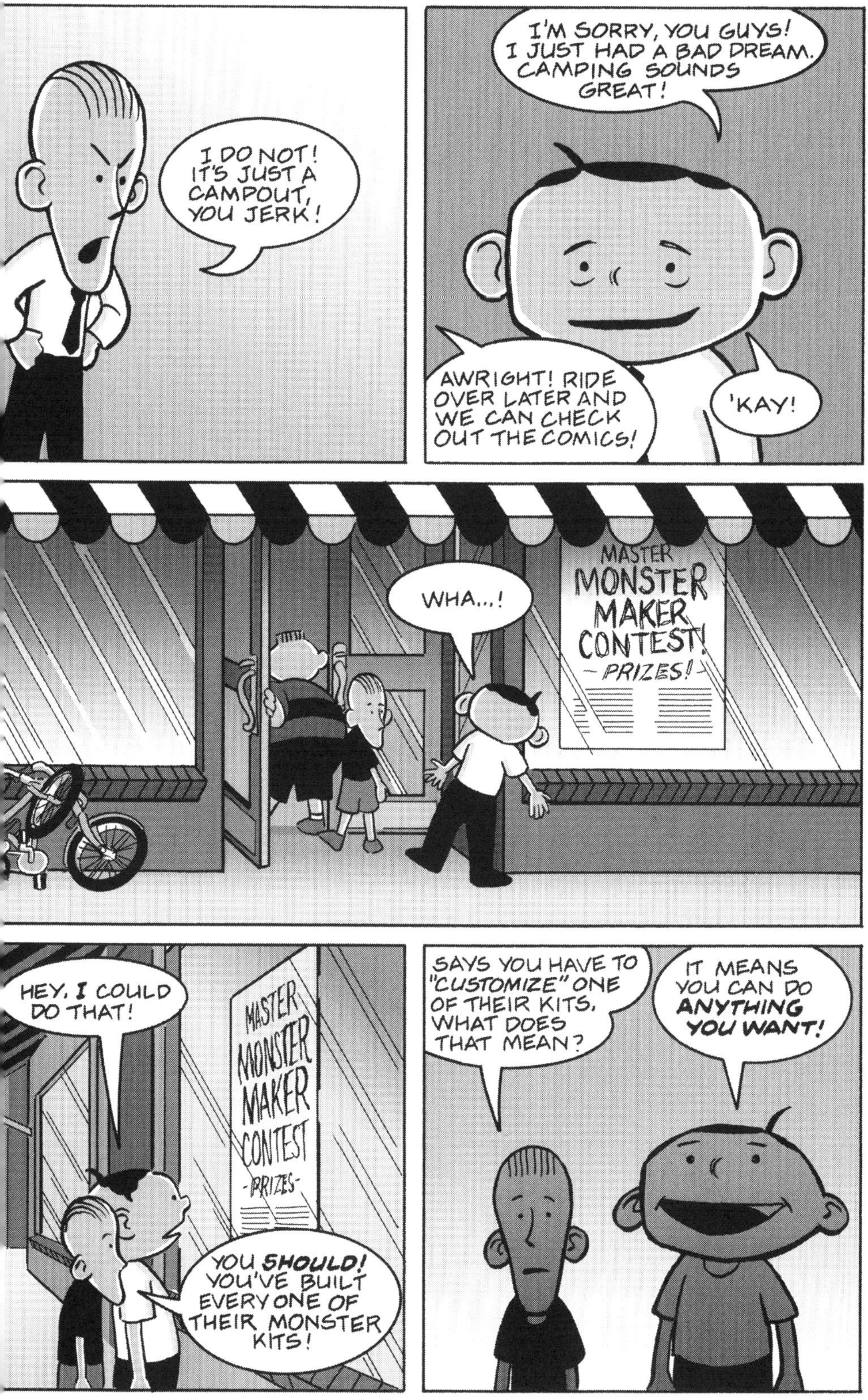
I DO NOT! IT'S JUST A CAMPOUT, YOU JERK!
I'M SORRY, YOU GUYS! I JUST HAD A BAD DREAM. CAMPING SOUNDS GREAT!
AWRIGHT! RIDE OVER LATER AND WE CAN CHECK OUT THE COMICS!
'KAY!
MASTER MONSTER MAKER CONTEST! -PRIZES!-
WHA...!
HEY, I COULD DO THAT!
MASTER MONSTER MAKER CONTEST -PRIZES-
YOU SHOULD! YOU'VE BUILT EVERY ONE OF THEIR MONSTER KITS!
SAYS YOU HAVE TO "CUSTOMIZE" ONE OF THEIR KITS, WHAT DOES THAT MEAN?
IT MEANS YOU CAN DO ANYTHING YOU WANT!

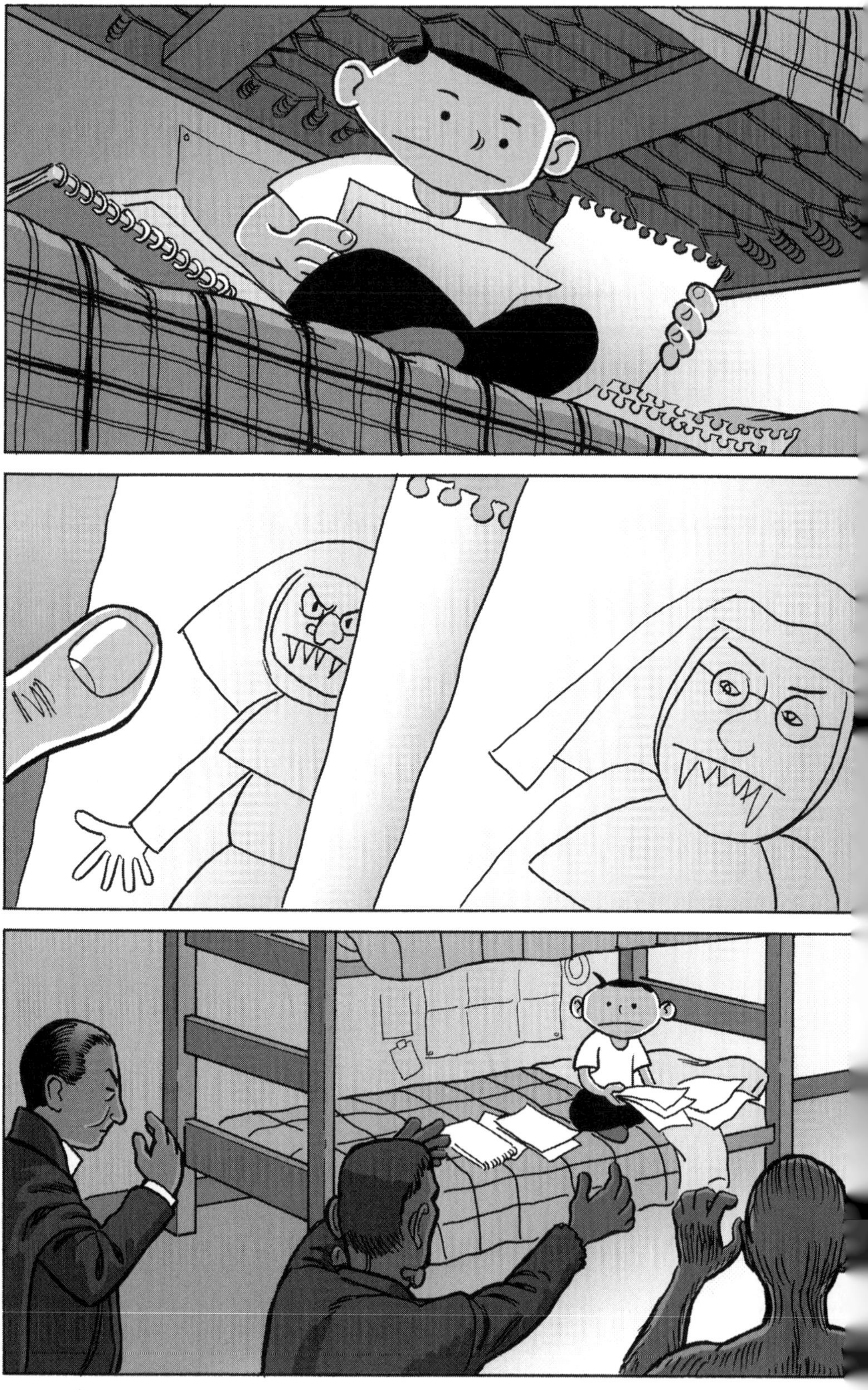

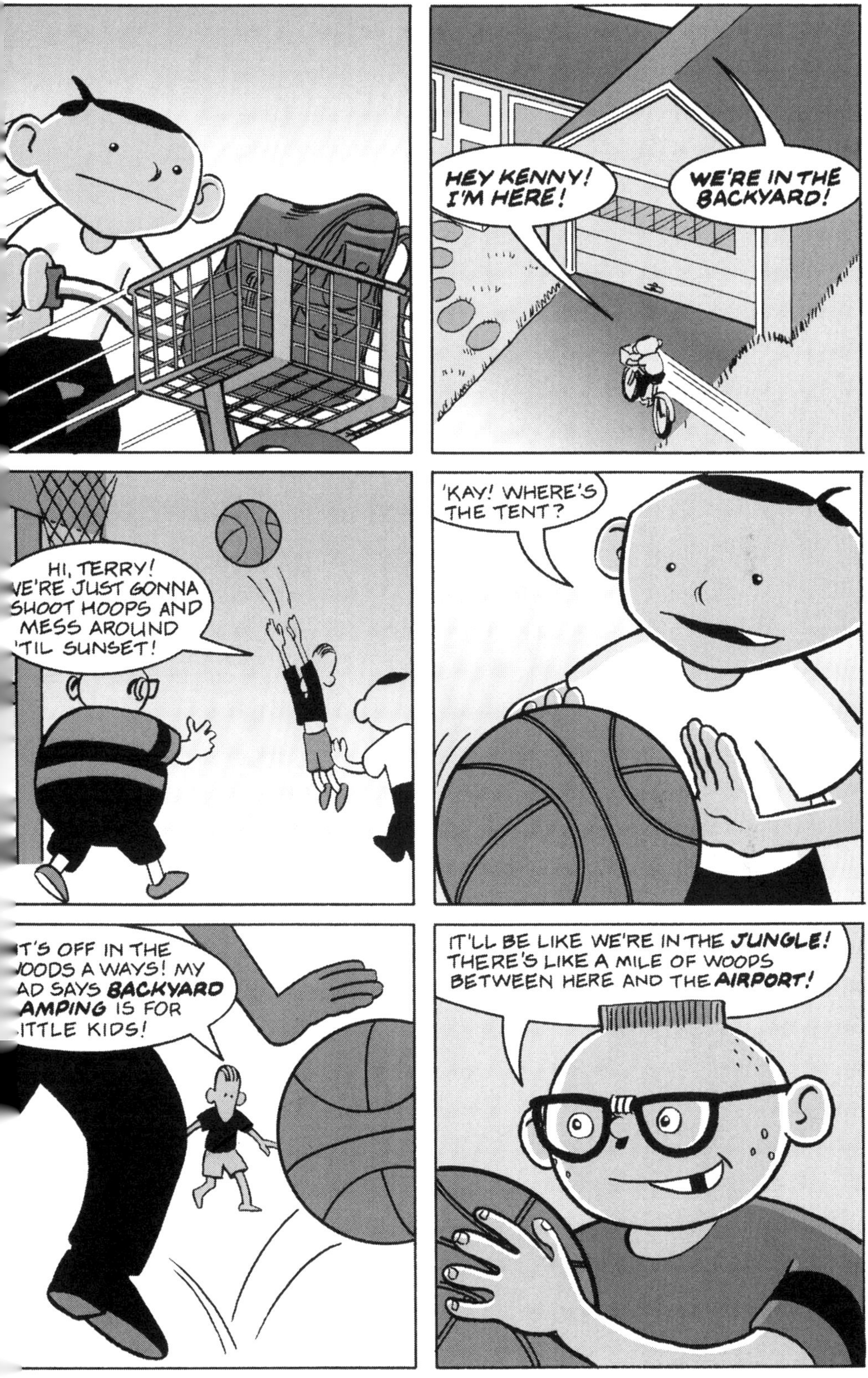
HEY KENNY! I'M HERE!
WE'RE IN THE BACKYARD!
HI, TERRY! VE'RE JUST GONNA SHOOT HOOPS AND MESS AROUND 'TIL SUNSET!
'KAY! WHERE'S THE TENT?
IT'S OFF IN THE OODS A WAYS! MY AD SAYS BACKYARD AMPING IS FOR ITTLE KIDS!
IT'LL BE LIKE WE'RE IN THE JUNGLE! THERE'S LIKE A MILE OF WOODS BETWEEN HERE AND THE AIRPORT!

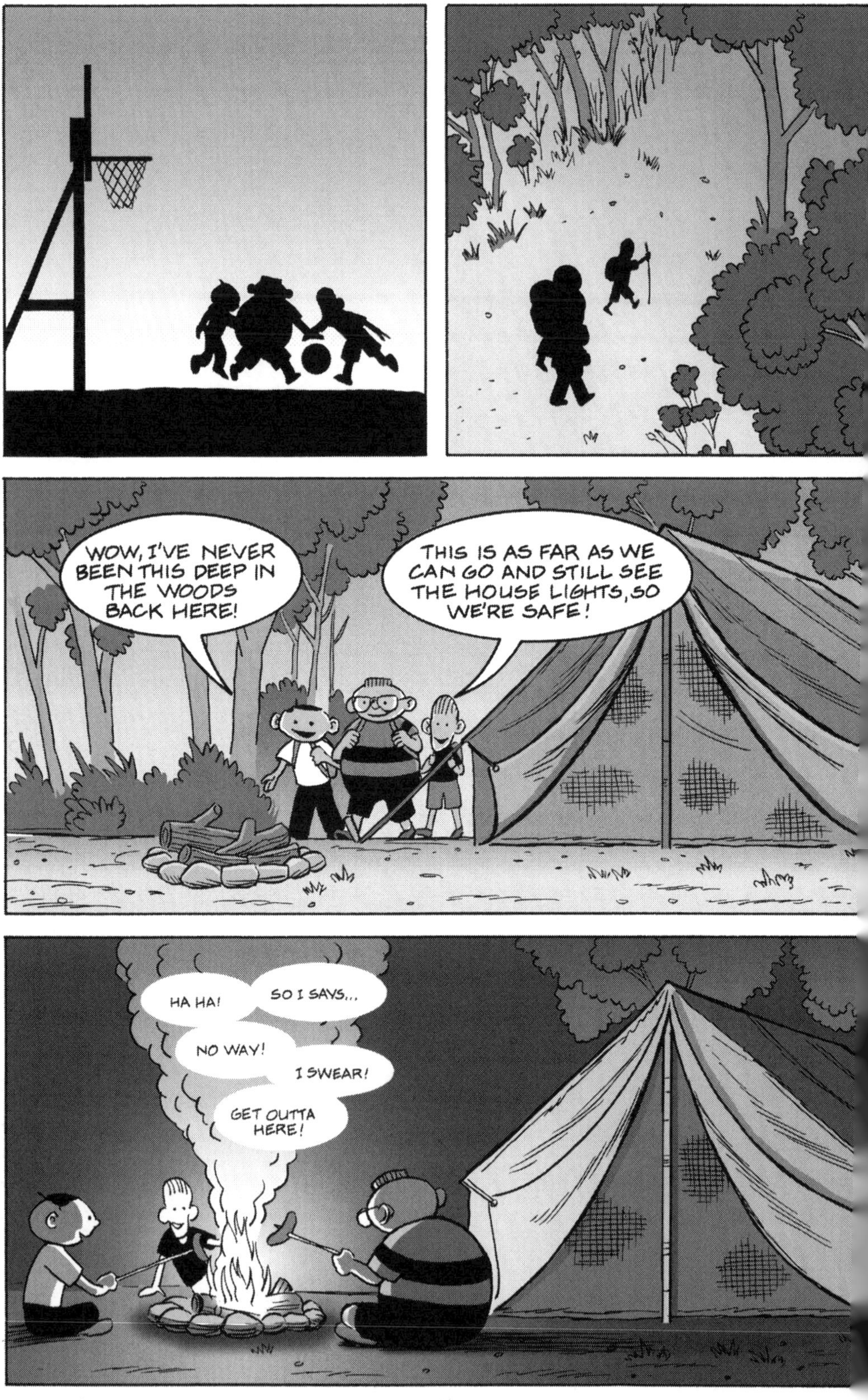
WOW, I'VE NEVER BEEN THIS DEEP IN THE WOODS BACK HERE!
THIS IS AS FAR AS WE CAN GO AND STILL SEE THE HOUSE LIGHTS, SO WE'RE SAFE!
HA HA!
SO I SAYS...
NO WAY!
I SWEAR!
GET OUTTA HERE!

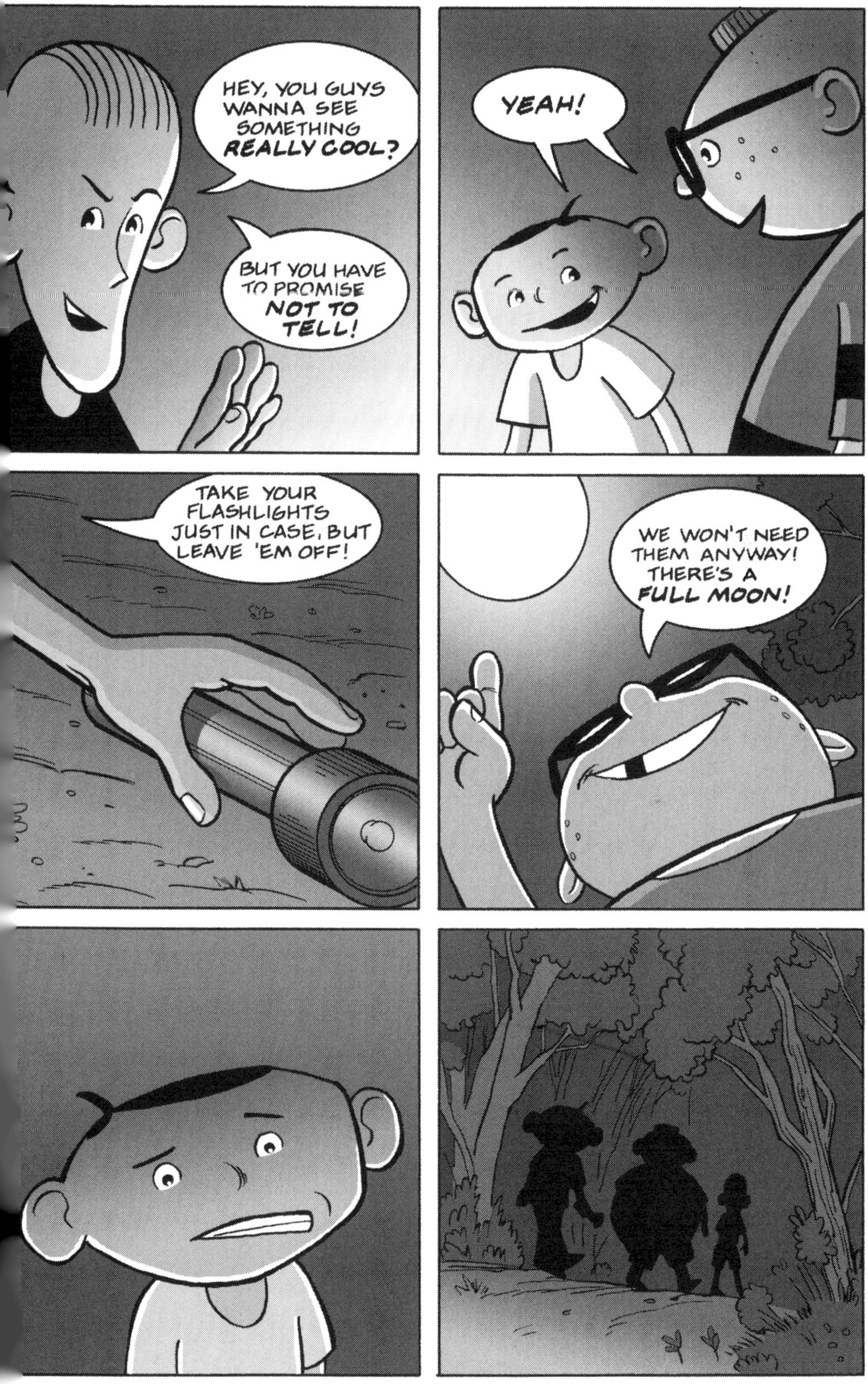
HEY, YOU GUYS WANNA SEE SOMETHING REALLY COOL?
BUT YOU HAVE TO PROMISE NOT TO TELL!
YEAH!
TAKE YOUR FLASHLIGHTS JUST IN CASE, BUT LEAVE 'EM OFF!
WE WON'T NEED THEM ANYWAY! THERE'S A FULL MOON!

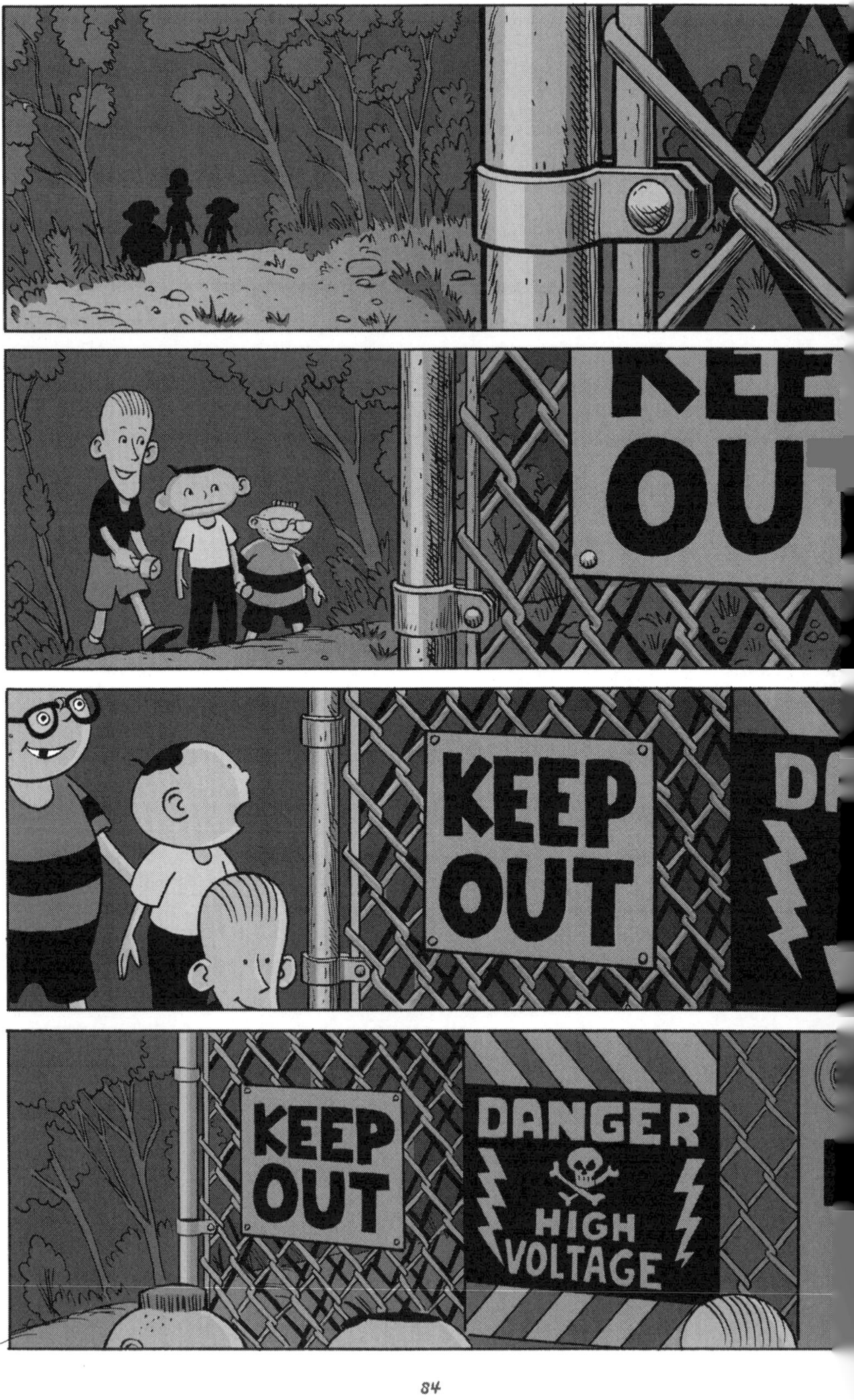
KEEP OUT
KEEP OUT
DANGER
HIGH VOLTAGE

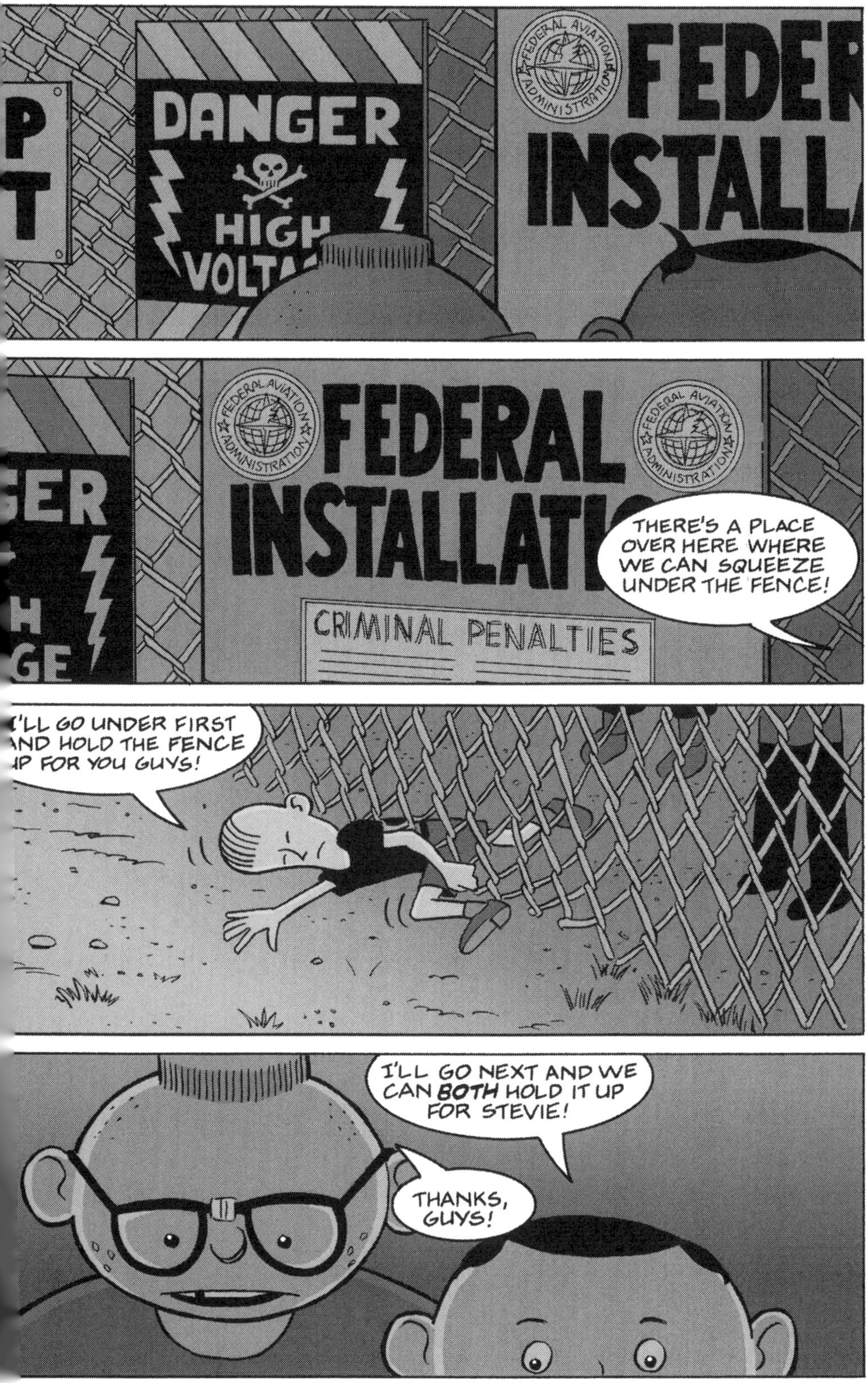
DANGER
HIGH
FEDERAL AVIATION ADMINISTRATION
FEDERAL
FEDERAL AVIATION ADMINISTRATION
THERE'S A PLACE OVER HERE WHERE WE CAN SQUEEZE UNDER THE FENCE!
CRIMINAL PENALTIES
I'LL GO UNDER FIRST AND HOLD THE FENCE UP FOR YOU GUYS!
I'LL GO NEXT AND WE CAN **BOTH** HOLD IT UP FOR STEVIE!
THANKS, GUYS!

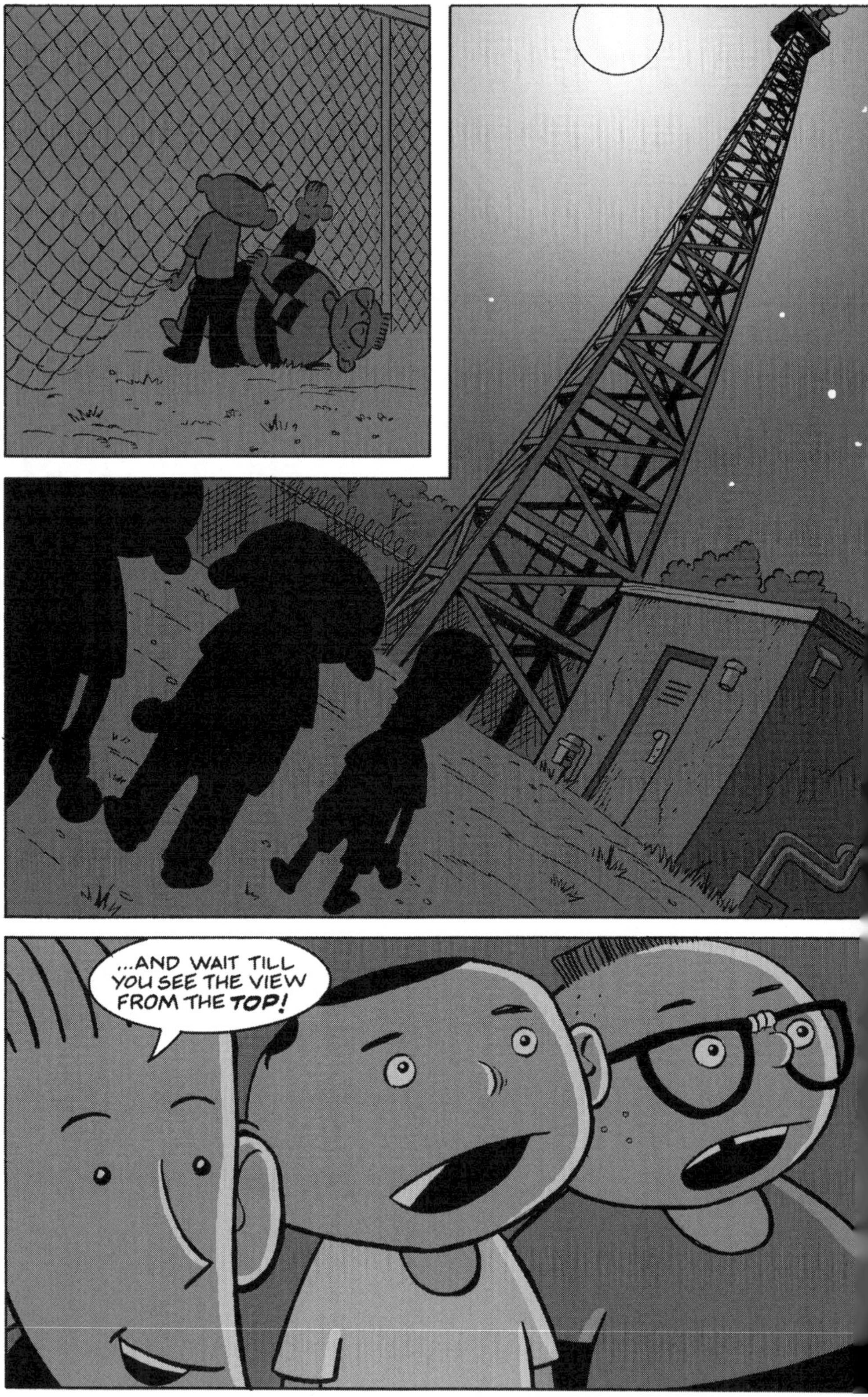
...AND WAIT TILL YOU SEE THE VIEW FROM THE **TOP!**

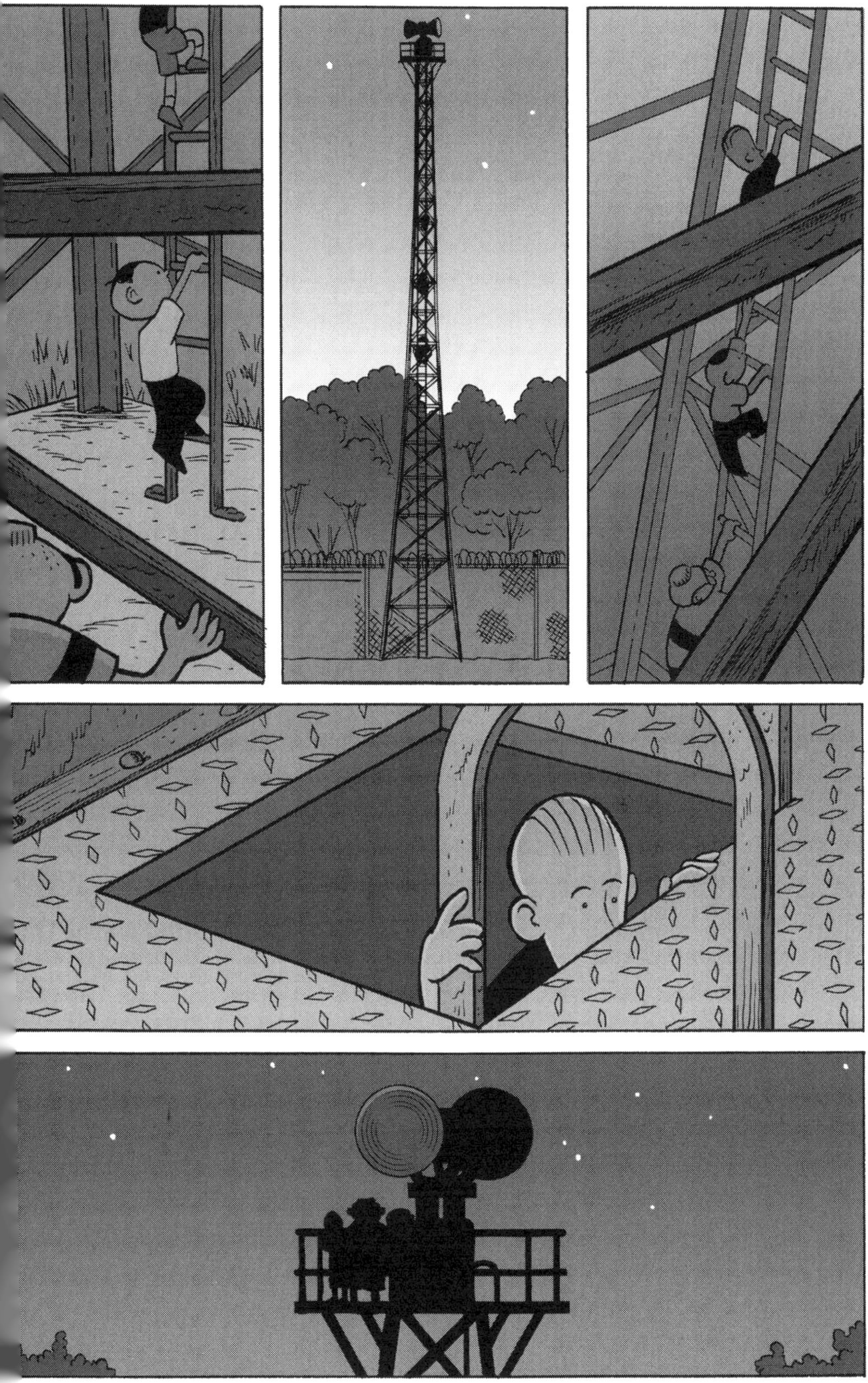

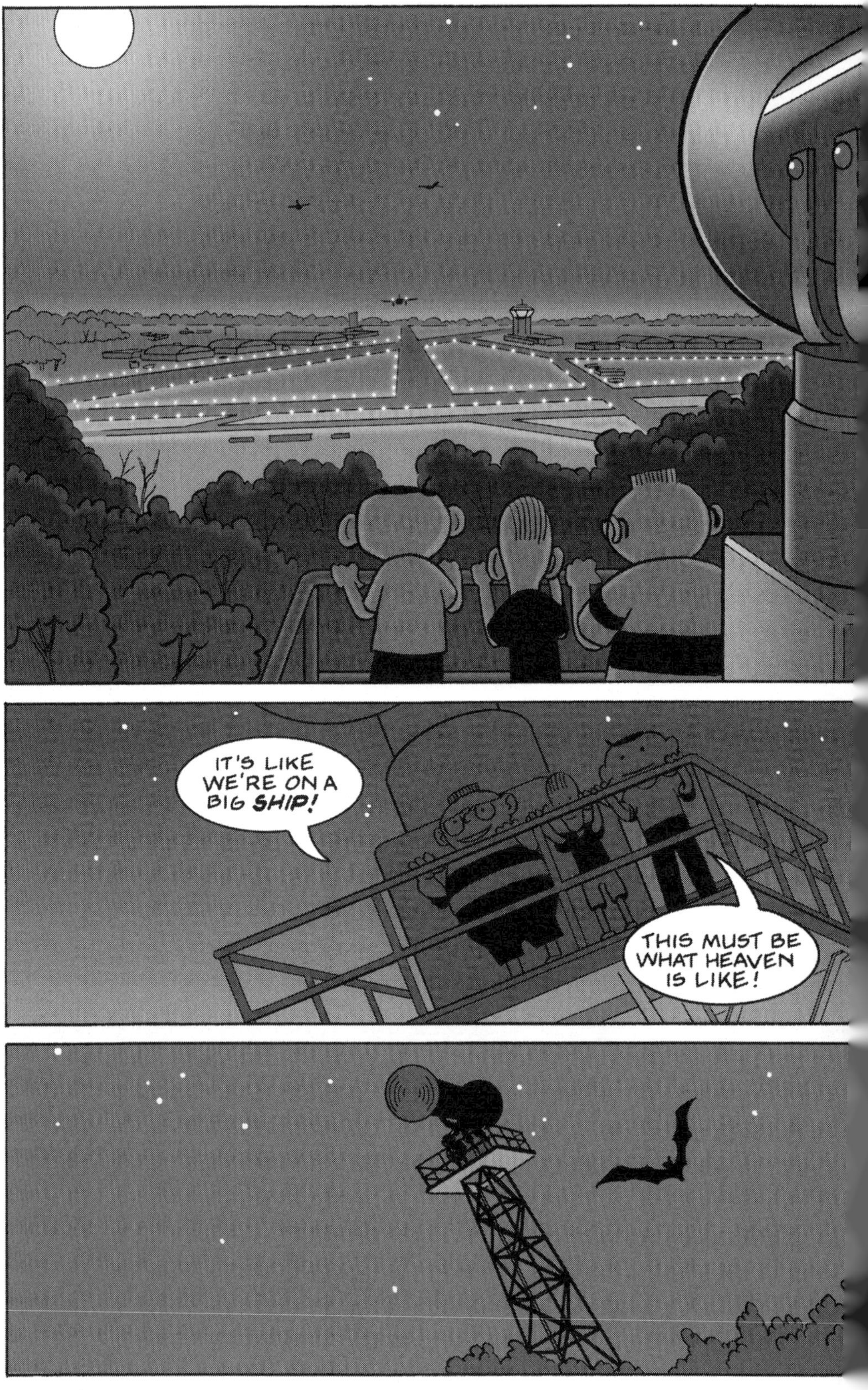
IT'S LIKE WE'RE ON A BIG SHIP!
THIS MUST BE WHAT HEAVEN IS LIKE!

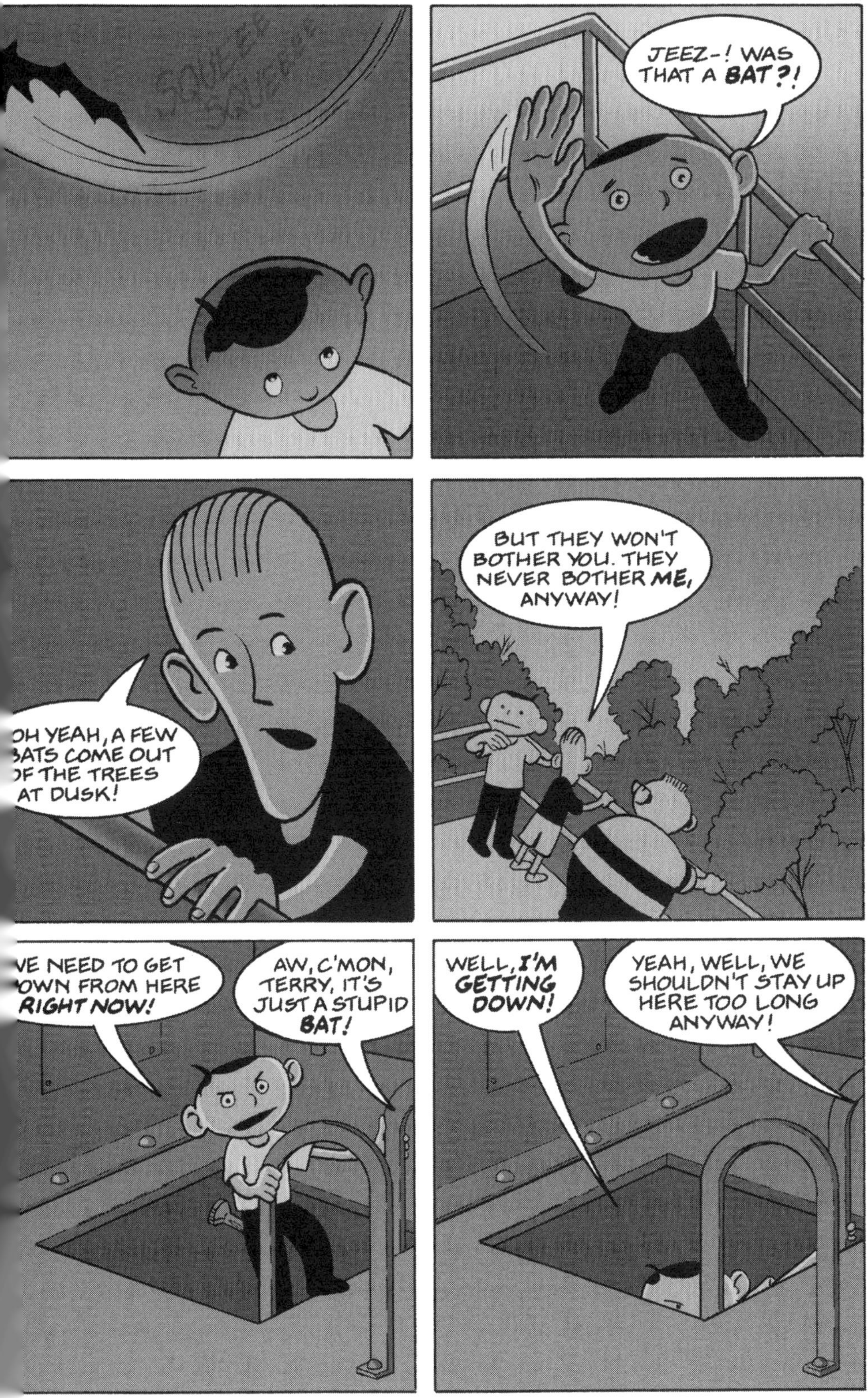

JEEZ-! WAS THAT A **BAT?!**
OH YEAH, A FEW BATS COME OUT OF THE TREES AT DUSK!
BUT THEY WON'T BOTHER YOU. THEY NEVER BOTHER **ME**, ANYWAY!
WE NEED TO GET DOWN FROM HERE **RIGHT NOW!**
AW, C'MON, TERRY, IT'S JUST A STUPID **BAT!**
WELL, **I'M GETTING DOWN!**
YEAH, WELL, WE SHOULDN'T STAY UP HERE TOO LONG ANYWAY!

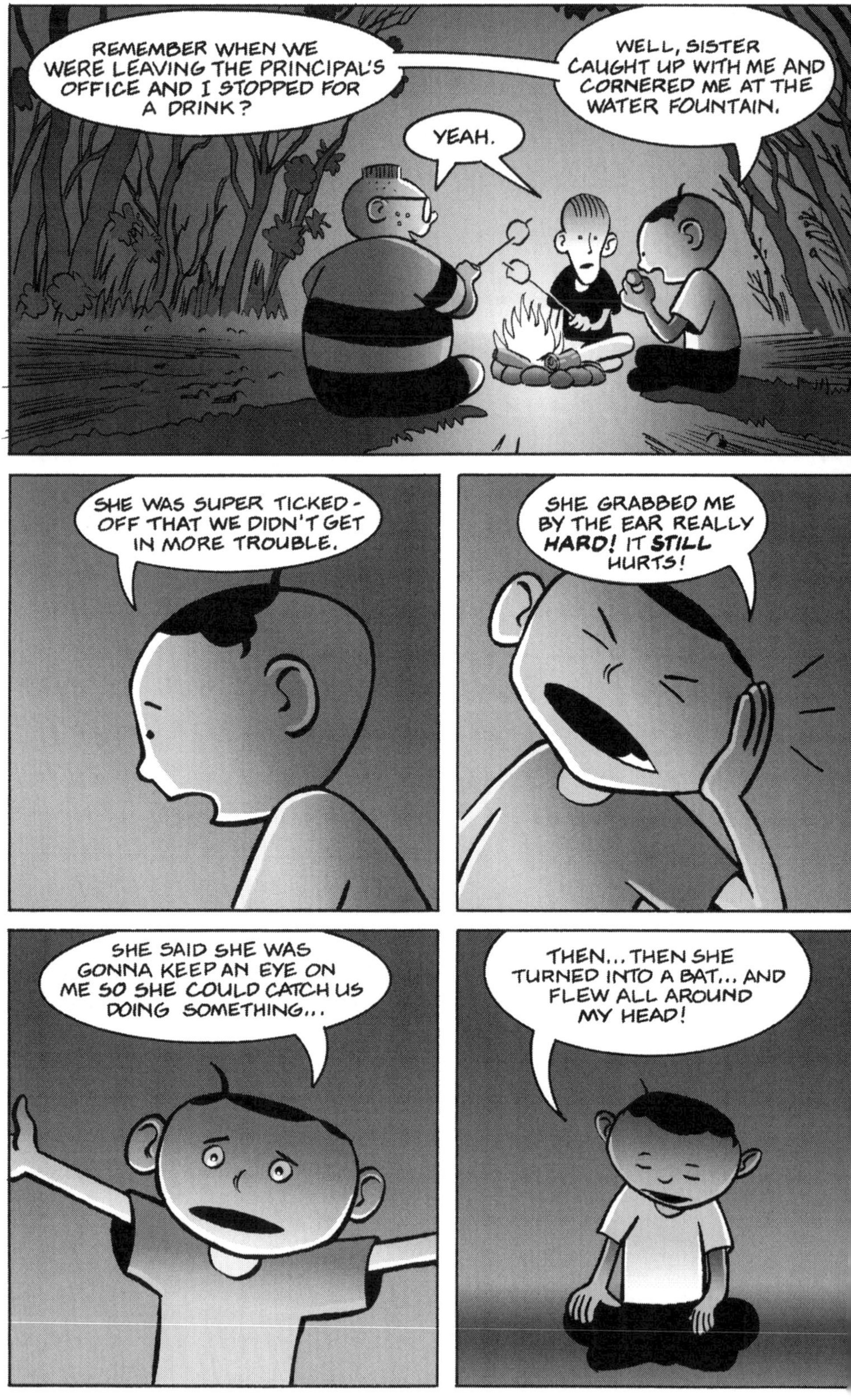
REMEMBER WHEN WE WERE LEAVING THE PRINCIPAL'S OFFICE AND I STOPPED FOR A DRINK?
YEAH.
WELL, SISTER CAUGHT UP WITH ME AND CORNERED ME AT THE WATER FOUNTAIN.
SHE WAS SUPER TICKED-OFF THAT WE DIDN'T GET IN MORE TROUBLE.
SHE GRABBED ME BY THE EAR REALLY HARD! IT STILL HURTS!
SHE SAID SHE WAS GONNA KEEP AN EYE ON ME SO SHE COULD CATCH US DOING SOMETHING...
THEN... THEN SHE TURNED INTO A BAT... AND FLEW ALL AROUND MY HEAD!

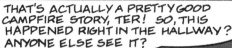

THAT'S ACTUALLY A PRETTY GOOD CAMPFIRE STORY, TER! SO, THIS HAPPENED RIGHT IN THE HALLWAY? ANYONE ELSE SEE IT?

WELL, THERE WERE A COUPLE OF GIRLS THERE! I *THINK* THEY SAW IT!

SO, WHAT, YOU THINK SHE'S A BAT AND SHE'S WATCHIN' US NOW?

WELL, THEN THE OTHER NIGHT I HAD A REALLY BAD DREAM WHERE SHE TURNED INTO A *BAT*, I MEAN FROM A *BAT* INTO A *NUN*...

WHOA, WHOA, WAIT! IS THIS ALL A DREAM NOW? WHICH PART IS WHICH?

SHE *REALLY* TURNED INTO A BAT!

WELL YOU *REALLY* SHOULDN'T FALL ASLEEP BY THE AIRPLANE GLUE!

HA! GOOD ONE!

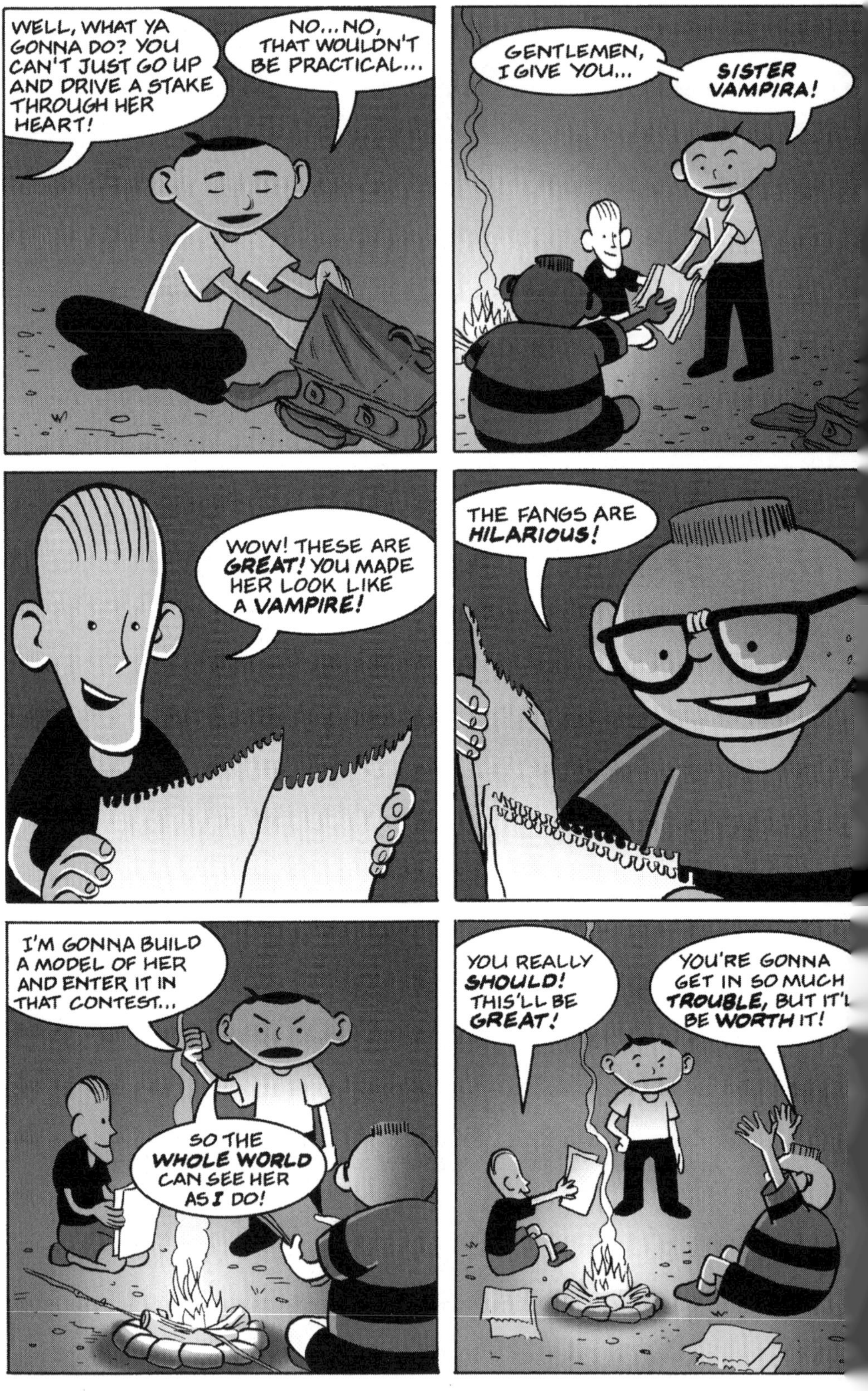
WELL, WHAT YA GONNA DO? YOU CAN'T JUST GO UP AND DRIVE A STAKE THROUGH HER HEART!
NO... NO, THAT WOULDN'T BE PRACTICAL...
GENTLEMEN, I GIVE YOU...
SISTER VAMPIRA!
WOW! THESE ARE GREAT! YOU MADE HER LOOK LIKE A VAMPIRE!
THE FANGS ARE HILARIOUS!
I'M GONNA BUILD A MODEL OF HER AND ENTER IT IN THAT CONTEST...
SO THE WHOLE WORLD CAN SEE HER AS I DO!
YOU REALLY SHOULD! THIS'LL BE GREAT!
YOU'RE GONNA GET IN SO MUCH TROUBLE, BUT IT'LL BE WORTH IT!

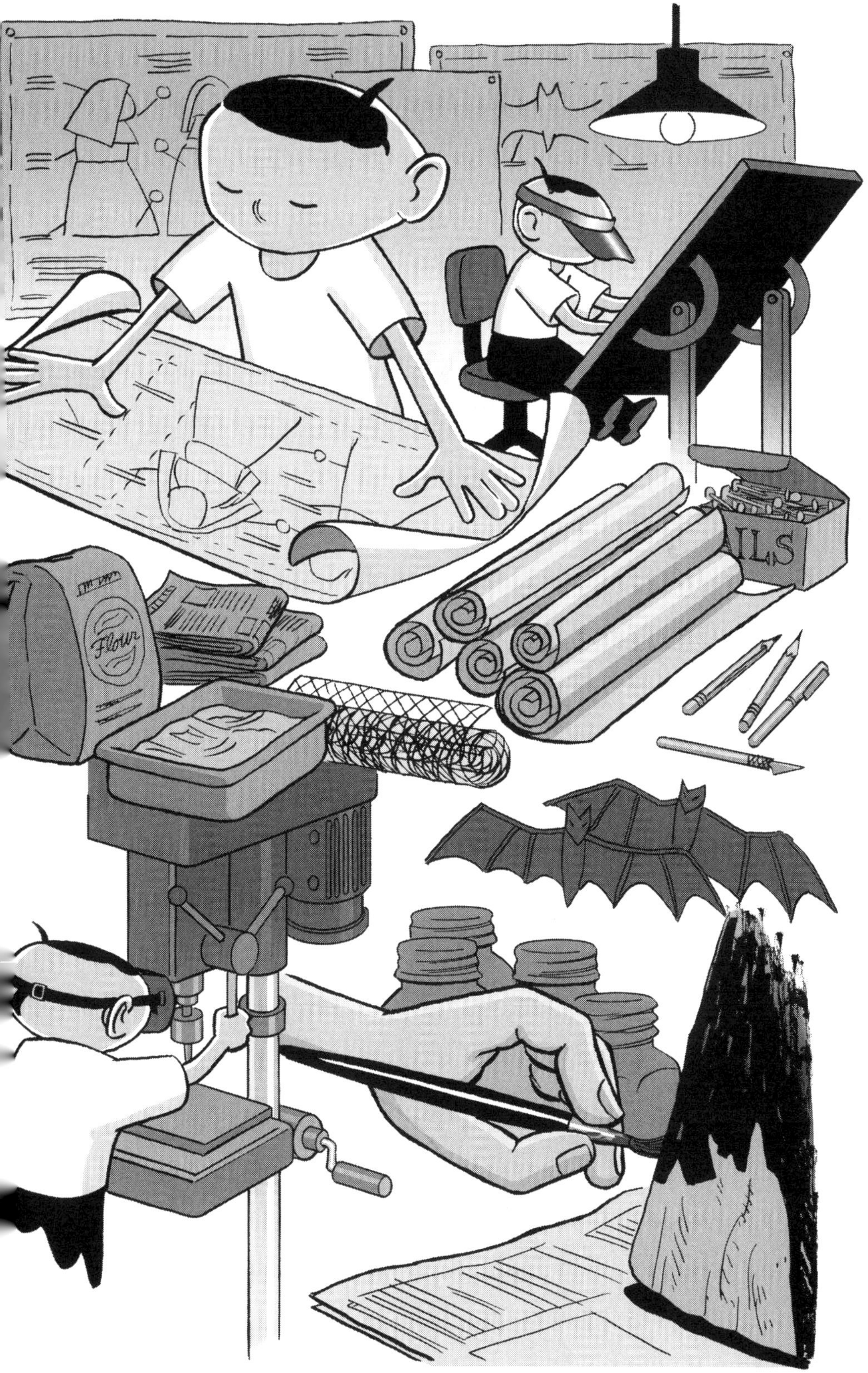
ILS
Flour

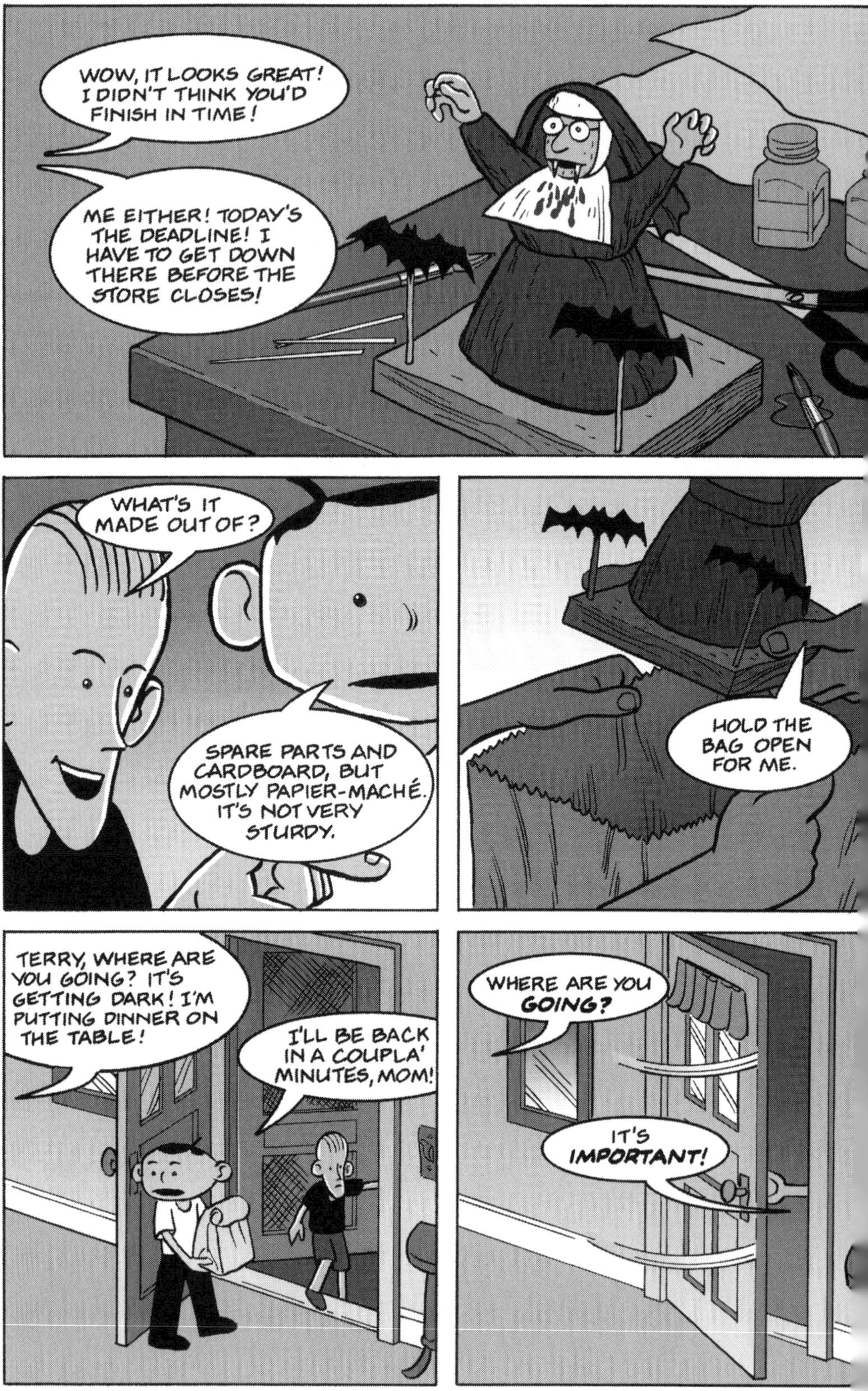
WOW, IT LOOKS GREAT! I DIDN'T THINK YOU'D FINISH IN TIME!
ME EITHER! TODAY'S THE DEADLINE! I HAVE TO GET DOWN THERE BEFORE THE STORE CLOSES!
WHAT'S IT MADE OUT OF?
SPARE PARTS AND CARDBOARD, BUT MOSTLY PAPIER-MACHÉ. IT'S NOT VERY STURDY.
HOLD THE BAG OPEN FOR ME.
TERRY, WHERE ARE YOU GOING? IT'S GETTING DARK! I'M PUTTING DINNER ON THE TABLE!
I'LL BE BACK IN A COUPLA' MINUTES, MOM!
WHERE ARE YOU **GOING?**
IT'S **IMPORTANT!**

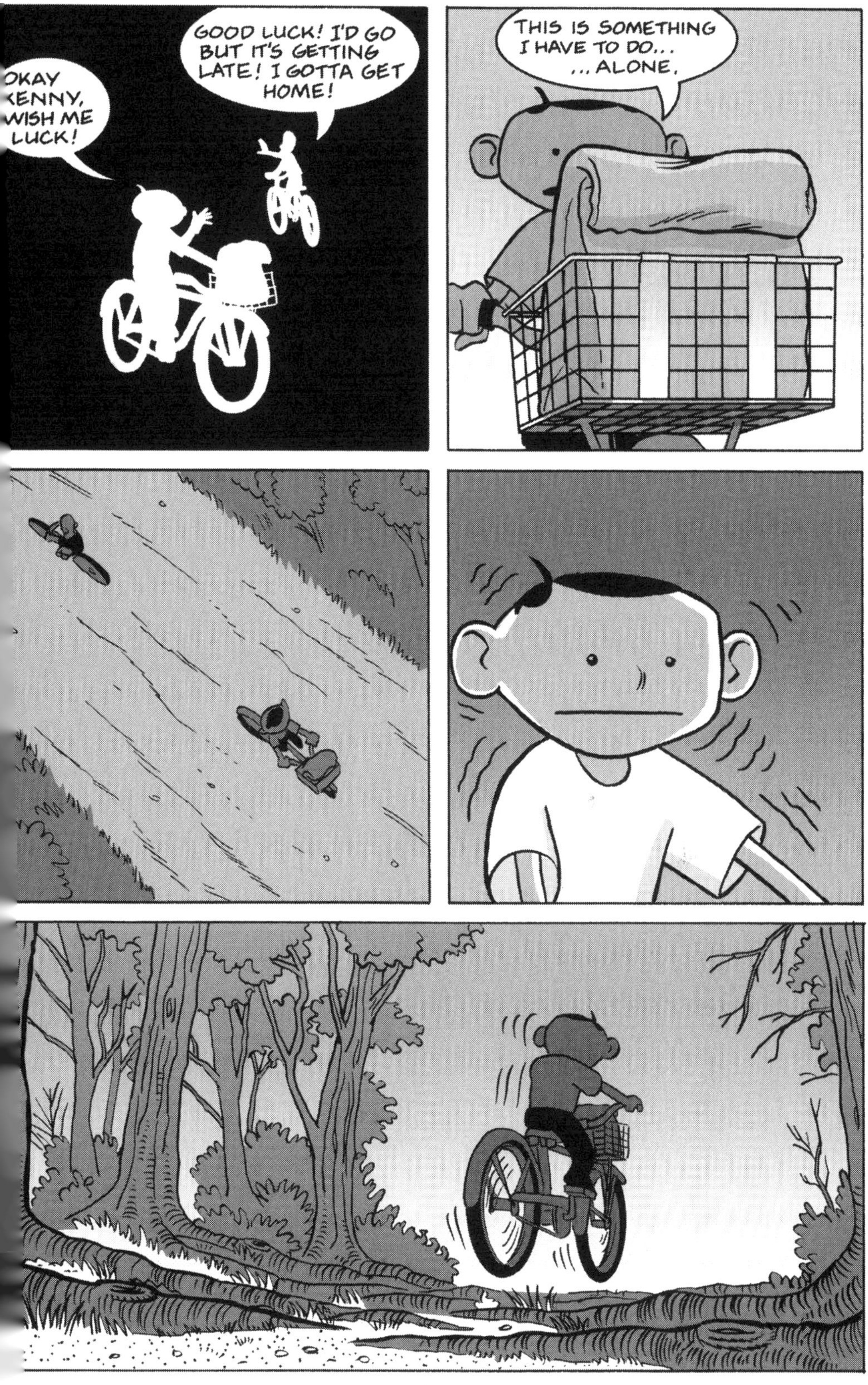
OKAY KENNY, WISH ME LUCK!
GOOD LUCK! I'D GO BUT IT'S GETTING LATE! I GOTTA GET HOME!
THIS IS SOMETHING I HAVE TO DO... ...ALONE.

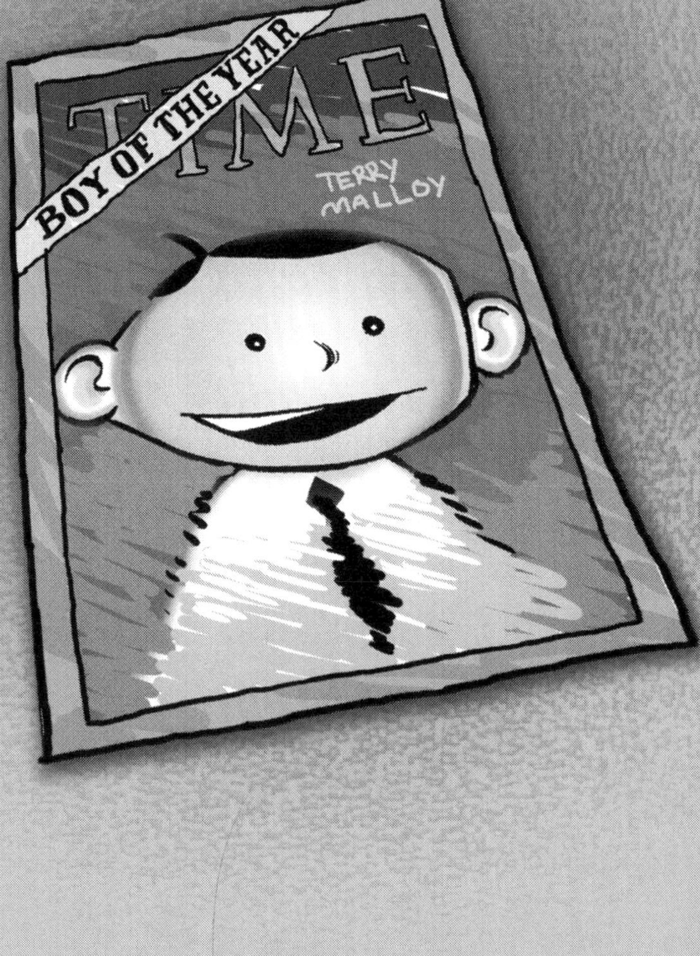
TIME
BOY OF THE YEAR
TERRY
MALLOY

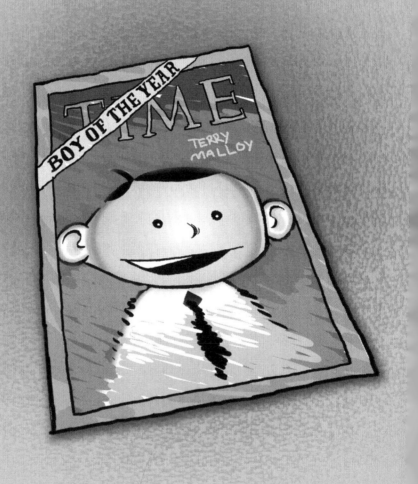

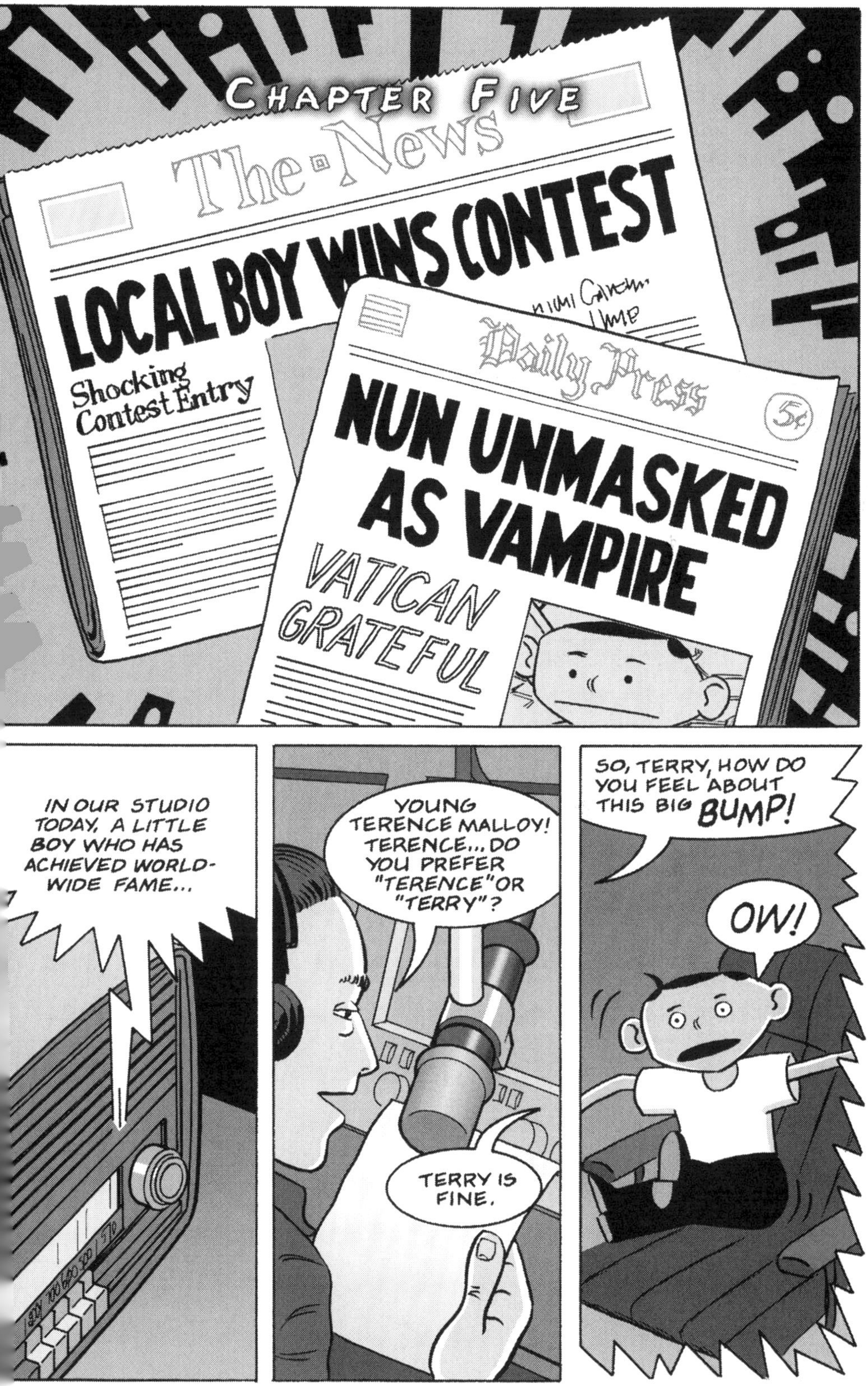
CHAPTER FIVE
The News
LOCAL BOY WINS CONTEST
Shocking Contest Entry
Daily Press
5¢
NUN UNMASKED AS VAMPIRE
VATICAN GRATEFUL
IN OUR STUDIO TODAY, A LITTLE BOY WHO HAS ACHIEVED WORLD-WIDE FAME...
YOUNG TERENCE MALLOY! TERENCE... DO YOU PREFER "TERENCE" OR "TERRY"?
TERRY IS FINE.
SO, TERRY, HOW DO YOU FEEL ABOUT THIS BIG BUMP!
OW!

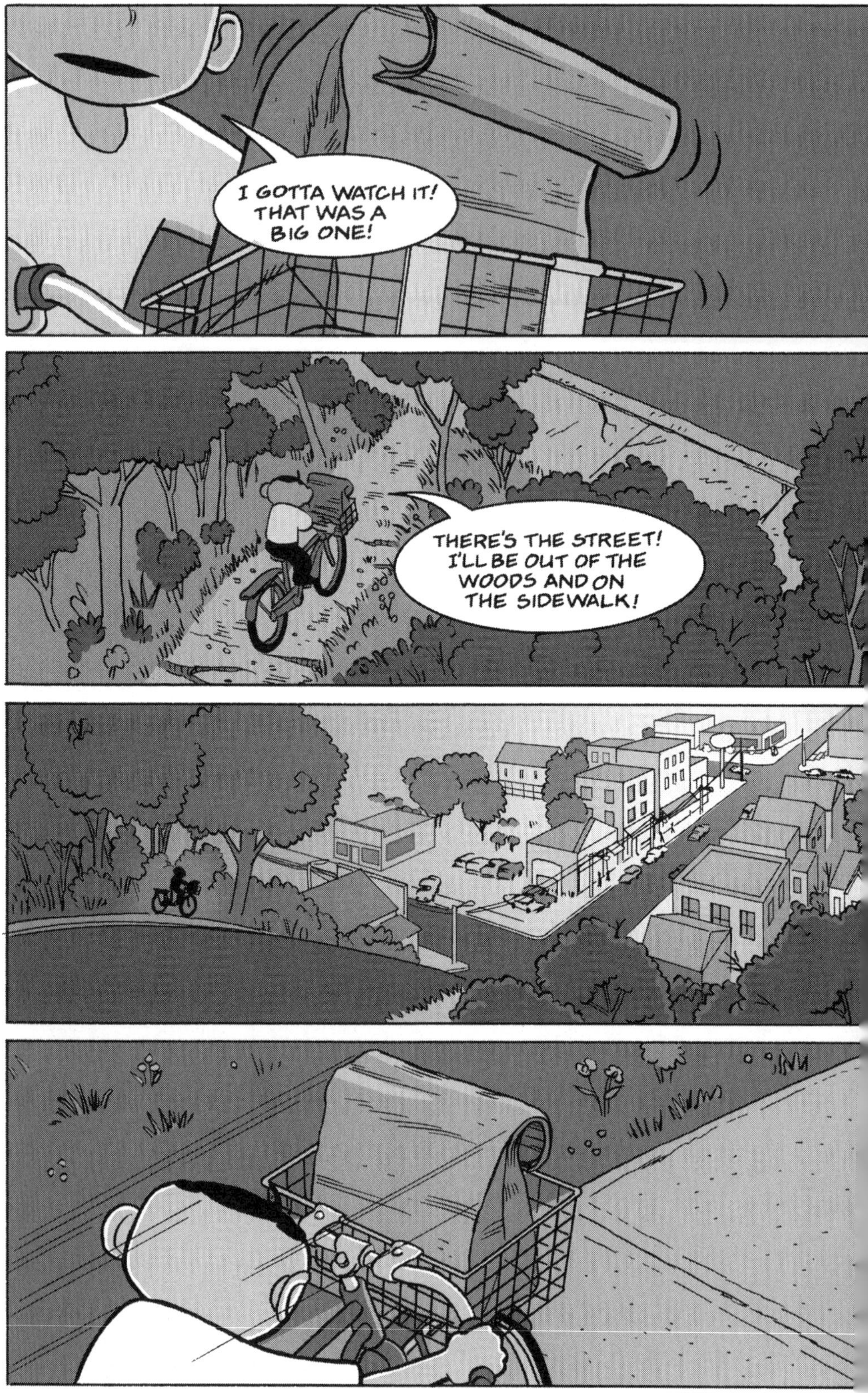
I GOTTA WATCH IT! THAT WAS A BIG ONE!
THERE'S THE STREET! I'LL BE OUT OF THE WOODS AND ON THE SIDEWALK!

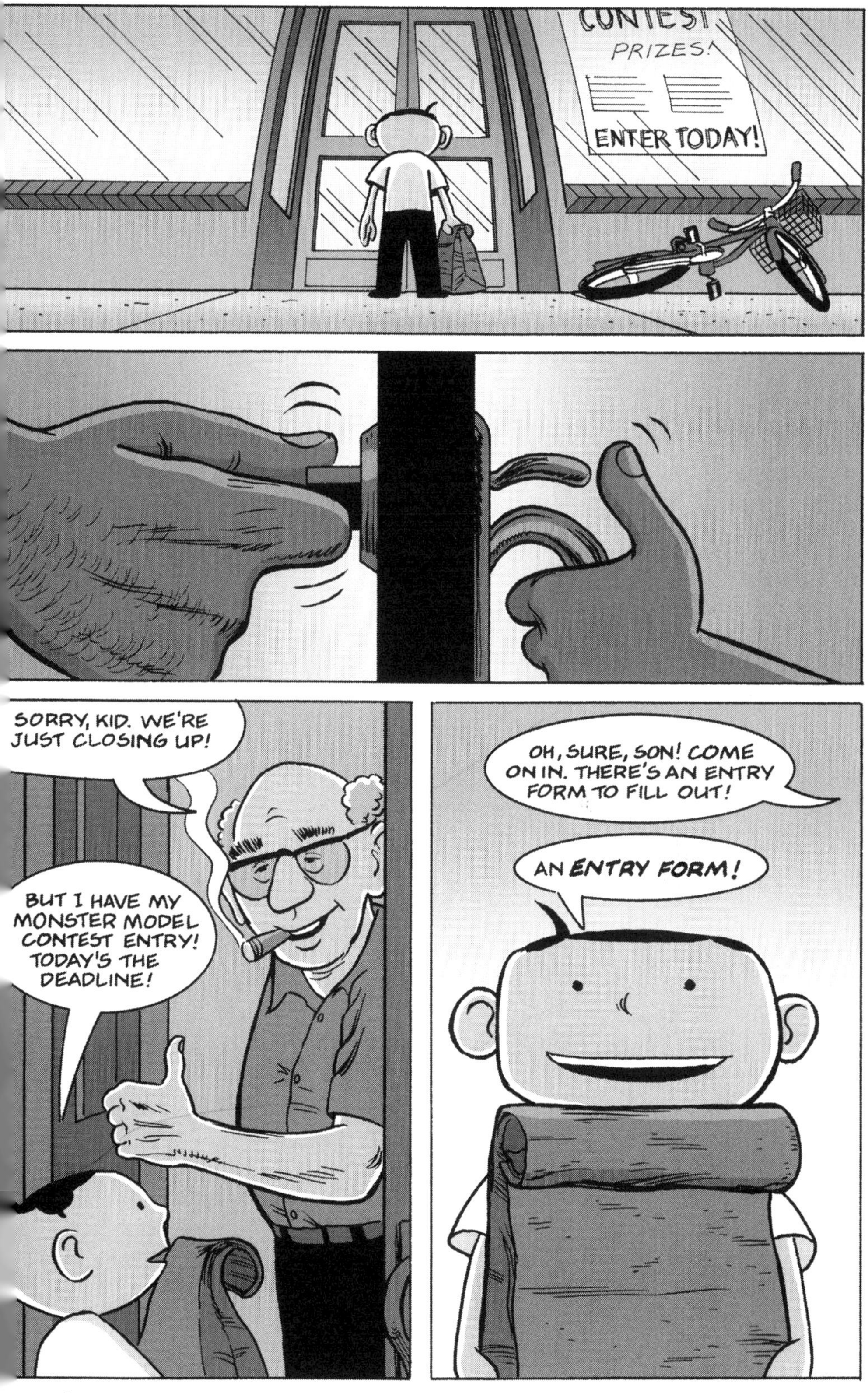
CONTEST
PRIZES!
ENTER TODAY!
SORRY, KID. WE'RE JUST CLOSING UP!
BUT I HAVE MY MONSTER MODEL CONTEST ENTRY! TODAY'S THE DEADLINE!
OH, SURE, SON! COME ON IN. THERE'S AN ENTRY FORM TO FILL OUT!
AN ENTRY FORM!

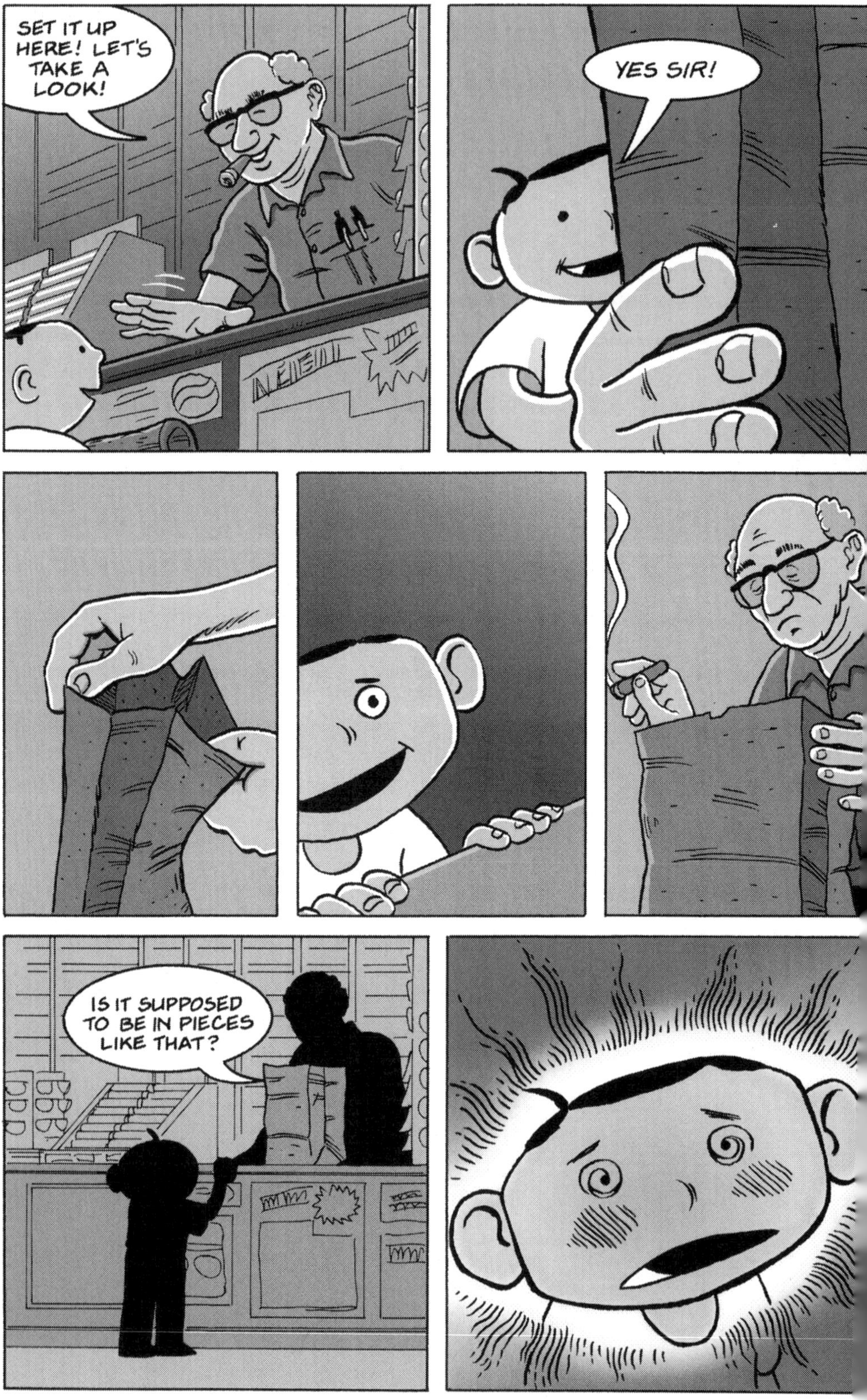
SET IT UP HERE! LET'S TAKE A LOOK!
YES SIR!
IS IT SUPPOSED TO BE IN PIECES LIKE THAT?

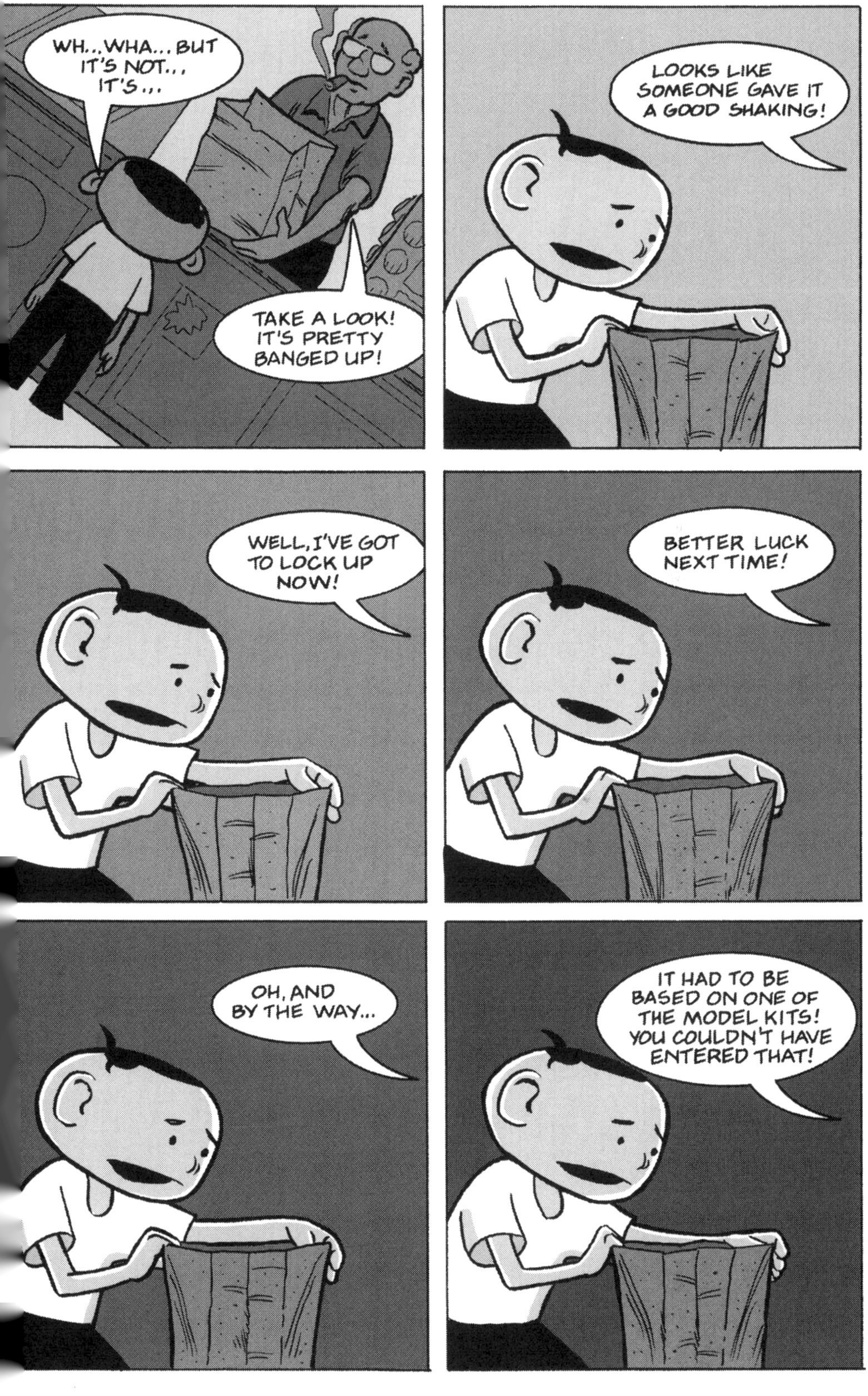
WH...WHA... BUT IT'S NOT..., IT'S...,
TAKE A LOOK! IT'S PRETTY BANGED UP!
LOOKS LIKE SOMEONE GAVE IT A GOOD SHAKING!
WELL, I'VE GOT TO LOCK UP NOW!
BETTER LUCK NEXT TIME!
OH, AND BY THE WAY...
IT HAD TO BE BASED ON ONE OF THE MODEL KITS! YOU COULDN'T HAVE ENTERED THAT!

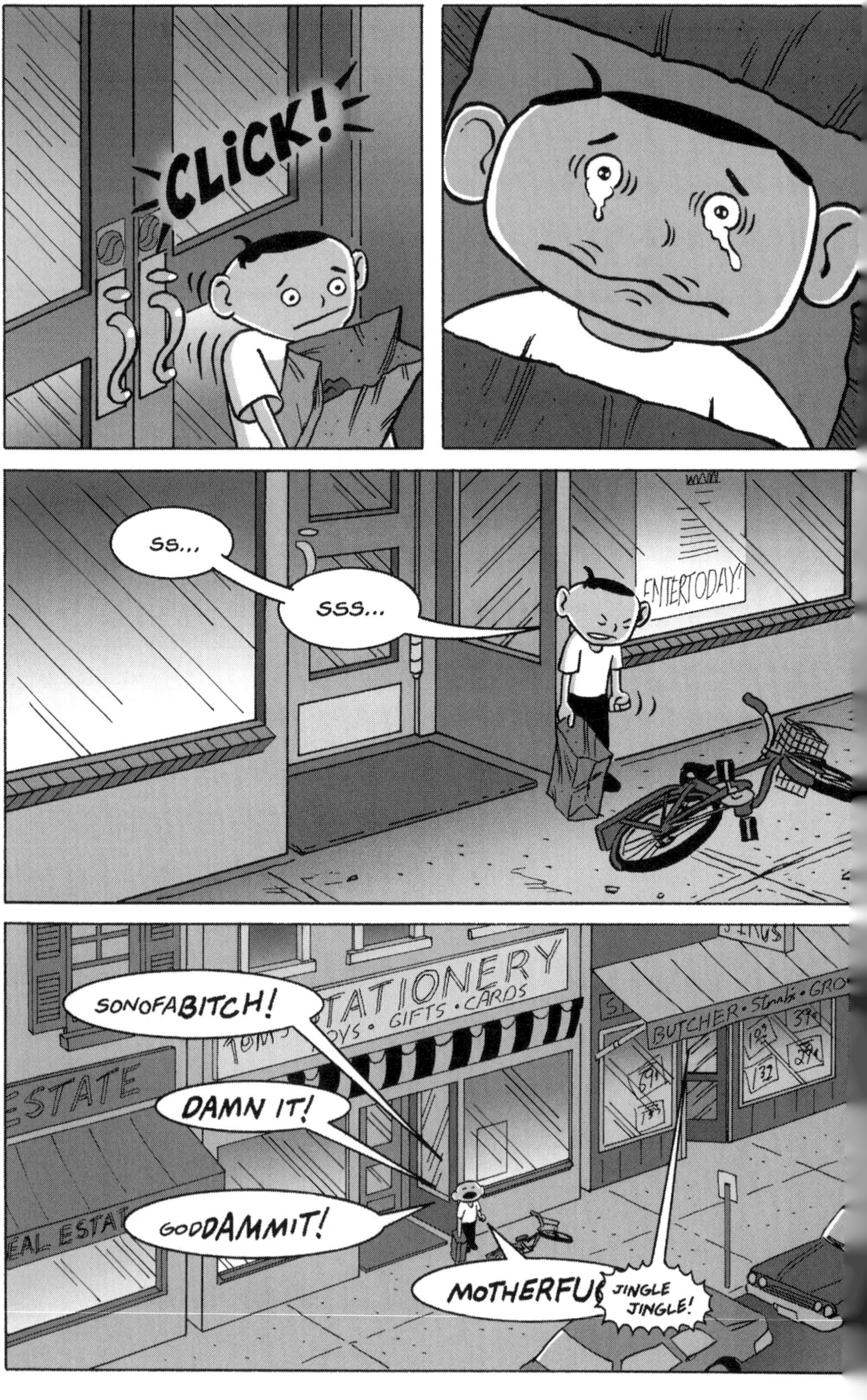
CLICK!
SS...
SSS...
ENTER TODAY!
STATIONERY
TOYS • GIFTS • CARDS
ESTATE
EAL ESTAT
BUTCHER
SONOFABITCH!
DAMN IT!
GODDAMMIT!
MOTHERFU
JINGLE JINGLE!

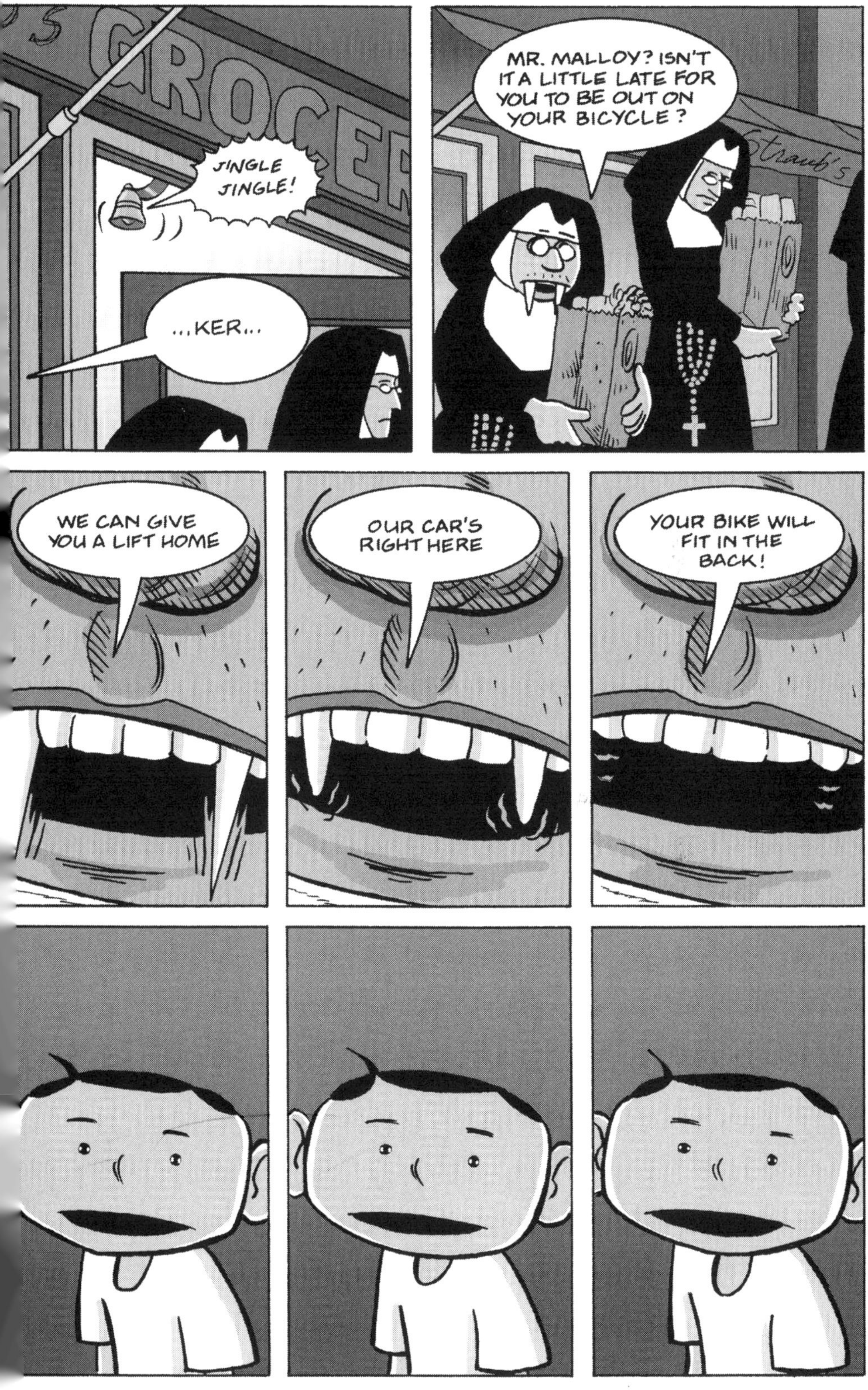
GROCER
JINGLE JINGLE!
...KER...
MR. MALLOY? ISN'T IT A LITTLE LATE FOR YOU TO BE OUT ON YOUR BICYCLE?
WE CAN GIVE YOU A LIFT HOME
OUR CAR'S RIGHT HERE
YOUR BIKE WILL FIT IN THE BACK!

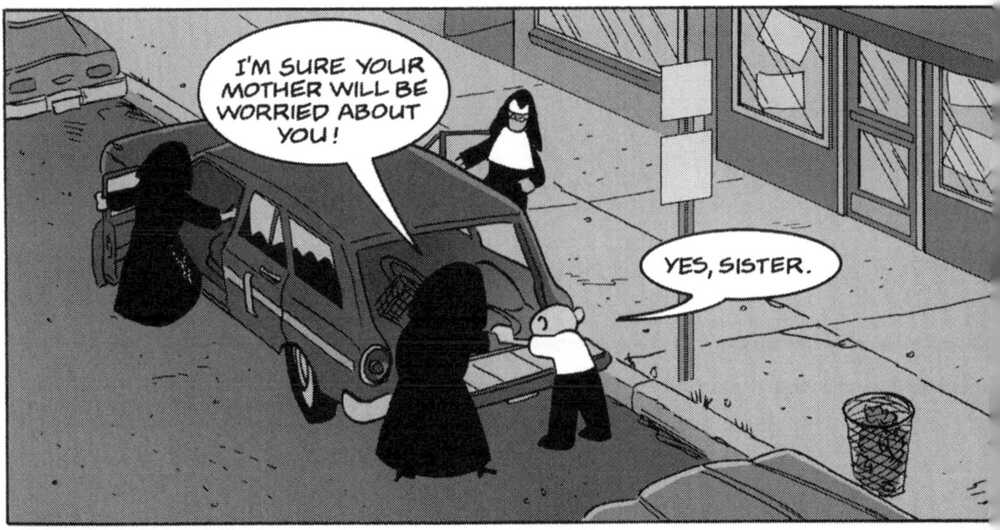
I'M SURE YOUR MOTHER WILL BE WORRIED ABOUT YOU!
YES, SISTER.

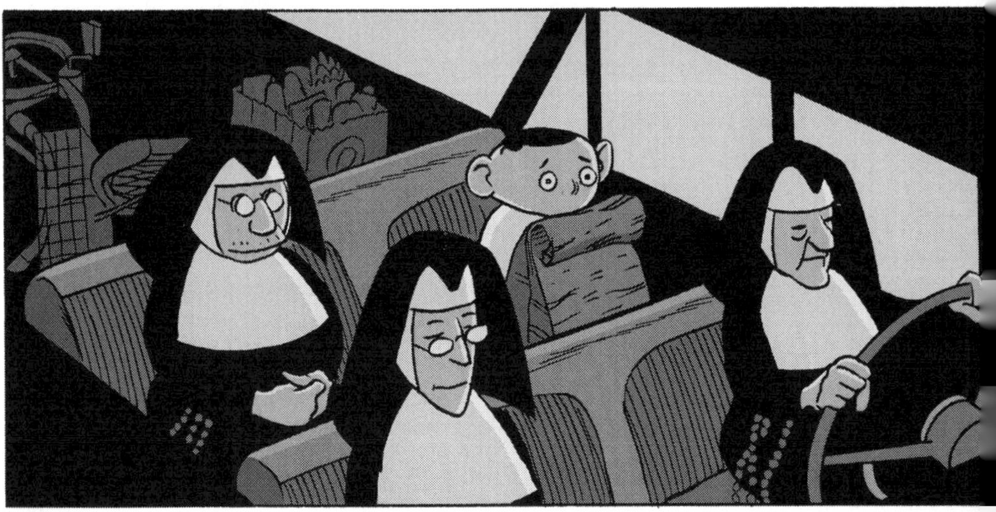

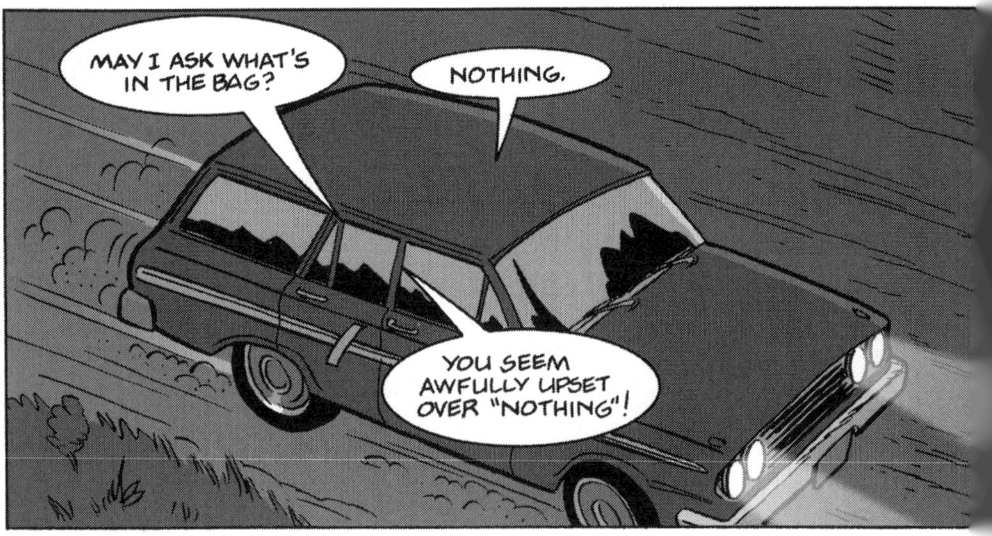
MAY I ASK WHAT'S IN THE BAG?
NOTHING.
YOU SEEM AWFULLY UPSET OVER "NOTHING"!

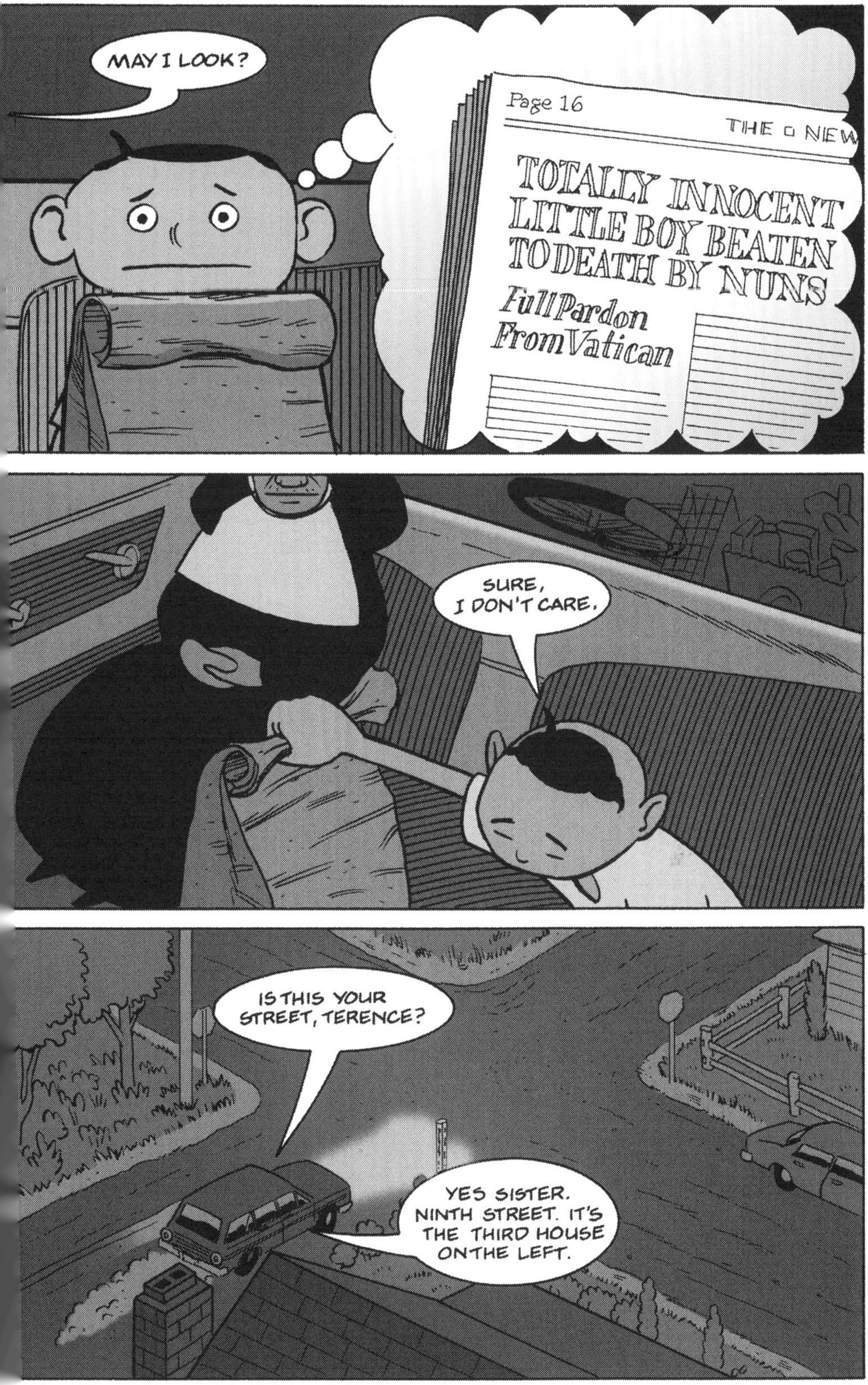

MAY I LOOK?
Page 16
THE NEW
TOTALLY INNOCENT LITTLE BOY BEATEN TO DEATH BY NUNS
Full Pardon From Vatican
SURE, I DON'T CARE.
IS THIS YOUR STREET, TERENCE?
YES SISTER. NINTH STREET. IT'S THE THIRD HOUSE ON THE LEFT.

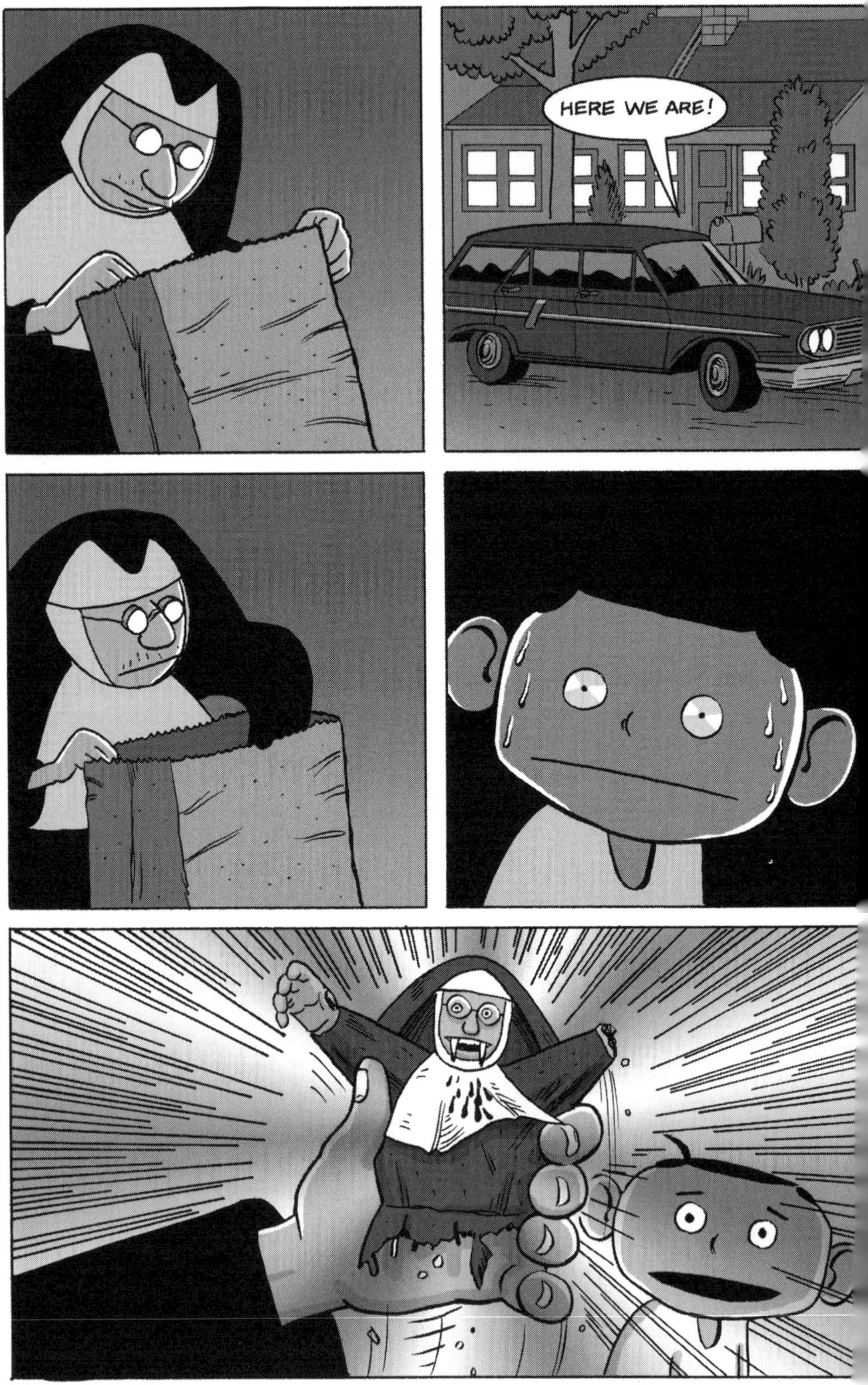
HERE WE ARE!

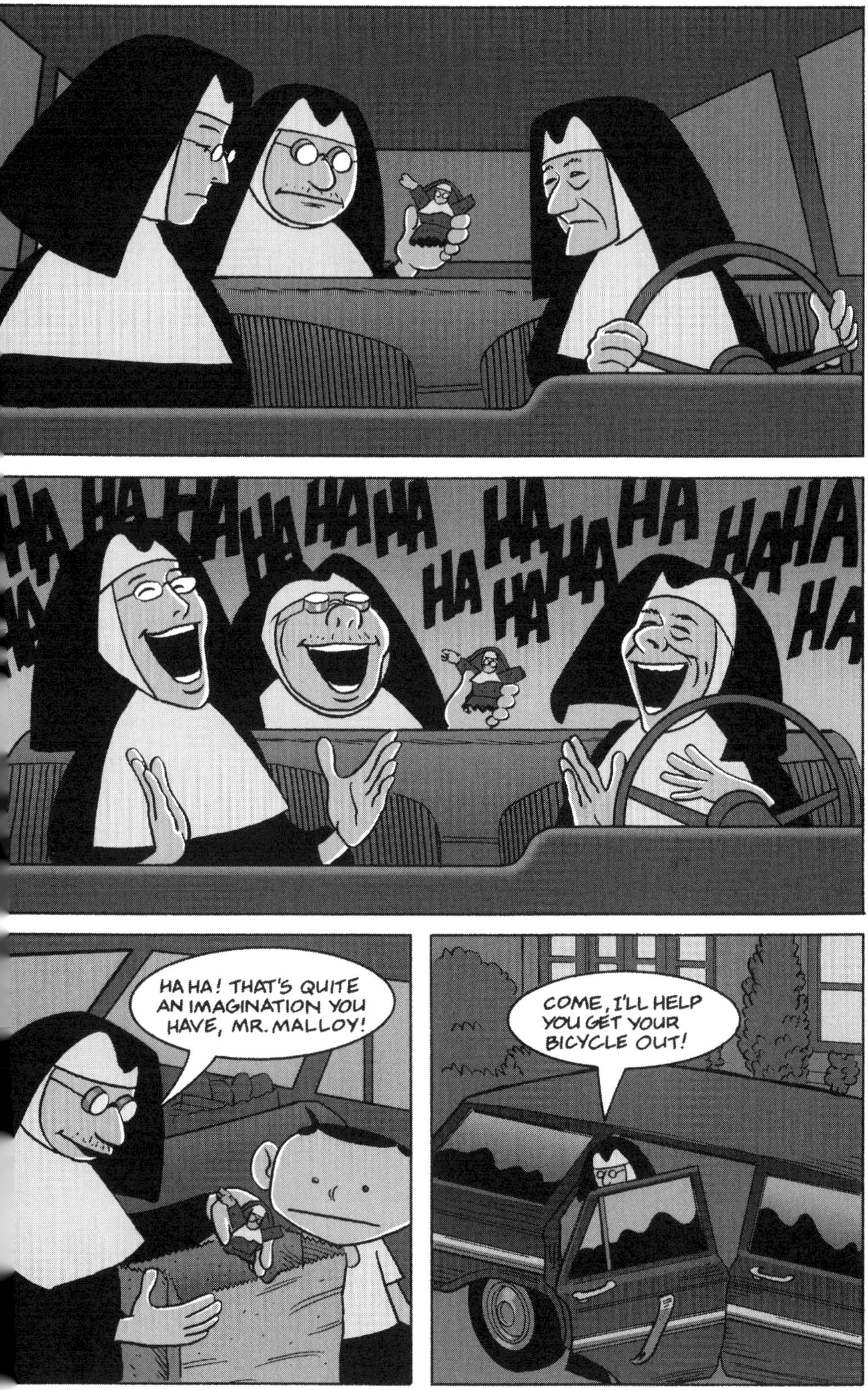
HA HA! THAT'S QUITE AN IMAGINATION YOU HAVE, MR. MALLOY!
COME, I'LL HELP YOU GET YOUR BICYCLE OUT!

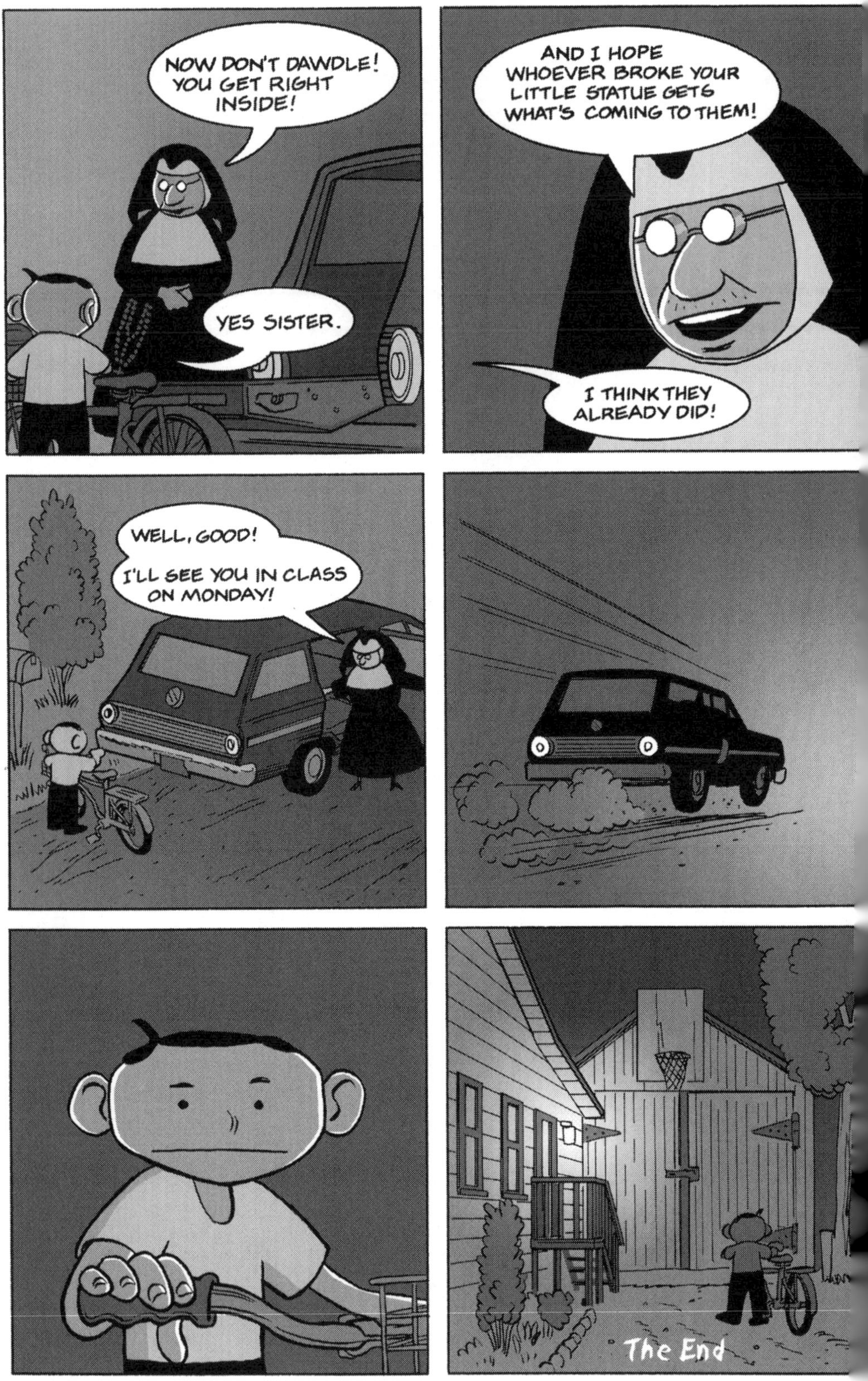
NOW DON'T DAWDLE! YOU GET RIGHT INSIDE!
YES SISTER.
AND I HOPE WHOEVER BROKE YOUR LITTLE STATUE GETS WHAT'S COMING TO THEM!
I THINK THEY ALREADY DID!
WELL, GOOD!
I'LL SEE YOU IN CLASS ON MONDAY!
The End

Made in the USA
Charleston, SC
27 October 2014